Disinformation
and
Misinformation

Disinformation, Misinformation, and the "Conspiracy" to Kill JFK Exposed

Armand Moss

Archon Books 1987

© 1987 Armand Moss. All rights reserved
First published 1987 as an Archon Book,
an imprint of The Shoe String Press, Inc.,
Hamden, Connecticut 06514

Printed in the United States of America

The paper used in this publication meets the minimum
requirements of American National Standard for Information
Sciences—Permanence of Paper for Printed Library Materials,
ANSI Z39.48–1984. ∞

Set in Times Roman by Brevis Press, Bethany, Connecticut.
Designed by Nora Jacobson.

Library of Congress Cataloging-in-Publication Data

Moss, Armand.
    Disinformation, misinformation, and the "conspiracy"
to kill JFK exposed.
    Bibliography: p.
    Includes index.
    1. Kennedy, John F. (John Fitzgerald), 1917–1963—
Assassination. 2. Public opinion—Soviet Union.
3. Soviet Union—Foreign relations—1953–1975.
4. Propaganda, Russian. 5. Press and politics—Soviet
Union. I. Title.
E842.9.M648 1987   364.1'524   87–1156
ISBN 0–208–02143–4 (alk. paper)

For Deirdre

Acknowledgments

I am indebted to Asimina Caminis, who took a rough manuscript written in a combination of French and English and made from it something readable. I would like to acknowledge the unstinting help of my bilingual wife. Without them, I would never have been able to bring my undertaking to fruition.

I express my gratitude to James Thorpe III, president of The Shoe String Press, Inc. This book has been greatly improved by his invaluable suggestions and his precious editorial assistance.

Contents

Contents

Introduction

> *In accordance with Stalin's orders, which are still obeyed, the United States is invariably portrayed as a country run by a handful of multi-millionaires . . . while . . . teams of gangsters, controlled by a corrupt police force, carry out their criminal activities with impunity.*
>
> —Boris Souvarine, "Le Mot-clef au Proche-Orient"

The Soviet Union, which sees itself as being at war with the capitalist countries, uses disinformation on a large scale. Its aim is to undermine the Atlantic Alliance; to force a weakened America to withdraw into isolationism; to dominate Europe and impose its system and will on every European country. Disinformation is basic to Soviet foreign policy; disinformation is the chief means by which the Soviet Union hopes to accomplish its geostrategic political goals without the need for major armed conflict or nuclear war.

According to the neutral language of lexicography, as defined by the *Oxford English Dictionary, dis-,* as in *disinformation,* is "a living prefix, with privative [negative] force . . . used with verbs, substantives [nouns], and adjectives, without regard to their origin." This definition characterizes use of the prefix etymologically as "with a substantive expressing the opposite, or denoting the lack or absence, of (the thing in question)."[1] *Disinformation* is different from *misinformation.* The prefix *dis-* calls to mind *reverse,* or *opposite,* and has connotations of irrevocability, whereas the prefix *mis-* merely indicates wrongness—something that can be corrected. *Displaced* persons rarely return home after a war, while a *misplaced* object is usually found. The *Soviet Concise Political Dic-*

tionary defines *disinformation* as "provocative, mendacious information brought forward as fact with the object of misleading public opinion, widely used by the capitalist press, radio, television, and other mass media; it is their favorite weapon in their anti-Communist propaganda and their slanderous campaign against socialist countries."[2] Even when defining *disinformation,* Moscow disinforms. Replacing "capitalist" with "Communist," "anti-Communist" with "anti-American," and "socialist" with "capitalist" straightens out the definition.

In the case central to this book, to say that the Warren Commission was formed to ascertain the facts about John F. Kennedy's assassination is to give information; to say that it did a poor job is misinformation; to say that it did not give the real story is disinformation. The object of this book is to analyze the disinformation process in action by showing how it worked—and worked with stunning, very likely unexpected success—in shaping European and American reaction to the murder of President Kennedy and in changing the way the United States was perceived abroad.

Since 1959 a department of the KGB has specialized in the conduct of "active measures" prejudicial to the United States in particular and the Atlantic Alliance in general. A classic measure is to concoct a story, trumped up in Moscow and full of falsehoods, concerning a real historical situation, and have it published in a foreign newspaper, preferably a non-Communist one. Tass, the Soviet news agency, then distributes the article, indicating its origin—thus distancing the story from its KGB source.

A typical example of Soviet disinformation, which spreads calumny about the United States and attempts to split Europe from America by warping a real historical situation, took place in April 1961, roughly coinciding with the Bay of Pigs invasion. This fiasco was not one to elevate American prestige or CIA credibility in Europe, and France—then a member of NATO—was particularly vulnerable to the KBG's disinformation directorate. The French army refused to accept President de Gaulle's reluctant decision to conclude the festering Algerian war by allowing the North African colony independence. There was open military revolt in French Algeria; the right-wing *Organisation Armée Secrète,* the metropolitan arm of the rebelling generals, brought France to the brink of civil war and was fomenting assassination attempts against de Gaulle. At this juncture the Italian Communist daily *Il Paese* "revealed" that Francisco Franco, the Fascist dictator of Spain, Antonio Salazar, the Fascist dictator of Portugal, and Allen Dulles, director of the CIA, were behind the generals' rebellion. The Tass wire carried the article in English, with a reference to its alleged Italian origin. A French non-Communist newspaper was taken in, and published an article based on the sensational disinformation, under the byline of a respected journalist, with the headline "Allen Dulles' Strategy." Tass then could and did distribute an article that had every appearance of informed indignation at news that the CIA was fomenting civil war in France.[3]

No responsible observer would claim this single instance of Soviet disinformation caused de Gaulle to withdraw from NATO shortly after he consolidated power at home—his suspicion of Anglo-Saxon leadership was legendary. Indeed, only a small number of the articles detrimental to the United States are directly planted by the KGB. Its aims are constantly and effectively served in Europe by apolitical people whose fluctuating anti-Americanism is fostered by the continuous spread of disinformation, much of it self-generated, and by Communists or fellow travelers who have been disinformed in their youth and speak or write with little prompting in the best interests of the Soviet Union. The well-meaning, the ill-informed, and the self-interested make their contributions.

The KGB encourages collaboration and knows how to get the active collaboration of fellow travelers. In 1979 a pro-Communist French citizen, Pierre-Charles Pathé, was caught by French Intelligence Department agents in the act of receiving money from a Soviet official. Pathé was publishing a 500-copy newsletter that was sent, often free of charge, to 139 French senators, 299 members of the Chamber of Deputies, fourteen embassies, and forty-one newspapers.[4] He wrote in his newsletter that the FBI wanted President Kennedy "out of the way"[5] and that his assassination represented "an essential aspect of American democracy."[6] Pathé was "a Parisian insider [who] knew people in public life across the political spectrum from de Gaulle to Mitterand."[7] He belonged to "a group called 'Movement for the Independence of Europe,' whose members have included a number of government ministers."[8]

This view of the Kennedy assassination is doubtless believed by just about everyone in the Soviet Union, ordinary readers as well as those whose job it is to propagate it. Most KGB agents, brought up with the conviction that capitalist regimes are rotten to the core, must sincerely believe that Lyndon Johnson, a group of rich Texans, the CIA, and the Mafia were accomplices in the assassination of President Kennedy. Their propagation of the conspiracy abroad was disinformation, whether the propagators believed it to be well founded or knew it to be false. Regardless of mere facts, in the Soviet version of Marxism the conspiracy was by historical necessity "objectively" true.

Numerous examples of disinformation put forth by the KGB have been given in recently published books and magazines. Generally, there is a specific KGB maneuver: a piece of false news planted somewhere, or a tendentious interpretation of some fact, and that is the end of it. The nature of the disinformation examined in this book is different; what we see here is ongoing, varied propaganda, which seized on every opportunity to present the absurd act of an isolated individual as an immense conspiracy bringing to light the alleged corruption of the United States' political structure. Thus does disinformation create myth.

A myth, in the strict sense of the term, comes into being in the course of time with the countless contributions of ordinary people who have no personal interest in distorting the facts—for example, the myths of primitive religions or the legends that abound in each country's history. There are other myths, of a different nature, too absurd to survive for long—for example, the myth of Mussolini or Hitler for Europeans in the prewar era, or the myth of Stalin for the Russians in the 1930s and 1940s (and for many Americans during the war years). Similarly, the myth of the conspiracy in the case of President Kennedy's assassination, in contrast to myth strictly speaking, did not arise spontaneously, did not develop naturally: it was elaborated, fostered, and became, for almost everyone, common knowledge—historical truth. The collective illusion was the result of subtle propaganda maneuvers and disinformation at the start, although as it gathered momentum, only limited direction from Moscow was needed.

The propagation of false news that followed the assassination, cultivated day after day, operated in the same way a contagious illness turns into an epidemic: people infected one another. It was enough for the Moscow experts to plant the poison in a few places, and thousands of individuals would then innocently infect masses of people with it. It was thus a special sort of disinformation campaign, whose aim was to distort, in the eyes of the whole world, a specific incident, and one that continued over a period of years.

In order to understand how disinformation was sown around the assassination, the reader should first have a thorough knowledge of the information available. This is contained in the 900 pages of the report published by the Warren Commission—which rests on the impressive work of all investigative agencies of the United States and whose only flaw is a misleading section on Oswald's background and character.[9] A large part of this book, therefore, will revise the misinformation unintentionally given by the commission on this subject. With this additional information at their disposal, the readers will then be shown how prejudiced, disinformed, and misinformed writers and newspeople disinformed or misinformed the European public, and then a growing segment of the American public. So much was written about the "conspiracy" that some readers will find it hard to recognize that they were mystified for over twenty years.

This book will show that not a line has to be changed in the *Warren Report* with respect to the essential facts. There is nothing in the report to justify the slightest criticism, except for the report's interpretation of Oswald's act. The commission's mistake here was to rely on the conclusions of Wesley J. Liebeler, the assistant counsel in charge of investigating Oswald's background and possible motives, who saw a "committed Marxist"[10] behind a mediocre young man chiefly interested in improving his lot, and whose every action was for personal reasons.

Failing to understand Oswald, this assistant counsel had to conclude that "no motives or group of motives [could] be ascribed to him"[11] and that "no one will ever know what passed through [his] mind during the week before November 22, 1963."[12] The crime remained unexplained, and many people were led to believe that something had happened that was too dreadful to be disclosed.

A revision of the misleading chapter of the *Warren Report* will make clear that President Kennedy was assassinated by a frustrated, insignificant individual who believed that his wife had just decided to leave him;[13] that he had lost his children as well, and to whom an extraordinary combination of circumstances had given the chance to show all the people who had never paid him the slightest attention and to show his wife, who made fun of his ideas,[14] that he was someone to be reckoned with.

Having established Oswald's motives, this book will show how amateur detectives, not realizing they were serving the Soviet Union, convinced many Europeans that President Kennedy had been the victim of a huge conspiracy involving a range of villains from rich Texans and the CIA to the Dallas police and the gangsters imagined to be at their command; that Lyndon B. Johnson knew what was being planned; and, that after the success of an assassination that gave him the presidency, he appointed a commission of inquiry instructed to protect the guilty parties. These Europeans wondered whether there was any security in being protected by a country so fallen into disarray and official immorality. Against the backdrop of the Vietnam War, so unpopular in Europe, and then Watergate, the criminal nature of which Europeans failed to understand and which they sometimes misinterpreted as a mere settling of accounts, the most absurd accusations were believed.

The allegations of those who proclaimed before any investigation had begun that the Dallas tragedy had a mysterious or scandalous side were the first attempts to denigrate America. Shortly after the assassination the *New York Times* pointed out that "in France particularly, people were listening to a Communist tale, spread by Communist newspapers" that Oswald was "part of a plot."[15] One French voter out of four chose the Communist candidate in those days. After the publication of the *Warren Report,* the *New York Times* stressed that conspiracy theories were "held intensively, particularly in Paris."[16] The first series of articles giving a complete conspiracy theory, written by a former member of the Communist party, Thomas Buchanan, was published in *L'Express,* the most influential French magazine.[17] The New York correspondent (Léo Sauvage) of the most important French daily, *Le Figaro,* was already writing a book about the "conspiracy" while the Warren Commission's investigation was still underway and before it had published anything.[18] The first interview accusing the Warren Commission of not seeking the truth was given by an American "progressive," Mark Lane, to one of the most respected French monthlies, also before the publication of the *Warren Report.*[19] This book, therefore, will give much attention to the propagation of the conspiracy story in France, which was and is a key target in the Soviet campaign to weaken or destroy the Atlantic Alliance.

Mark Lane, who declared that "practically the only way to inform the American people" was "to speak in Europe,"[20] had been able, while in England, to gain the confidence and backing of Nobel Prize–winner Bertrand Russell. One of nine books on the issue[21] published in Germany, Switzerland, The Netherlands, and England by a writer *persona grata* in Moscow, Joachim Joesten, bore the title *The Case against Lyndon B. Johnson in the Assassination of President Kennedy.*[22] Paralleling the development of the disinformation campaign in Europe, the number of Americans who believed in the "conspiracy" grew rapidly.

In the process of analyzing the anti-American campaign, this book will show that the Kennedy assassination had not been premeditated and was, one might venture to say, an accident. Since there was no conspiracy, nothing will ever come to light that could add to the available documentation. As a final account of the assassination, this book is thus also addressed to those interested in contemporary American history.

Chapter 1 examines the comments of the media in the weeks following the assassination, and chapter 2 examines the beginning of the separate but complementary forms of disinformation—one by independent individuals, the other by Soviet professionals—between those early weeks and the publication of the *Warren Report.*

Chapter 3 shows how the Warren Commission was organized and how it functioned, pays homage to the quality of its work, and explains how it was led to declare itself incapable of uncovering Oswald's motives. Chapters 4 and 5 examine all the points on which the Warren Commission was mistaken. These chapters determine the real reasons behind Oswald's trip to Europe after his discharge from the Marine Corps, his decision to stay in the Soviet Union, and his attempt to get a visa for Cuba. The effect of Oswald's dyslexia and of quarrels with his wife on his psyche are analyzed, correcting the portrait of Oswald drawn by the commission.

Chapter 6 discusses the propagation of the conspiracy story in Europe and shows how it flourished, thanks to the disinformation process, after the publication of the *Warren Report.* Chapter 7 shows how the myth spread in the United States, leading to the creation of the second commission of inquiry, the House Select

Committee on Assassinations, whose function was to examine whether the misinformation or disinformation that had so disturbed public opinion had any basis. Its work is examined in chapter 8.

The most successful books on the assassination "conspiracy," published between the time the possibility of a second investigation was mentioned in the media in 1975 and the time the Committee on Ballistic Acoustics, established by the National Research Council in 1980, disproved the presence of a second sniper—and therefore definitively destroyed the conspiracy theory—are reviewed in chapter 9, as are the comments of the media upon the twentieth anniversary of the Kennedy assassination. In conclusion, chapter 10 sums up the body of misinformation and disinformation examined in the preceding chapters.

1

Disinformation in 1963

Twenty years ago the Dallas tragedy was called the event of the century; it appears now that the label was justified, not because of the event itself, but because America began to lose its prestige immediately after President Kennedy's death. Those who, even before the investigation began, cried scandal or alleged that there was more to his assassination than the public was being told, succeeded in planting the first doubts in Europe as to the United States' right to preeminence.

William McKinley, the twenty-fifth President of the United States, had also been struck down by an assassin. For Americans born after 1960, John F. Kennedy is a figure hardly more exciting than McKinley, and many of their elders—who saw him and Jacqueline Kennedy as the prince and princess in a glorious fairy tale—have since come to understand that his untimely death prevented him from achieving greatness.

History books yet to be written, even if they devote many pages to his presidency, will give only a few brief sentences to the last day of his life. The confusion surrounding his assassination, however, will be thoroughly examined in the chapters on the relations between the United States and Europe. And it will be explained that if Oswald was described as the instrument of a powerful group of conspirators or as a scapegoat, and that if the distinguished members of the Warren Commission of official inquiry were accused of taking part in another conspiracy—a conspiracy to hide the truth—it was for one reason. America's enemies knew that that theory's acceptance would erode the prestige of the United States in Europe and would call its system of government into question at home.

At the time of the Kennedy assassination, there were a fair number of Europeans who automatically and unquestioningly followed the Communist party line. Soon others, who knew that scandal and mystery sell, wanted to cash in on the tragedy. The media published false information and proposed the most absurd hypotheses. They failed to see the implications of the conspiracy theory and, playing into the hands of the Communists, stigmatized Dallas and discredited Washington. Sensationalist coverage of the event, ridiculing or denouncing the United States, was all the more persuasive when it appeared in conservative newspapers such as *Le Figaro,* or magazines such as *L'Express,* the most important French weekly. The public trusted respected journalists who cried scandal; the ramifications of this scandal, the journalists said, were such that Washington had no choice but to cover its tracks. Books written on the subject, which will be briefly reviewed later, had a profound effect on public opinion. Even well-intentioned Europeans began to question the United States' national unity and the integrity of her leaders. The French and the Germans listened more sympathetically to the neutralists, hostile to the United States, who were demanding the withdrawal of U.S. troops from Europe, and who were unconcerned by the possibility of the United States returning to its discarded policy of isolation.

On November 24, 1963, two days after the assassination, *Pravda* published a piece that set the tune: "The more details are reported, the darker and more shameful this entire story becomes. . . . It brings to mind other, of course much less important, acts of bands of gangsters whose connections often lead to very high-placed, extreme right-wing circles of their protectors."[1] And on November 26 readers of France's Communist daily, *L'Humanité,* were told: "We are confronted with a political crime that was long in the making, and with a far-reaching conspiracy plotted by American extremists who wish to give their country's policy a new direction, pointing towards war and fascism."

Several circumstances had caused the Soviet Union to intensify its efforts to undermine the Western bloc in 1962: American ascendency in Europe seemingly firmly established then; the monitoring of Soviet air space by the U-2 until 1960; the exodus of East

Germans that led to the building of the Berlin Wall; the obvious deterioration of Soviet relations with China; and the withdrawal of Soviet missile bases from Cuba. The job of Soviet propaganda services was to convince the United States' allies that union under the leadership of a "decadent country" could have disastrous consequences for them. General de Gaulle had suffered humiliations during the war years at the hands of those he called the "Anglo-Saxons," and among his entourage it was considered acceptable to criticize the United States—although at the time of the Cuban missile crisis, General de Gaulle had immediately expressed solidarity with the United States. An intensified anti-American campaign would bear fruit especially in France. The misinformation published in the foreign press in the first weeks after the assassination was the basis for the disinformation that followed.

The situation had been clear from the outset. Early newscasts reported that the assassin was an employee of the Texas School Book Depository, from where the shots had been fired. His name was Lee Harvey Oswald. Witnesses placed him on an upper floor of the building at the time of the assassination, and he had stayed behind after the other workers had gone to lunch; the evidence included his rifle, found between two rows of cartons. Immediately after the shots rang out, he left the building. After stopping by his lodgings to pick up a revolver, he shot and killed a cruising patrolman, J. D. Tippit, who had challenged him. He ducked into a movie theater to flee his pursuers and was arrested there.

The day after the assassination more incriminating evidence was found that pointed to him as the killer. The handwriting on a mail order for a rifle to be shipped to a post office box he had rented was identified as his. His wife confirmed that he owned a rifle similar to the one found. He had walked into the Texas School Book Depository in the morning with a long brown package.[2]

Oswald was gunned down on Sunday, November 24, while being moved to the county jail—in front of a camera crew that filmed the scene for millions of viewers. On the next day the *New York Times* was able to give out accurate information on his murderer. Jack Ruby was a small-time operator in the nightclub and gambling world. He had had several brushes with the law in Chicago and Dallas for minor misdemeanors, but he did not have a record of any felonies; between 1949 and 1963 he was arrested eight times by the Dallas Police Department on suspicion of carrying a concealed weapon, for violating liquor laws, for permitting dancing in his club after hours, for simple assault (he was found not guilty), for ignoring traffic summonses.[3] He was described as neurotic and excitable at all times. Strong emotions and loyalties were the mark of the man. He had a reputation for kindness and generosity. As a young boy in Chicago, he would strike anybody who would disparage President Roosevelt. He loved every president. He had a desperate yearning for social acceptance. Several friends of his confirmed that after the shooting he was very, very nervous, "very upset, almost on the verge of collapse."[4]

On November 26 the media gave out more details concerning Ruby. He was no angel, but he was not a criminal. One of his friends was sure that Ruby thought killing Oswald would make him a hero, and another said that when he got something in his mind, it just built up and built up. He was uncontrollable when angry.[5] The important Paris evening newspaper, *France-Soir*, however, described him as a small-time drug dealer for the Mafia with a long criminal record. *Le Figaro*, the influential morning newspaper, spoke of how he had managed to get into police headquarters on the evening of the assassination, how he had mingled with journalists from other cities and distributed invitations to his nightclub. Further information was published about his past: he had worked as a salesman of novelty items; he had scalped tickets at theaters and sports stadiums.[6] The evening newspaper *Le Monde* confirmed that he was known for his impulsive temperament and that his need to make himself noticed was general knowledge.[7]

None of this fits the portrait of the typical professional hit man who agrees to kill only when he can cover his tracks; his victim's body is found in a restaurant or on a sidewalk, and he always has an alibi. It was obvious that Ruby was not a professional killer nor the sort of man to be involved in a conspiracy to kill the president. Why would a man of fifty-two consent to spend the rest of his life in prison without ever being able to collect the payoff he would have been promised?

He was so sentimental he "cried like a baby" when one of his dogs was hurt.[8] That morning he had left a dog in his car when he went to the Western Union office to send a money order to one of his employees.[9] Coming out of Western Union, he saw a small group of people gathering in front of police headquarters and walked over to see what was going on. He acted spontaneously, impulsively, when by pure chance he found himself face to face with the president's assassin. He never left home without his revolver because he always carried all his money—a thick roll of bills—on him, probably in order to impress other people. His role in the course of events was the intrusion of a not terribly bright, impulsive passerby into the tragedy.

Between the Friday of the assassination and the Sunday of the murder, few people considered the possibility of Oswald's having accomplices, aside from the Soviet propagandists who immediately seized the opportunity to vilify the United States. It was only when Ruby stepped into the picture that the public began to have doubts about what had really happened. As it was then essential to ascertain whether Ruby's involvement was limited to the final seconds of Oswald's life, the investigators left no stone unturned in their study of his background and associations; his character and interests are scrutinized in an appendix to the *Warren Report*.[10]

If Ruby had been involved in a conspiracy, he would surely have met or called at least one accomplice after the president's assassination. The commission drew up a minute-by-minute account of his activities during the seventy-two hours preceding Oswald's murder and questioned all the people with whom he had had the slightest contact. Many of those with whom he had had dealings even in the distant past gave detailed information about him. The testimony given by friends, acquaintances, and employees indicates that Ruby was simpleminded, uneducated,[11] that he was acting on impulses[12] and was unable to plan anything in advance,[13] that he thought he was a businessman, rightfully respected. He believed that it was somehow his duty to correct any wrong he saw.[14] He used the word class quite often; everything had to have class.[15]

His nightclub was a cheap place with a small orchestra and three or four striptease dancers, where coffee, beer or Coca-Cola were served; but as a friend of his observed admiringly, Ruby was living in the sparkling world of theater people. In the afternoons Ruby tried to find and promote gadgets that would make him wealthy.

When Ruby learned of the president's death, he wept and sobbed. He closed his nightclub out of respect and was indignant that his competitors remained open. That evening, having succeeded in entering police headquarters between two journalists with press cards pinned on their coats, he had tried to show off, to make himself useful.[16] He was said to have been carried away by the excitement of history. Later on he demonstrated an exercising device he was trying to promote to a group of employees at a newspaper office.[17]

After the assassination the FBI and the sheriff's office received anonymous telephone calls in which threats to kill Oswald were made. One policeman told Ruby, "They should cut this guy inch by inch into ribbons," and a striptease dancer commented: "In England they would drag him through the streets and would have hung him."[18] In this lynch mob atmosphere it appeared to Ruby that if somebody crushed "the complete nothing, the zero who would kill a man like President Kennedy,"[19] everyone would applaud.

On Sunday, November 24, Oswald was to be transferred at 10:00 A.M. Ruby left his apartment shortly before 11:00. At about 11:20, having walked over to the police department to satisfy his curiosity, Ruby noticed after standing there for a while that a policeman stationed at the top of a ramp leading down to the basement was looking the other way. He walked down the ramp.[20] After a few moments Oswald emerged.

In the Chicago neighborhood where Ruby grew up, street fights were a frequent occurrence, and the police officer vaguely represented might and right, respectability and success. One of Ruby's acquaintances from his youth said that Ruby had a deep respect for law enforcement, that if he had been somewhat larger physically, he would have liked to have become a police officer.[21] "You could call him a frustrated policeman," said a friend immediately after the murder. At his interrogation, Ruby said that his heart was with the police department and that he had hoped there would someday be an opportunity for him to help the police in a battle, to become part of it.[22]

On the eve of the president's assassination, Ruby talked about opening another club and was looking for a financial backer. Twelve hours before shooting Oswald he had agreed to meet a friend for dinner the following evening.[23] The morning of the shooting of Oswald, Ruby had read in the newspaper "a heartbreaking letter" written to the president's little girl. Just three minutes before shooting Oswald, he had been standing in line at the Western Union office, patiently awaiting his turn, as he had had nothing else to do. "You killed my President, you rat," he shouted at Oswald as he fired.[24] Ruby felt that the police would envy him for getting the chance to destroy the Communist; he was the one who was doing what everyone had been wishing for; he expected to be congratulated.

In the early days after the assassination, the inefficiency of the protection given the president by the Secret Service, as well as the incompetence of the Dallas police, the protests of innocence by Oswald, who had neither the appearance nor the comportment of a killer, the strangeness of Ruby's appearance on the scene—all of these factors led the public to think, justifiably enough, that the ramifications of a conspiracy would be rapidly uncovered. Articles and books were quickly published that brought out into the open the inconsistencies in the statements made by the Dallas police, the district attorney, and the doctors in Dallas. In the week following the assassination, the Justice Department was already worried about the publicity given to the comments of the Dallas police, which were taken as the official explanation of the event. And the disinformation process began by making Ruby out to be the lowest sort of mobster—a hit man working for the Mafia, the Dallas police, the CIA.

On Sunday, before Oswald's death had been announced, political analysts invited by Soviet radio discussed the significance of the assassination. The guilty parties were "influential groups of politicians" whose backers were "big monopolies, especially those connected with the production of arms and oil interests abroad." It was they who, "foaming at the mouth, opposed the solution of the Negro problem in the spirit of the twentieth century." Jean-Paul Sartre was quoted as an authority: "The murder shows the fanaticism to which the racial struggle in the United States leads."[25]

Soviet foreign broadcasting is received clearly in many countries. For years European and American false news about the "conspiracy" the Kremlin judged useful for propaganda purposes was broadcast in scores of languages.

East German commentaries echoed the statements made by the Soviet Union: "The land of unlimited opportunities has demonstrated to the world that even the impossible is possible there . . . that it is the land where murder and assassination reign. . . . Who are these gentry who let a police officer be killed because he most likely knew too much about the instigators of the assassination? Kennedy became a victim of the same North American freedom which he himself extolled as the ultimate good . . . this kind of freedom that they would like to force upon us with the aid of NATO and the atomic threats of Bonn."[26] *L'Humanité* also described the chain of events as a plot masterminded by the police.

The *New York Times* report on the reaction in France said: "The murder of Lee Harvey Oswald . . . has caused many friends of the United States to question the internal stability of Europe's protector. Another effect is that a normally prudent people are at least listening to a Communist tale, spread by party newspapers, that Oswald was eliminated as part of a plot." In London, said the newspaper correspondent, everything that happens in the United States "is put on the scales that forever weigh the United States' right to lead the Western world."[27]

After Oswald's death the Soviet press was prompt to spell out the party line. On November 26 *Pravda* announced: "It was done by the same people who prepared and committed the assassination of the President, done by the same 'ultras.' . . . The city authorities in Dallas who organized Oswald's transfer from one jail to another acted in the way that the protectors and accomplices of gangsters— who have many times covered up the traces of dark deeds—usually act in the U.S.A." *Izvestia* concurred: "Oswald apparently understood what awaited him when he saw Ruby. Weren't these two men linked in the same plot, the same scheme? And weren't people of the Dallas Police Department involved in the plot? All the circumstances of President Kennedy's tragic death give grounds to the belief that the assassination was conceived and executed by ultra-right-wing fascist and racist circles."[28] The next day *Pravda* said: "Ruby was only executing someone's desire, relying in this on the active cooperation of the Dallas police. . . . They are covering the traces in Dallas. . . . This is being done by purely gangster methods." *Izvestia* claimed that "the reactionary figures who murdered Kennedy undoubtedly personified the savagery and banditry of the political mores of the U.S., the sensational character of the press, the corruption of the police," that the event "recalled the worst moments in human history, the time of the coming to power of fascism in Germany."[29] Tass, the telegraphic press agency, distributed the Soviet version: "Oswald could not have planned and carried out such a murder alone."[30] This version was improved the next day: "It was not Oswald who assassinated the President but somebody else carefully protected by the Dallas police."[31]

Cuba followed immediately with a Foreign Ministry statement: "The assassination was a provocation against world peace perfectly and minutely prepared by the most reactionary section of the U.S. Powerful forces of reaction in the U.S. are using all resources and influence to cover up the intellectual authors and the true motives behind the assassination."[32]

On November 26 *Le Monde* reported that three cartridge cases and the brown paper in which the rifle had been wrapped were found on the sixth floor of the Book Depository, near a carton of books the sniper had used as a seat and others he had used to prop up the rifle. The report stated that a photograph found among his things showed him brandishing a rifle, with a revolver tucked into his belt—the rifle that had been used to assassinate the president and the revolver that had killed Tippit.[33] *Le Monde* also raised the possibility that the police had carefully chosen in advance a suspect who could be convicted of the crime, while protecting the true assassin, and that Oswald could not have been the only person to shoot the president. It added that General Charles de Gaulle was right, that it was dangerous for a country to allow its security to depend upon a distant country, however powerful that country might be.[34] Speculations and rumors were already being publicized; for instance, *Paris-Presse* said that according to the FBI, Oswald had an accomplice beside him at the window of the Book Depository.[35] *Le Figaro* justifiably accused the Dallas police of giving out contradictory information but wrongly accused them of knowingly telling outright lies.[36]

The public was informed very early that Oswald, having left the United States for the Soviet Union at the age of twenty, had been a worker in Minsk and had returned home two years later with a wife and child. The first time he was questioned, he denied being a Communist but had called himself a Marxist. *L'Express* was vehement: "Lee Oswald, known to the police everywhere, but allowed to pass by the Dallas police. . . . Are the Texas magnates and their police force capable of setting America ablaze the way the Reichstag fire did Germany? . . . There is so much overwhelming evidence against Oswald that it is not plausible."[37] *L'Humanité* saw the affair as having been in the works for a long time, plotted by American extremists, whose "cover up" had "a troubling resemblance to the Reichstag fire." Instead of quoting the French Communist paper, *Pravda* published an opinion voiced by the general secretary of the French Socialist party: "Hitler did the same thing in his time. All this is too reminiscent of the burning of the Reichstag."[38]

L'Express sent a couple of journalists to Dallas. A startling headline announced that they had uncovered the conspiracy, without a thread of evidence in the article to back up this claim.[39] "Perhaps some day a plot will be discovered but the climate we found in Dallas is just as deadly as any plot."[40] The translation of a long portion of the article, the one describing the "deadly climate," appeared in *Izvestia*.[41]

Five weeks after the assassination, *Paris-Match* noted: "It is scarcely an exaggeration to declare that the affair is on its way to being filed and classified in America . . . while . . . in Europe, it remains by far the main subject of conversation. . . . The explanation given, that Ruby, a police informer, the proprietor of a house of ill-repute, a pimp, and a professional gangster killed Oswald in patriotic indignation, is found laughable. . . . It justifies the suspicion of a desperate cover-up . . . from the White House to Murder Inc."[42] *Le Monde* said that nothing could happen in Dallas without the consent of a hierarchy controlled by "seven key leaders."[43] *Stern* assured its readers that Oswald had been killed because "he was on the verge of telling the truth."[44]

General de Gaulle commented privately:

> This is the story of two races which are unable to get along. This is the way things always happen in countries where racial hatreds clash.[45] The police is in collusion with the extremists. . . . The falsehood consists of trying to make people believe that this guy acted out of exaltation and love for Communism. . . . They were keeping him around in case they needed him. . . . The guy ran away because he must have been on his guard. . . . They were going to kill him on the spot, but things didn't go as planned. He defended himself. A policeman was killed.[46] The police went and found an informer who couldn't refuse to cooperate with them, who was in their power.[47]

General de Gaulle added that his views had been proved correct:

"America is less and less a stable, dependable country."[48] People believed General de Gaulle had reached this conclusion from confidential information received by French intelligence, but he was just expressing a personal opinion. His view was soon known. A Broadway theater in the United States that was showing a play on the "conspiracy" quoted one of his public statements in its advertising.

If many of the French drew the same conclusions from what they were hearing, the work of the Soviet propaganda services proved useful. France withdrew from NATO in March 1966; it may have been in part a consequence of reasonings similar to those of General de Gaulle.

Day after day, evidence of Oswald's guilt—of his guilt alone—continued to build up. Tests showed that the bullets had been shot from his rifle, which had been left during the two preceding months in the house of Ruth Paine, a friend who had offered shelter to his wife and child. No one besides Oswald could have taken the weapon; his fingerprints were on it, on the paper in which it had been wrapped, and on the cartons of books he had moved.[49] If he had been innocent, there would have been no reason for him to leave the scene immediately and to kill the police officer, J. D. Tippit.

Tippit, it was said, had no valid reason to challenge Oswald; the description of the assassin transmitted on the police radio was too vague. However, ten minutes after the assassination, Oswald had been recognized on a bus, on which he rode for a few minutes, by a woman who had been his landlady for a week. She described him later: "He looked like a maniac; he was dirty. He looked so bad in his face, and his face was distorted."[50] A man of this appearance walking down a residential street in the middle of the day would certainly seem suspicious to a patrolman. Oswald would have been approached by Tippit that day even if no description of the president's killer had been given on the radio. The meeting between them took place three-quarters of an hour after the assassination. Tippit had heard nothing but talk of the assassination on the radio that was his link to headquarters.

As for the "racists" who were accused by the foreign press of being behind the plot to assassinate John F. Kennedy, they could not have cared less what happened to him: desegregation had started with Dwight D. Eisenhower, was carried on by Kennedy, and in the event of his demise, would be implemented by Lyndon Johnson, who would automatically succeed him and apply the Democratic party's platform. President Kennedy's opponents could hardly think, therefore, that eliminating him would change the course of events. Looking back to the 1930s, President Roosevelt's enemies were convinced the country would be saved if the man they called "the Bolshevik" and "the warmonger" were not leading the country. Millionaires and isolationists were thoroughly frustrated, but it did not occur to any of them to resort to extreme measures to get a president they hated removed from office.

Conspirators would not have chosen Oswald or Ruby, but a professional like James Earl Ray, Martin Luther King's assassin, who, after his discharge from the army, had spent fourteen out of twenty years in prison.[51] They would have given the killer a rifle comparable to the one Ray said he had received $700 to purchase.[52] Oswald's rifle had cost about $20;[53] it had no sling, and he made one himself with a makeshift strap.[54]

Oswald had been hired to work in the Texas School Book Depository several weeks before the assassination, before it was known that the president would one day be in a motorcade under its windows. Le Figaro said, as did L'Express, that the evidence of his guilt was "too massive, too perfect, really, not to give one the impression that it had been made to order."[55] (In other words, a suspect is probably guilty when the evidence of his innocence is massive, perfect.) Le Figaro added that Oswald's behavior, if he was guilty, lacked "psychological plausibility"; while the correspondent for Le Monde, using the same phraseology, said that the official version of the event had "a certain psychological plausibility": "We can see Oswald only too well, the unstable man with his obsessions, whom neither Russia nor Cuba would accept in spite of his primary leftism, a man whose citizenship the United States refused to revoke—that is, somebody no one takes seriously—who wants to destroy what embodies the framework of society, status, happiness. . . . As for Ruby, he dreams only of respectability, of 'class,' of identification with those he admired. Why, given the inexcusable failings of the local police, should we see more in the confrontation between Oswald and Ruby than the chance meeting of two warped loners who had literally gone mad?"[56] This was a wise judgment, considering that it was made one week after the assassination, when everybody believed that Oswald had deeply rooted political convictions.

European newspapers of different shades of opinion—and which liked to editorialize, as shown in the preceding pages—were not necessarily influenced by their own political bias in their interpretation of the event. There were Europeans, true friends of the United States, who were immediately convinced that a conspiracy would be revealed, while other Europeans, who admired Russia, saw the inanity of the conspiracy theory. The aim of the Soviet propagandists was to convince as many foreigners as possible that they should add "something is rotten in America" to their pronouncement "there is a conspiracy," thus joining their Communist fellow countrymen.

The disinformation technique is clearly revealed in the series of articles on the assassination found in the weekly *New Times* (Novoe Vremia) published by the International Information Department of the Communist party (*Novoe Vremia* is represented as being published by *Trud*, the organ of the labor unions.) Most anti-American disinformation is disseminated throughout the world by the foreign editions of *Novoe Vremia*. The articles are written according to the instructions from above—like all foreign affairs articles in the Soviet Union.

New Times, which describes itself as "a Soviet weekly of world affairs," is not a magazine in the usual sense of the term. The only advertiser is the Soviet government. *New Times'* function is to distribute pro-Soviet and anti-American propaganda; the success of this unprepossessing periodical is not measured in terms of money, but rather by the decrease of American prestige and the increase of Russian influence in the world. (The distribution—in the political world only—of the French pro-Soviet newsletter described in the introduction of this book was modeled on the distribution of *New Times*—to persons of importance, in different fields, who could influence public opinion in their country.)

New Times announced in its first issue (January 1956) that it was published in Russian, English, French, German, Spanish, Polish, Czech, Romanian, Hungarian and Swedish. (Over the years, Portuguese and Italian replaced Romanian and Hungarian.) *New Times* may be obtained anywhere in the world, from the few stores or firms that handle Soviet books and publications as agencies or correspondents of Mezhdunarodnaia Kniga (International Books) —some of which seem to be normal commercial enterprises. There are five of them in the United States and three in Great Britain. Other countries have generally between one and four stores where Soviet publications may be found. For example, Malta, Singapore, and Egypt have one store; Iran, Syria, and Hong Kong have two or three. It would seem that the number of outlets depends more on regional conditions than on the importance of the country in the eyes of the Soviet Union. (There are two outlets in Japan, but twenty-one, a surprising number, in India.) Subscriptions may be placed with all those stores.

Editions of *New Times* in other international languages are distributed in the same way in French-speaking, Spanish-speaking, or other countries. The Russian edition is read in the Soviet Union and in its client states where the study of Russian is obligatory in schools, and where Russian is replacing English as the international language.

New Times indicates the party line to Communist parties everywhere—jointly with the monthly review *Problems of Peace and Socialism,* and with *International Affairs,* also organs of disinformation. (In the issue of *New Times* that published the voluminous report to the Twenty-seventh Congress delivered by Gorbachev, the editor stressed that the problems dealt with were "associated with the further strengthening of socialist cooperation.")

In 1978 the CIA "cited the following estimates of annual Soviet expenditures for key foreign propaganda outlets during the latter years of the 1970s: Tass, $550 million; Novosti Press Agency, $500 million; *Pravda,* $250 million; *New Times,* $200 million; and Radio Moscow foreign service, $700 million."[57] The Soviet dissident Stanislas Levchenko, who was before his defection the *New Times* correspondent in Tokyo,[58] said that for the most part the *Times* correspondents are, as he himself was, KGB agents; their job was their cover.[59]

It is easy to follow the development of the campaign of lies and calumny after the assassination of President Kennedy by examining in chronological order the *New Times* articles devoted to the subject. The reason for concentrating on the reading of *New Times* in this book is that it is like having laid out before us instructions given by the Soviet Union's Central Committee of the

Communist party to *New Times* over the years, on the matter of presenting the assassination. In other words, it gives the complete story of the Soviet disinformation on the event. Studying other Soviet publications that do not specialize in anti-American propaganda would give only part of the story of Soviet disinformation on the matter; and former issues of *World Marxist Review,* the English-language edition of *Problems of Peace and Socialism,* and *International Affairs* are not found as easily as *New Times.* The study of European publications would demonstrate only the end result of the disinformation process.

The first *New Times* article concerning the assassination was published on December 11, 1963.[60] (The president was killed on November 22, 1963.) *New Times,* like Tass, often uses as its point of departure quotations, with the reference, of misinformation and disinformation found in books and newspapers published abroad, preferably in the United States, thus giving them worldwide distribution. This article was a mixture of irresponsible rumors and willful disinformation trumped up by the Kremlin.

This writer will not attempt to correct all the misinformation or to refute all of the disinformation published. To review all the contradictory allegations made by the conspiracy theorists and explain why they are wrong would require thousands of pages. The writer will limit himself to the consideration only of the major allegations. The task is to establish the basic facts and then show how they were distorted, how disinformation worked in a particular case, and how effective it is. (If the writer's rectifications contribute to correcting the general view of the event, it will be an added beneficial result of his research.)

The opening sentence of the *New Times* article reads: "Immediately after Kennedy's death the Dallas police, who had so signally failed to safeguard their country's President, hastened to release their version of the crime."[61] The Dallas police did not release any version of the crime. The district attorney, Henry Wade, and several police officers gave, individually, their personal impressions when interviewed. Whenever they mentioned the possibility of a conspiracy, they presumed it had been organized by the Soviet Union; Americans who believed right from the start that Oswald had accomplices accused only Russia or Cuba.

According to *New Times,* Oswald was a godsend, a newcomer with no relatives or friends. The Soviets thought it wise to ignore that he was married, that his wife and daughter were Russian. As for the assertion that he was a newcomer, the fact is that on his return from Russia he had lived on the outskirts of Dallas at his mother's, near his brother; he settled in Dallas not too long afterward. *Le Monde* was quoted: The police had prepared a suspect beforehand, but *New Times* neglected to mention that *Le Monde* had also said that the version of Oswald's guilt, and of his being the only guilty party, had a certain psychological plausibility. The only papers mentioned in support of the claim that the Dallas police version had been greeted with unconcealed irony were the *Courrier de Genève* and *Al Akhbar*. The *New York Journal-American* was quoted: "Because of what had happened in Dallas, Americans felt ashamed and a little afraid." The ineffectiveness of the Secret Service, whose job is to protect the president, and the Dallas police's inability to protect Oswald were the reasons for American shame and uneasiness.

New Times launched a few falsehoods that were later repeated—or imagined independently—by the partisans of a conspiracy theory. For instance, "experts on firearms have vouched that there could not have been only one man firing at the President," and "Oswald had dropped hints that he had been in the Soviet Union as an American secret agent." Direct accusations followed such statements: "That excesses and acts of terrorism were in preparation in the South against Federal authorities and that the preparers were ultra-reactionaries and racists was known to the whole world." It was thus no longer a question of a conspiracy against the president but, rather, of the beginning of a rebellion against Washington. Texas had its share of political organizations whose platforms were absurd, just as California had its religious cults that were no less absurd. None of the Texas organizations were composed of secessionists or terrorists. According to *New Times,* "Kennedy himself received warnings from all quarters not to go to Texas."[62] This was not the case. The *Dallas Times-Herald* had called upon its readers to welcome the president with dignity and courtesy. The president of the Dallas Chamber of Commerce asserted that citizens would greet the president with warmth and pride. And indeed the president received an enthusiastic reception; the last words he heard were spoken by Texas Governor John B. Connally's wife: "Mr. President, you can't say that Dallas does not love you."[63]

New Times then compared the "frame-up" of Oswald to the "frame-up" of Van der Lubbe, the Dutchman accused of setting the Reichstag fire, "who was branded a Communist by the Nazi police." The ultraright-wing organizations were listed in the article, including the John Birch Society and the National Indignation Convention, unknown to this writer. The guilty parties were denounced: H. L. Hunt, "the multimillionaire oilman," and General Edwin A. Walker, "führer of the American ultras."

"Anyone familiar with life in present-day America," continued *New Times,* "knows of the existence there of a powerful triumvirate: politicians-police-gangsters." This statement complied with Stalin's instructions, as can be seen in the epigraph to this book's introduction. "That triple alliance finds reflection in everything, in daily events, in the press, even in art and literature." The *Daily Herald* was quoted: The ultrareactionary organizations would easily find crack marksmen among their members.

More lies followed. Oswald was "known to the police who kept an eye on him" and he had been "interviewed by an FBI agent a few days before the President's death." The FBI agent actually had made a visit to the home of Ruth Paine to interview Marina Oswald, who, soon to give birth to her second child, had moved in with the Paines when Oswald tried to go to Cuba. Oswald wanted to ask the agent to leave his wife alone and had unsuccessfully tried to see him. The visit took place after Oswald's pro-Castro activities in New Orleans were reported to the FBI office in Dallas. *New Times* continued: "After killing Tippit, [Oswald] apparently lost his head. Was it because he learned that he was to be made the scapegoat for the President's murder?" (This assertion would later be used by all those who tried to resolve the contradiction implicit in the murder of a police officer by a harmless young man who had been merely an innocent spectator of the president's assassination three-quarters of an hour earlier.)

The Dallas police were aware that there was some risk involved in moving Oswald to the county jail. An armored car had been provided. The chief of police had promised newspeople that Oswald would be transferred at a time when they could take pictures. In order to demonstrate that the police had decided to have Oswald killed, however, *New Times* claimed that hospital workers had been alerted to stand by. The article then refers to the appearance of "the sinister figure of the Chicago gangster Ruby, nicknamed 'Sparky' . . . an individual with a rich criminal past and a no less criminal present . . . who wiped out Oswald in the typical gangster fashion, by shooting his victim in the stomach." After this the police announced his case 'closed' which meant closing the case of the President's assassination as well. It was, of course, not closed. FBI agents interrogated Oswald as early as one hour after his arrest, again the next day, and once more before he was killed. (Their reports are on pages 612–25 of the *Warren Report*.) The FBI and other agencies kept hundreds of agents on the case for months as investigators for the Warren Commission, and the case was closed only in 1982.

Finally, *New Times* distorts (as many others would do in the future) the contents of a letter sent by the acting attorney general, Nicholas deB. Katzenbach, to the White House—"We must dispel all suspicions and remove all doubts"—implying that this was proof there were plans to cover up the affair.[64] (See chap. 9, below, for comments on Katzenbach's letter.)

Carelessness, disorder, negligence, and *chaos* were words found over and over again in the description of conditions at police head-quarters. Oswald's questioning was impeded by journalists who hung around in the hallways, invaded the offices, took over the telephones. The television crew made the decisions. (They had the arrangements for Oswald's transfer to another jail changed on the grounds that they needed a better angle from which to film him as he walked past.) The correspondent for *Le Figaro* stated that the information the journalists received was not always clear.[65] It consisted of incomplete and unconnected statements by witnesses or the police, which, to make matters worse, were often unfounded or misinterpreted by the journalists. This correspondent had wired on the day of the assassination that nobody knew how Oswald had been arrested, that he had killed two policemen, and that he was a deserter from the Marine Corps.

Bystanders who had seen nothing and knew nothing appeared on television screens throughout the world, saying whatever popped into their heads: "I now realize that many of the words I frantically took down from the mouths of witnesses during the next few hours were the production of imagination, shock, confusion or from something much worse—the macabre desire of some bystanders to be identified with a great tragedy, or to pretend greater firsthand knowledge of the event than they actually possessed."[66]

The arguments in support of the conspiracy theory came from incoherent statements made by the man in the street or from unfounded opinions expressed at police headquarters and at the hospital where President Kennedy had been taken. The local authorities were legally in charge—they tried to prevent the body from being taken out of the hospital and their jurisdiction[67]—but only for a short time. The Dallas police and the Dallas district attorney were completely out of their depth in dealing with such an extraordinary event. They became the center of attention for the entire world for three straight days, which further impaired their ability to function efficiently. Moreover, they felt obliged to cooperate with the swarm of reporters who had descended on Dallas.

2

Disinformation in 1964

Some of those who persistently cast doubt on the integrity of the investigators, whether they stigmatized the least important FBI agent or the chairman of the Warren Commission, were blinded by their political bias—which could have been nothing more than an automatic antiestablishment position. The particular blindness, for example, of Professor G. Robert Blakey, the chairman of the second investigative commission, the House Select Committee on Assassinations, was his obsession with the idea of the Mafia's involvement. Similarly, Wesley J. Liebeler, junior assistant counsel of the Warren Commission, was blinded by his obstinacy in seeing Oswald as committed to Marxism or communism.

Among the books that attacked the conclusions of the Warren Commission over the years were some published with the backing of the Soviets, if not entirely fabricated by them. The others, at least in the United States, were generally written by people who sincerely believed they had uncovered the truth; some of them may have been enticed by the prospect of material gain. All too human in their refusal to backtrack from a position rooted in the rumors of the first few months, they helped to build up the conspiracy theory, while those who did not believe the theory became increasingly indifferent with the passage of time.

The press campaign to make the assassination appear to have been fomented by the extreme right with the assistance of the Dallas police, the FBI, and the CIA, and later covered up by the

Warren Commission, started in Europe months before the publication of the *Warren Report*.

In February 1964 *L'Express* published a series of articles signed "T. Buchanan" under colorful headlines: "Oswald Did Not Kill," or "The No. 1 Assassin Was Wearing a Policeman's Uniform." Thomas Buchanan, an American, had been dismissed from his job at the *Washington Evening Star* in 1948, when it was discovered that he was a member of the Communist party.[1] He had left the United States and was living in Paris at the time of the assassination. A friend of his, a former member of the French Communist party,[2] had shown Buchanan's comments on the assassination to a co-editor of *L'Express,* Françoise Giroud.[3] The series was presented as a brilliant demonstration of the facts.[4] The Texas School Book Depository, Thomas Buchanan wrote, belonged to the city of Dallas; this meant Oswald was a municipal employee, hired despite his subversive opinions, which would have been impossible unless a fairly highly placed authority had intervened on his behalf. (The Texas School Book Depository was a privately owned and run business; Oswald was a nobody who happened to be on the spot, and no one cared about his opinions.)

Thomas Buchanan believed, or pretended to believe, that the railroad overpass ahead of the motorcade was off-limits to the public.[5] (Two policemen were standing guard on it, and thirteen railroad employees had positioned themselves there waiting for the motorcade to pass.)[6] He also claimed that the front windshield of the car had a small round bullet hole in it.[7] (No bullet had penetrated the windshield; a small residue of lead was found on the inside of the glass, probably from the impact of a fragment of the fatal bullet that had grazed the windshield from inside the car.)[8] He said that Oswald was a very bad shot[9] (he was an excellent marksman);[10] that the police had blocked all the exits of the building immediately after the last shot had been fired[11] (the exits were blocked approximately four minutes after Oswald had walked away)[12] and that an order to pick Oswald up had been issued at 12:30 P.M., a minute after the assassination.[13] (Oswald was arrested at 1:50 P.M. for the murder of Patrolman J. D. Tippit and taken to police headquarters before any warrant had been issued.)[14]

Constructing a scenario based on these statements, Thomas Buchanan said there had been two assassins, one on the overpass—the "hole in the windshield" proved it—the other having been

29

taken by Oswald to the depository the night before the assassination—being a "bad shot," Oswald could only stand guard.[15] He stated that there had been four accomplices: a policeman to allow Oswald to escape from the building—since "immediately" after the assassination no one had been allowed to leave it—another to issue the order to pick up Oswald,[16] an order Thomas Buchanan had to dream up in order to justify the appearance of the third accomplice, Patrolman Tippit. The fourth one was "a plain-clothes officer in an automobile whose mission was to follow Oswald." At an agreed signal, Tippit was supposed to arrest Oswald, "induce him to pull out his pistol, then kill him in self-defense; instead, Tippit had been assassinated and slain by Oswald."[17] Perhaps, Buchanan conjectured, Tippit had been the assassin lying in wait in the building, and Ruby the one posted on the overpass. Buchanan wrote: "The assassin no. 1 left the scene of the crime alone in a police car and we will have occasion to speak again of a police car occupied by a single patrolman." That "single patrolman" supposedly was Tippit. As for the second assassin, "Ruby had stayed alone in a room which gave onto the overpass and the depository."[18]

Thomas Buchanan's readers also learned that Oswald shared a post office box with a certain Hidell, "whose true identity no one ever bothered to check into."[19] (Very early on it was known that "Hidell" was the name chosen by Oswald for a forged selective service card and the one he used to order both his rifle and revolver.) Buchanan added that Ruby was a former gangster from Chicago who had once strangled another gangster, "Needlenose."[20] (This allegation may have been taken from an article in the French newspaper *L'Aurore*.)

Thomas Buchanan's version, which *L'Express* called the "official theory," goes as follows. A single bullet was shot from behind "at an angle of 45°," passed "through the President's head," "disintegrated " on the floor of the car, then "made a small round hole" on the windshield and reappeared "almost intact" on the president's stretcher.[21] (The bullet went through the President's neck, wounded Governor Connally, who was sitting in front of him, and was found on Connally's stretcher; it had been fired at an angle of 21° or less.)[22] The killer on the railroad overpass "had left his rifle behind."[23] (The reader is reminded that two police officers and thirteen railwaymen were on the overpass.) Thomas Buchanan deleted the most absurd of his allegations in the American edition of his book, which was published after the *Warren Report.*

The last of Buchanan's *L'Express* articles claimed that Dallas was run by a council composed of 250 prominent citizens headed by a seven-member group, all of whom had enormous fortunes and wielded tremendous power. Thomas Buchanan implied that the rich and powerful oilman, H. L. Hunt, "who had moved the Texas millionaires to give McCarthy financial backing," was the soul of the conspiracy.

The articles were reproduced practically everywhere in the world,[24] wrote Buchanan. The book that followed—*Who Killed Kennedy?* [25]—was published in seventeen countries, according to him.

The preface to Mark Lane's book, *Rush to Judgment,* [26] another source of disinformation, published in the summer of 1966, was written by the Oxford University professor Hugh Trevor-Roper. It was Trevor-Roper who, twenty years later, would bear most of the responsibility for the scandal surrounding Hitler's forged diaries, which he had declared to be authentic "on the strength of one afternoon's glimpse at the material."[27] Professor Trevor-Roper later recognized that Mark Lane's intentions were "suspicious" because he was politically "pretty far to the left,"[28] but by that time Mark Lane had become the best known of the many authors of books on "the conspiracy."

Less than a month after the assassination, Mark Lane had published a long article entitled "Oswald Innocent?" in the *National Guardian,* a "progressive" weekly according to its masthead, which had shown its political position in its first issue in 1948 with an article entitled "The Marshall Plan Brings Chaos and Starvation into the World." The following year the *National Guardian* declared that the Soviet Union "carried the hope of mankind" and that the United States was a police state. In the issues appearing in 1963, the year that interests us, it carried advertising for the New York School for Marxist Studies.

In his article Mark Lane relied heavily on statements made by stunned and overwhelmed policemen, taken down on the day of the assassination, thus spreading rumors that had already been proved false. He had spent a few weeks in Europe before the *Warren Report* was published. Claiming that he had useful information to give the investigators, he was allowed to testify. All he had to offer the Warren Commission was hearsay and gossip. "Were you getting evidence in Europe?" he was asked. "No," he answered, "I found that practically the only way to inform the American people is to speak in Europe."[29] Oswald's mother had originally authorized him to represent her, which enabled him, even though it soon ceased to be the case, to present himself in Europe as the family lawyer. He was thus able to attract a credulous audience.

During his trip he had been able to win the confidence of several prominent personalities who set up the "Who Killed Kennedy Committee" in England. In France he gathered together lawyers and legal experts.[30] Jean-Paul Sartre's magazine, *Les Temps modernes,* interviewed him; his allegations showed a singular capacity for telling the most extravagant stories and making people believe them.

From among the hundreds of false assertions to be found in Mark Lane's written or oral statements, we have chosen to focus on those mentioned during the interview—without omitting any of them, as these are the assertions the interviewer obviously considered the most persuasive. They can be found in almost all the articles or books by the Warren Commission's detractors, along with Lane's other allegations, year after year. "Oswald was deprived of the assistance of legal counsel";[31] "the major witness of the policeman's murder," during a telephone conversation he taped, gave him "a description of the murderer which did not fit Oswald's description."[32] Mark Lane tried, "without success, to locate her after the telephone conversation; 'she had disappeared' ";[33] "a photograph shows a man with an uncanny resemblance to Oswald standing in front of the School Book Depository at the very instant the assassination took place, but the police refused to reveal his identity and the Warren Commission has no intention of penetrating his incognito"; "a policeman swore under oath that the weapon found in the School Book Depository was a Mauser, while it was an Italian rifle"; "Oswald was given the paraffin test, there was no trace of nitrate on his face"; "Oswald was arrested for the murder of Tippit, who had been killed at 13:00, but the description of Tippit's murderer was broadcast by the police at 12:43."[34] (These allegations are disproved in *WR,* 144, 201, 552, 560, 644, 645, and *WR* 7:499.)

"I had managed," Mark Lane explained, "to get myself summoned before the Commission to present my documents and provide it with certain information on secret meetings in Dallas at which had been present, among others, Ruby, Officer Tippit and the man who had had anti-Kennedy advertisements published in one of the city's newspapers."[35] (This third man was Bernard Weissman, who explained to the commission during his questioning that he had published the advertisements for business reasons, in an attempt to curry favor with the wealthy Republicans of Dallas.) Mark Lane did not have any documents to give the commission. Chief Justice Earl Warren commented at the end of Mark Lane's second testimony: "We heard that when you were here in March . . . hopefully you would be able to tell us . . . [something] concerning the so-called meeting between Jack Ruby and others in his nightclub. And we have been pursuing you ever since with letters and entreaties to give us that information. . . . Here we pay your expenses from Europe, bring you over here and without telling us at all that you won't answer that question, you come before the Commission and refuse to testify."[36]

The story about the meeting had been invented by an irresponsible journalist or by Mark Lane himself. The commission wanted to hear him testify behind closed doors, Mark Lane asserted, but it finally agreed to give him a public hearing.[37] In fact all witnesses were given the choice of a public or a private deposition,[38] and only Mark Lane requested a public hearing; it was part of his publicity campaign. The commission decided, he concluded, that the content of his deposition "would be classified as 'top-secret,' and I knew from experience that the newspapers would not print any of it." Chief Justice Warren had reminded Mark Lane during the second deposition that like other witnesses he had been free to discuss his first testimony "before the press, and the radio, and the television."[39]

As for the "top-secret" classification, the deposition given by each witness was at the witness's disposal,[40] and all were marked "top-secret." Moreover, all of the depositions were published in the twenty-six volumes that came out shortly after the report itself. "Top-secret" is meaningless; even the White House menus are top-secret.

Obtaining the backing of *Les Temps modernes* was a real coup. The interview gave Mark Lane authority in European intellectual circles. The conspiracy myth began to grow in France on its own, not requiring much effort on the part of the Kremlin.

An article on the "conspiracy," by Bertrand Russell, published in London, gained wide attention and lent more credibility to Mark Lane. It was entitled "16 Questions on the Assassination."[41] Bertrand Russell mentioned that he was indebted to Lane for much of his information.[42] These "questions" rested on speculations, rumors, or false statements that the *Warren Report* demolished. (The pages that dealt with them—before the article was published—are as follows: for question (1) 475–80; (2) 254–58; (3) 101–5; (4) 61–195; (5) 472; (6) 447; (7) 31–40; (8) 52–60; (9) 79–117; (10) 66–67; (11) 647; (12) 560–62; (13) 651–52; (14) 175; (15) 125–28 and 647; (16) 654.)

That a respected signature should appear at the end of an article that was a rehash of easily refutable arguments can be explained by the fact that Bertrand Russell's confidential secretary was a certain Ralph Schoenman, who became the head of the London branch of Lane's Citizens Committee of Inquiry. Schoenman was an American citizen whose passport had been stamped "valid only for return to the United States" after he had made an illegal trip to China.[43] "Futile efforts to make a Russell documentary under the corrupting influence of Lane" are described by Emile De Antonio, a filmmaker who collaborated with Mark Lane and deposited his files with the State Historical Society of Wisconsin.[44]

Bertrand Russell had a statement published posthumously, dissociating himself "from many of his secretary's statements and actions on his behalf."[45] Schoenman's influence, like Mark Lane's, might already have been making itself felt in 1964.

A letter to the editor published by the *New York Times* three months before the Bertrand Russell article reads as follows.

> Your June 1 account of the speculation run rampant in Europe concerning the assassination of President Kennedy was much needed. Unfortunately, four months of travel and talk in Europe leads me to doubt with your reporters whether even the most thorough refutation by the Warren Commission of the wildly absurd theories prevalent there will have any effect.
>
> The plot-seeking mentality which pervades so many Eu-

ropean countries and the totality of ideological commitment which governs judgment in many quarters there prevent a dispassionate consideration of the evidence by a large number of people. The usual epithet "naive" frequently hurled at Americans by Europeans can hereafter be taken lightly, given the incredible example of European credulity and even gullibility in this matter.[46]

The Warren Commission had investigated Thomas Buchanan's background. It knew that the *National Guardian* was a "progressive" publication, that the names Bertrand Russell and Jean-Paul Sartre commanded respect, and that *L'Express* and *Le Figaro* were widely read. The commission did not foresee that the conspiracy story would finally come to be believed in the United States. It neglected to enlighten the public in good time about the "suspicious intentions" of Thomas Buchanan and Mark Lane, whose assertions soon appeared in the disinformation campaign of the Soviet Union. (As the years passed it was sometimes difficult to decide whether their disinformation should be classified with the disinformation by well-meaning or commercially minded people in the Western world or with the anti-American disinformation.)

3

Information and Disinformation

The Kennedy assassination, the most documented event in history, is also, oddly enough, the one about which the most nonsense has been published. Had Oswald been a fanatic, a terrorist, he would have gloried in his crime, but he protested his innocence. Therefore, the conclusion had to be, for those who did not believe him, that he was a hired assassin or, for those who believed him, that he was the victim of a Machiavellian plot. The fact is that when Oswald came to his senses after his arrest, he felt sure he would be able to extricate himself from his ghastly situation. He always believed he could easily outsmart anybody, and he was sure the police would be unable to prove his guilt.

Many years have gone by, and it is hard to realize how intense feelings were throughout the entire world at the time. The United States was at the apogee of its power, and its resources seemed inexhaustible. Its young and successful president, a symbol of the country itself, fascinated everybody. That such a charismatic life had been shattered by the willful act of an insignificant little man was too preposterous to be believed. This would explain in part why a section of the public so readily accepted the theory that John F. Kennedy had been the victim of high-level enemies (for the American rightists, the intelligence department of a hostile country; for the European leftists, Texas millionaires or anyone else their tabloids—unwittingly serving the Kremlin—could conjure up). This may also explain why some commentators, following the commission's interpretation, made of Oswald an emulator of

Herostratus, who burned the famous Ephesus Temple in order to immortalize his name, whereas his act was merely the final gesture of a man defeated by life.

The Warren Commission's report shows that Lee Harvey Oswald, "a misfit and a loner," killed the president and confirms that Ruby, overcome by his emotions, impulsively took it upon himself to play judge and jury. All the essential documentation can be found in the report and the twenty-six volumes of hearings and exhibits published by the Warren Commission. The seven members of the commission had ultimate responsibility for the investigation, but the actual research was handed over to fourteen assistant counsels. Their role was first to sort out the information they received from professional investigators belonging to various federal agencies—principally the FBI, which submitted over 2,300 reports—then to obtain additional information by hearing testimony from witnesses, and finally to write their reports.[1] These lawyers divided their work into six areas and worked in pairs. Wesley J. Liebeler was the junior lawyer assigned to study Oswald's background and to bring to light motives for the crime. His findings are set forth in chapter 7 of the report.

Each chapter went through six or more substantial redrafts, with different persons assuming editorial responsibility at different times.[2] Liebeler, however, "did most of the original work"[3] on the section on personal motive, and it was agreed that he would "assume responsibility" for this section.[4]

The possibility of a conspiracy was examined in chapter 6 of the report which ended with this statement:

> Based upon the investigation reviewed in this chapter, the Commission concluded that there is no credible evidence that Lee Harvey Oswald was part of a conspiracy to assassinate President Kennedy. Examination of the facts of the assassination itself revealed no indication that Oswald was aided in the planning or execution of his scheme. Review of Oswald's life and activities since 1959 . . . did not produce any meaningful evidence of a conspiracy. The Commission discovered no evidence that the Soviet Union or Cuba were involved in the assassination of President Kennedy. Nor did the Commission's investigation of Jack Ruby produce any grounds for believing that Ruby's killing of Oswald was part of a conspiracy.[5]

The commission had to resolve the contradictions that were the product of witnesses' imagination or faulty memory and was led to publish much worthless information. Ludicrous tales can be found in the volumes containing the exhibits—for example, the one in a report from the FBI to the commission stating that someone asserted that Ruby was Oswald's father.

In its zeal to cover every possible scrap of evidence, the commission provided its critics with weapons to use against it. All anyone had to do to cloud the issues was to pick out some information the commission had rightly found useless after close examination. The critics did not trouble to look at the commission's reasons, given in the report, for rejecting incorrect information.

On the other hand, certain witnesses of limited intellectual capacity gave testimony in which mistakes were so obvious that the commission did not consider it essential to publish their declarations with the other exhibits. The commission's critics used these omissions to accuse it of having discriminated among the testimonies.

Any collective work is marked by discussions and refinements. The work of the commission was no exception. For instance, after reading the galley proofs of chapters 4 and 6, Liebeler sent to the general counsel four memoranda, totaling approximately 14,000 words, in which he suggested many changes on minor points. (He chiefly objected to "the quality of the written work.") He assumed his suggestions were accepted,[6] which meant that many pages had to be reset at the last minute. Furthermore, there was a time limit that made it impossible to present a well-coordinated report or to eliminate the many repetitions. The report has 816 pages, as well as 60 pages of references in double columns.

The *Warren Report* contains three separate biographies of Oswald. The first one was written by the assistant counsel in charge of the investigation of a possible conspiracy; the second study was written by the assistant counsel looking into Oswald's possible motives; the third, entitled "Biography of Lee Harvey Oswald," is Appendix 13—alone totaling approximately 35,000 words and based on a wealth of available documentation. In actuality, Oswald was a man of small ambitions before his return to the United States, without the qualifications for advancement. He dreamed only of escaping the condition of unskilled worker that was his prospect. But the investigators saw this mediocre man as a gifted man who "started to read Communist literature" at fifteen, "studied Marxism" at seventeen,[7] and who, at twenty, decided to live his life in accordance with his ideas. ("His ideas" did not motivate him; he wrote in his diary that he returned to the United States because he could spend his money nowhere, because there were "no nightclubs or bowling alleys" in Minsk, where Moscow had sent him and where he received the privileged treatment given to defectors.)

Just before his twentieth birthday Oswald had found himself in Europe, his savings wiped out. Because he had miraculously extricated himself from an impossible situation, he began to think he was a remarkable man who deserved better than his current lot in life. For fifteen months after his return to the United States, he played the part of a learned scholar, of a future statesman, and little by little he came to believe he was the person he tried to appear to be.

Liebeler was mistaken about Oswald. J. Lee Rankin, general counsel for the Warren Commission, was questioned by the House Select Committee on Assassinations. In the course of his testimony he described the atmosphere inside the commission: "Now with regard to Mr. Liebeler you have to recognize that he was an extreme conservative in a rather hot bed of liberals on our staff and he early became disenchanted with some of the others, not really about the investigation but they had a lot of crackpot liberal ideas as far as he was concerned and he had a lot of crackpot conservative ideas, radical conservative as far as they were concerned."[8]

Liebeler saw in Oswald's "Marxism" the key to his doings. He mentioned this "Marxism" several times in his text of chapter 7; "his commitment to Marxism or Communism,"[9] "his attachment to Marxist and Communist doctrines,"[10] "his reading of Communist literature,"[11] "Oswald studied Marxism after he joined the Marines,"[12] "Oswald's interest in Marxism,"[13] "Oswald's commitment to Marxism or Communism."[14] Liebeler believed that Oswald had gone to the Soviet Union and had later dreamed of going to Cuba because he was politically committed. Not understanding Oswald, Liebeler could not see that his "defection" had not been premeditated. Nor did he want to see that Oswald's wife, by rejecting him on the eve of the murder, determined the course of events. In accepting Liebeler's conclusion and viewing Oswald as a "Marxist" drawn to the Soviet Union since adolescence, who was indignant about his country's policy toward Cuba, the Warren Commission inadvertently fueled the conspiracy theory. It gave credibility in Europe to the stories that had made Oswald into a heaven-sent scapegoat, and in America, to those that alleged he was working for the KGB or the Cuban political police.

"Others," the commission stated, "may study Lee Oswald's life and arrive at their own conclusions as to his possible motives."[15] This may have been an admission on its part that the interpretation of his character offered in the chapter "Background and Possible Motives" was open to discussion or even wrong. That chapter tries to present Oswald as an exceptional individual, fanatically militant, envious of the immortality achieved by great criminals. His case was in reality a textbook case for the psychologists, and not for the criminologists. An exact analysis of his character would have solved the alleged mystery of his crime.

What got in the way of the commission's understanding of him was that it clung to its preconceived ideas. It failed to see, after studying the documentation gathered, that the facts contradicted these ideas. It did not realize that the point to elucidate was the time the idea of assassination had taken shape in Oswald's mind.

Historians, familiar with critical analysis of documentary material, should have been in charge of chapter 7 of the *Warren Report*. They would have been better qualified to draw Oswald's portrait than lawyers skilled in interrogation, examination, and cross-examination, whose special skills were useless, since the subject of the inquiry was dead and buried.

The establishment of a presidential commission was an unprecedented move. J. Edgar Hoover, the FBI director, thought that it was a reflection on him and that the reputation of the FBI was tarnished by having the investigation taken out of his hands. Perhaps to demonstrate that he would in any case be the center of the investigation, he submitted a summary report to President Johnson as early as December 9, 1963. Some errors, "which had resulted simply from a lack of complete knowledge," were found in it when it became public. The critics wrote book after book about the contradictions between this early FBI report and the *Warren Report* but did not mention that the commission made it clear that "the correction of earlier assertions of fact . . . is a normal part of the process of accumulating evidence."[16]

If the commission, during the course of its investigation, did not let it be known through "reliable sources" that many of the rumors flying around were false, it was probably because it thought the publication of its report would put the public's doubts and questions to rest once and for all. Moreover, the commission, which was set up in December, had to devote itself first to reviewing twenty or thirty thousand documents, and it did not begin to take depositions until February. Only in June did a spokesman give some information to the press.

The main objective was to uncover Oswald's motives, but it was of course impossible to discover "reasons" behind an absurd and gratuitous act. The investigators tried in vain to explain why Oswald had committed the crime; they should, instead, have tried to understand what had brought him to that point.

After having read the manuscript of chapter 7, Dr. Howard P. Rowe, senior consultant in psychiatry at the Mayo Clinic, gave Liebeler valuable information on Oswald's dyslexia. The commission's investigators may have thought that their legal backgrounds had not given them the sort of expertise required to understand the mind of an apparently sane man who differed from ordinary political assassins, all of whom exulted in the success of their carefully planned crime. Did they believe that mental health experts would be able to help them? Did they meet with other psychiatrists? If so, one can imagine the sorts of things the investigators were told from reading the articles appearing in the specialized journals at the time. One of these journals asked three psychoanalysts with different theoretical leanings to give their interpretations.[17] The Freudian Dr. Joseph Katz thought that in shooting at the president, Oswald was aiming for his mother, that if he had not killed her, it was because it was "too much akin to penetrating her sexually and this he could not face at any cost."[18] The Adlerian Dr. Heinz L. Ansbacher knew that after his explanation, "the reader would ask what [he] had added to the existing newspaper and magazine accounts," and quoted in conclusion a sentence from another Adlerian Dr. Robert W. White. "Adler's ideas have gone into the stream of contemporary thought and have become the accepted clinical common sense of our time."[19] For the Jungian Dr. Ira Progoff, Oswald was "in the grip, in the fateful moment, of something that seized him. It was as though he was not Lee Harvey Oswald but Sir Mordred . . . the outcast of society consigned by destiny to kill the hero, King Arthur, and to be killed in return."[20]

For the *Bulletin of the New York Academy of Medicine,* "President Kennedy was the composite of Lee's parental images, fundamentally a mother figure with a super-imposed father figure."[21]

There was no need to resort to experts in depth psychology. Explaining Oswald was easy enough. Whatever he said or wrote give sufficient information about him. His assertions could be easily checked against testimony from the people who met him. When he bragged or lied, his ignorance and his self-satisfaction were easy to detect. Those who met him in the marines, in Moscow, in Dallas, whose testimonies or affidavits were published in the report's Hearings and Exhibits, were examined and sometimes reexamined by hundreds of investigators, month after month.

Let us look at a few testimonies out of these thousands and thousands of pages. A fellow marine said, "You could sit down and argue with him for a number of years . . . and I don't think you could have changed his mind."[22] One of the press correspondents Oswald met in Moscow said, "He did respect words, long words. . . . He was not qualified for a technical discussion of economics. . . . He seemed in some ways well-read, [but] he often used words incorrectly as though he had learned them from a dictionary."[23] The consular official who saw him in Moscow wrote, "I recall a strong impression that he used simple Marxist stereotypes without sophistication or independent formulations."[24]

Once Oswald was invited by a cousin of his, who was in a seminary, to give a talk on the USSR; his aunt was surprised that he did not prepare anything. "Oh, don't worry about me," he said, "I give talks all the time." He told her too that he did not have to learn anything, that he knew "everything." (He explained to his listeners that communism did not work, capitalism did not work, and that between those two systems there was socialism, and that socialism did not work either. His lecture was a success.)[25]

George De Mohrenschildt, a Russian-born American, the only person who stayed in touch with Oswald and his wife after all their other acquaintances in Dallas had given them up, was able to give the commission an idea of Oswald's ignorance: "Possibly he was seeking for something, but knowing what kind of brains he had, and what kind of education, I was not interested in listening to him, because it was nothing, it was zero."[26]

Oswald, according to those who met him, showed little understanding of what he had read. For example: "He believed in the perfect government, free of want and need, and free of taxation, free of discrimination, free of any police force, the right to be able to do exactly what he pleased."[27] And: "He seemed to have perhaps read quite a lot of political philosophy, but when it came to really understanding it, he couldn't present a very good case for it."[28] And also: "They asked him a question, something about comparative economics, and he gave some kind of stupid answer [that] more or less confirmed my opinion that he didn't know much about it."[29]

What had been uncovered about Oswald's childhood, his marriage, and his views made it easy to draw the right conclusion: he had stumbled unthinkingly, blindly, into becoming a defector without desiring to defect. On the eve of the president's visit to Dallas, Marina Oswald, not caring what her husband felt, had let him think that she wanted a separation, that he was losing his children as well as his wife.

Oswald's frustration had its roots, however, in his dyslexia, which was shown in his writings. And the commission's initial error consisted in failing to attach any importance to the long letter it received from a doctor giving a detailed description of dyslexia and explaining that Oswald, unaware of the nature of his difficulty, was seriously handicapped. This disability prevented him from spelling words correctly. But liking to hear himself talk, reading difficult books—without understanding them—he always thought that if he got a chance to go to a good school, he would learn how to spell and then become a newsman, a writer, a politician.

Oswald's writings, according to the *Warren Report,* "give some insight into his character."[30] The commission did not see that the most significant part of his writings was not their content; one look at the spelling, and an examination of Oswald's early years, offered the key to his disappointments and resentments, as well as his efforts to compensate, his need to impress others, and his lack of authenticity.

The commission's more serious error, however, was to believe that Oswald had left the United States in order to defect to the Soviet Union. He did not intend to go there; he wished only to become a true student somewhere in Europe.

The day after the assassination the *New York Times* said that Marxism was a religion for Oswald, that he had studied it and thoroughly immersed himself in it for five years.[31] The commission was unable to rid itself of the image of Oswald created by the media before it had actually begun its work. The image was of a politically committed man, who had left the United States at the age of twenty for the country of his dreams. The commission was even convinced that Oswald had studied the laws concerning repudiation of his American citizenship in advance,[32] while all he had to do to find out how to lose his nationality was to read his passport. The following statement appears in all passports: "You may lose your United States nationality by being naturalized in, or by voting in the elections of a foreign state; by taking an oath or making a declaration of allegiance to a foreign state; or by serving in the armed forces or accepting employment under the government of a foreign state."

The only thing Oswald did was to tell an American consul that his allegiance was to the Union of Soviet Socialist Republics.[33] It was not a formal declaration made to Russian authorities.

4

Misinformation
on Oswald's Background

It might help at this point to summarize Oswald's background; it will be examined in further detail in the following chapters. First, an overview of his life would be useful.

Lee Harvey Oswald was born in New Orleans in October 1939, two months before his father died. His mother put him in an orphanage when he was three years old and took him out the following year, as she was going to remarry. Since Mrs. Oswald moved often, Lee went from school to school; he changed schools twelve times in ten years. Mrs. Oswald was divorced when he was eight years old. They lived in New York in 1953–54. After a while Lee refused to go to school and was sent, as a truant, to a city facility, the Youth House, for psychiatric observation.

Lee completed the seventh grade with low but passing marks in all his academic subjects.[1] Back in New Orleans he left school at the age of sixteen by presenting to the school authorities a note written by him to which he had signed his mother's name. He tried to enlist in the Marine Corps, claiming that he was seventeen years old, the minimum age for enlistment, but he failed and got a job as an office boy. He enlisted the following year, in October 1956. He was in basic training for ten months, spent fifteen months overseas, and was then assigned to an air force base in California. He was discharged on September 11, 1959, went to Fort Worth and left for Europe on September 20. He presented himself in Moscow, in October, as a student. He had a tourist visa valid for six days; he hoped to get a scholarship to a Soviet university or technical school, but he was ordered to leave Russia at the expiration of his visa. Having already run through all of his money, he saw only one way for him to remain in the Soviet Union, and that was to fake a suicide attempt. To further convince the authorities, he went to the American embassy and said he wanted to renounce his citizenship. He left his passport with the consular official who received him.

He was finally accepted by the Russians, given a Stateless Persons identity card, and sent to Minsk where he worked in a factory. One year later he realized that life in the Soviet Union would never be pleasant and asked the American embassy to return his passport. He then met the girl he married, Marina Prusakova. He did not tell her until after they were married that he hoped to return to the United States. The formalities took more than a year. A child was born in February 1962. The three of them arrived in Fort Worth, Texas, where Oswald's mother and brother lived, in June 1962. Because he wanted to reimburse the State Department as soon as possible for the loan that had permitted their return, part of his salary was earmarked for the payments, which left very little for living expenses. Oswald found life in the United States quite different from what he had expected.

On April 10, 1963, he took a shot at General Edwin E. Walker, "an active and controversial figure in the political scene,"[2] and missed. A few weeks later he left for New Orleans, where he hoped it would be easier for him to find a good job than it had been in Fort Worth and Dallas. In the spring he was beginning to think of going to Cuba to seek a better life. The only way for an American citizen to go to Cuba was via Mexico. He arrived in Mexico on September 21 and applied to the Cuban consulate for a transit visa to Cuba. When his application was rejected, he got angry and was told off by the Cuban consul.

He returned to Dallas on October 3. He was discouraged; his unemployment benefits had run out and he had to find a job. He was hired by the Texas School Book Depository on October 16. His second child was born on October 20. The quarrels between Oswald and his wife had begun immediately after they arrived in the United States. After what was to be their last row on November 21, Oswald thought that his wife wanted to leave him and that he would lose his children too. On the following day he set out for the book depository with his rifle.

Dr. P. Rowe wrote to the commission as mentioned above about the effect Oswald's dyslexia had on his personality, but the commission did not give Dr. Rowe's analysis the attention it deserved. Oswald had a reading disability that explained in large part his "estrangement from people," "his diffident truculence during school years," and his "unwarranted estimation of his literary capacities."[3] For instance, Oswald wrote "offial" for "official," "plug" for "plunge," "patrioct" for "patriotic," "opions" for "opinions," "unsursen" for "insurance," "indepence" for "independence," "sensenlionilizism" for "sensationalism," "naturiclists" for "naturalistic," "tremonuso" for "tremendous."

In the severe cases, explained Dr. Rowe, "there is also a difficulty with the reading and counting of numbers and hence with calculation.[4] Indeed, it was found that the young Oswald had trouble not only in English grammar but also in arithmetic; on the other hand, he was above the average for his age group in arithmetical reasoning.

At thirteen Oswald was found to have "superior mental resources"; his I.Q. indicated "intellectual functioning in the upper range of bright normal intelligence."[5] Dr. Rowe wrote that a person of Oswald's intelligence "would be acutely conscious of [his] limitation and consequently chronically frustrated in [his] efforts to circumvent the disability."[6]

After Oswald learned how to read—at the age of eight or nine—he read everything he could get his hands on. Intellectually superior to his family and to his milieu, he thought he could outshine them all by immersing himself in difficult texts. His disability was to haunt him all his short life. Whenever he had to write an important letter, he managed to avoid mistakes by looking up every word in the dictionary and not using the words he was unable to find. He was once seen addressing the same envelope ten times, in order to get it right.

The commission received Dr. Rowe's letter in September 1964, after the report had already gone to press. Wesley Liebeler recommended that a reference to Oswald's disability be "set forth in the text."[7] Only half of the paragraph he sent the general counsel was inserted: "It has been suggested that this misspelling of names, apparently on a phonetic basis, was caused by a reading-spelling disability from which Oswald appeared to suffer. Other evidence of the existence of such a disability is provided by the many other misspellings that appear in Oswald's writings, portions of which are quoted below."[8]

This did not make much sense; to say that misspellings are an indication of a spelling disability is not very illuminating. Moreover, Oswald had conquered his reading disability early; only his inability to spell remained.

Oswald's problem with dyslexia continued to be ignored by the general public. Consequently some supporters of the conspiracy theory claimed that only those sentences containing misspelled words—sentences Oswald had written in haste—reflected his own efforts, whereas those sentences containing no mistakes—written when he applied himself—had been dictated to him.

Because of his dyslexia, Oswald was unhappy in school. Unable to follow what was going on, losing ground rapidly, he was left to himself by his classmates as well as by his teachers. He reacted by withdrawing and was considered "a loner." Seen as dull or inattentive, he was ridiculed or punished. The feeling that he was being unfairly treated was certainly the source of his pessimistic view of the world.

When Oswald was thirteen, he moved to New York with his mother for one and a half years. After a few months he played truant two days out of three. As previously mentioned, he was sent to the Youth House, a city institution for "juveniles who appeared to require psychological observation or guidance," where he remained three weeks. He was questioned and tested by a social worker, a psychologist, a psychiatrist, and a probation officer. None of them understood what his problem was. He told them that school took up too much of his time and that he was better off spending it looking at magazines, watching television, or reading. He acknowledged having fantasies about being all-powerful and being able to do anything he wanted.[9]

Instead of holding lengthy interviews, the Youth House staff should simply have asked him to write something. They elaborated endless reports on his case, using the habitual clichés: serious personality damage,[10] need for a father figure . . . emotional isolation; personality pattern disturbance with schizoid features and passive aggressive tendencies";[11] impoverishment in the social and emotional areas,[12] [incapacity] of constructing an effective ego-defense.[13] They did not try to figure out the reasons for his discomfort or his rebelliousness.

More lucid than the adults who tested him, the young boy said he needed only "remedial" help.[14] Years later he said that in his youth he had wanted the chance to study, and his mother could not afford to put him in a private school like his brother. He continued to cling to the belief that a good school with good teachers would fix everything, hence his repeated but vain efforts to enter some kind of school or college.

His mother did not understand why there was so much of a fuss about something as unimportant as refusing to go to school.[15] She was a selfish, conceited, stubborn person—and Lee took after her in many ways. To give the reader a glimpse of her and an idea of Oswald's milieu, here is a passage from her testimony; it refers to Oswald's stay in Russia. He had written to her, before leaving for Minsk, that he did "not wish to contact [her] again," and he had kept his word. She apparently believed that he had been sent to the Soviet Union by the government and that if she complained to those who had given him his orders, he would be reminded by them of his filial duties.

I arrived at the station eight o'clock in the morning and I called the White House. A Negro man was on the switchboard, and he said the offices were not open yet, they did not open until nine o'clock. He asked if I would leave my number. I asked to speak to the President. And he said the offices were not open yet. I said, "Well, I have just arrived here from Fort Worth, Texas, and I will call back at nine o'clock."

So I called back at nine o'clock. Everybody was just gracious to me over the phone. Said that President Kennedy was in a conference, and they would be happy to take any message. I asked to speak to Secretary Rusk, and they connected me with that office. And his young lady said he was in a conference, but anything she could do for me. I said, "Yes, I have come to town about a son of mine who is lost in Russia. I do want to speak—I would like personally to speak to Secretary Rusk." So she got off the line a few minutes. Whether she gave him the message or what I do not know. She came back and said,

"Mrs. Oswald, Mr. Rusk"—so evidently she handed him a note—and Mr. Boster was on the line —"that you talk to Mr. Boster who is special officer in charge of Soviet Union affairs"—if I am correct. And Mr. Boster was on the line. I told him who I was. He said "Yes, I am familiar with the case, Mrs. Oswald." He said "Will an eleven o'clock appointment be all right with you?" This is nine o'clock in the morning. So I said—this is quite an interesting story—I said, "Mr. Boster, that would be fine. But I would rather not talk with you." I didn't know who Mr. Boster was. I said, "I would rather talk with Secretary of State Rusk. However, if I am unsuccessful in talking with him, then I will keep my appointment with you."[16]

Mrs. Oswald saw no difference between the top and the bottom of the ladder; she went to tell her little story to the president as another would go to discuss it with a petty official. Her son went to kill the president as another would go to a neighbor and kill him.

In her deposition she made erratic statements, one of them being, "My son could have shot the President, and he could have been involved. I am not the kind of mother to think that he is perfect and could not do it."[17]

> *There is a . . . large amount of material available in Oswald's writings and in the history of his life which does give some insight into his character and, possibly, into the motives for his act.*
>
> *Warren Report,* chap. 7, p. 375

The chapter of the *Warren Report* entitled "Lee Harvey Oswald: Background and Possible Motives," analyzes Oswald's motives "in terms of [his] character and state of mind." The erroneous interpretation of his background, however, made it impossible to understand why he had committed his crime. The commission wrongly believed that he had decided to go to the Soviet Union long before his discharge from the Marine Corps, that he had gone to Moscow because of "his commitment to Marxism and Communism"[18] (or to "Marxism or Communism"[19]), and that afterward, his attempt to go to Cuba in September 1963 was "another act which expressed his hostility toward the United States and its institutions as well as a concomitant attachment to a country in which he must have thought were embodied the political principles to which he had been committed for so long."[20] He was a Marxist in words only, his defection to the Soviet Union was not premeditated, and his interest in Cuba was motivated by his feeling that he could have a better life there than in the United States.

The first task, then, is to seek the real reasons behind Oswald's departure for Europe after his discharge and to show that his "Marxism" had nothing to do with it.

He enlisted in the Marine Corps at seventeen. He was "very well versed, at least on the superficial facts of a given foreign situation," and he got into discussions with the officers about foreign affairs, about which they were less knowledgeable than he was. He wanted to show that he knew more than those in command.[21] Pleased with himself for voicing political opinions that set him apart from the other marines, he thought they were impressed by his knowledge and saw him as the thinker of the group. Had he had any education, he would have tried to dazzle his comrades with "advanced" ideas on art or literature as well. His need to be noticed, admired, would only grow.

After the assassination and the publication of a wealth of information about his stay in the USSR, some fellow marines were interviewed, and the image of Oswald having bought a Berlitz Russian conversation book, joking about it, speaking English with a deep Russian accent, calling them "comrades," was revived. It was Cuba, however, not the Soviet Union, that attracted him. He had learned some Spanish in school, and he sought out the company of another marine who was of Puerto Rican origin, Nelson Delgado. Castro had come into power in February and was not yet unpopular in the United States. Delgado explained to the commission:

> So we were thinking. I speak Spanish fluently and he's got his ideas of how a government should be run, you know, the same line as Castro did at the time. . . . So we would go over there. . . . We were going to become officers. . . . And we would talk about how we would do away with Trujillo and things like that. . . . He started actually making plans, he wanted to know, you know, how

to get to Cuba and things like that . . . so he started applying himself to Spanish, he started studying. He bought himself a dictionary, a Spanish-American dictionary. He would come to me and we would speak in Spanish. You know, not great sentences but enough. After a while he got to talk to me, you know, in Spanish.[22]

Oswald had told another marine that after his discharge, he would go to Cuba and work as an army instructor. On his passport application, completed just before his discharge, the list of the countries he would visit began with Cuba and the Dominican Republic (where he would have the opportunity to "do away with" Trujillo).

The other countries he listed were England, France, Switzerland, Germany, Finland, and Russia. In his three-year hitch, he had saved about a thousand dollars out of his pay—it seemed to him to be a lot of money. At that time, many young Americans were going to Europe, thinking they could manage on "$5 a day." Oswald believed he could do it too. He put on his passport application that the purpose of his trip was "to attend the College of Albert Schweitzer, Chur, Switzerland, and the University of Turku, Turku, Finland, to visit all countries as a tourist." He had seen an advertisement for the Churwalden school in March—he was to be discharged in December—and had mailed his $25 registration fee for the spring term. On his application form for "Vocational Interest (if decided upon)" he wrote that he wanted to be "a short story writer on contemporary American life."[23] He named two fellow marines as references. Thus, at least three marines knew of his plans. Delgado said in his testimony, "Out of the service [Oswald] was going to Switzerland, he was going to a school [that] was supposed to teach him . . . in six months what it had taken him to learn in psychology over here in two years, something like that."[24]

Oswald thought that being a real student for a few months would suffice to enable him to become part of the intelligentsia. He told his mother that he was hesitating between "going to a university, writing a book, or joining Castro's army."[25] He would choose among these possibilities after returning to the States. Mrs. Oswald said in her testimony that her son should not have left a sick mother, but that what was important to him was to have a better life than he had in Texas.

On the freighter Oswald shared a cabin with a young American who was going to study at a French university. Comparing his prospects with his fellow voyager's, he realized his project was too ambitious, for he told the young man he was "going to travel around in Europe and possibly attend school in Switzerland if [he had] sufficient funds."[26] He also told a couple who were the only other passengers aboard that the purpose of his trip was to attend a university in Switzerland. When he arrived in England, he declared to the British Immigration Service that he intended to stay for one week.[27] And then he suddenly decided to call off his European trip to get a Soviet visa in Helsinki and to go from Helsinki to Moscow, a decision triggered by a simplistic interpretation of the new United States–Soviet Union relationship. (The way from Le Havre to Helsinki or Moscow is through Paris and not through London.)[28]

It is necessary to think back to the political climate of the summer of 1959 to understand his change of plans. Oswald, who considered himself an expert in international affairs, arrived in England after eighteen days at sea, without news of what was going on in the world. On his arrival he learned that Soviet Premier Nikita Khrushchev's trip to the United States, which marked a reversal of policy, had been a great success. Peaceful coexistence and cultural exchanges were the order of the day. Khrushchev had arrived on September 15. On the nineteenth the media indicated that both countries were ready to reach an accord on the number of exchange students, to be between sixty and eighty-five. Oswald had left the United States on the twentieth. He may have read about the exchange student policy, and the idea of replacing Switzerland with Russia may have already crossed his mind in New Orleans. It was only in London, however, that he thought he could be accepted as a "state-supported student" in the Soviet Union.

It is easy to understand how he came to this conclusion when one checks the newspapers he may have read in London. On the day of his arrival, for example, the *New York Herald Tribune,* European edition, contained an article entitled "Khrushchev Says That a Completely New Situation Has Taken Shape without Any Precedent." Newsstands sold American magazines of the preceding weeks that may have alluded to the exchange of students. An American press correspondent who had been in Moscow at that time told the investigators that "the once-closed Soviet Union had just burst wide open to hordes of invading foreign tourists," and that large groups of them "chattered and milled" around the reception desk of the correspondent's hotel.[29]

It was now clear to Oswald that he would not have "enough funds" to be able to go to the Swiss college. As his dream was only to acquire knowledge in order to improve his lot, he saw himself enrolling with little trouble in a university where there was no tuition and where all expenses were paid, then returning to the United States with the magic diploma—the value of which he had learned in the Marine Corps—the diploma that enabled men he found less clever than himself to order him about.[30] The best way out of his predicament was to go straight to Moscow.

The investigators of the Warren Commission did not ask Marina Oswald whether or not she knew the reasons for Oswald's trip to Russia. When she gave her deposition to the second commission, the House Select Committee on Assassinations, fifteen years later, she was questioned on this point. "He said that being young, he just wanted to see—I mean he read something about Soviet Union and he wanted to see for himself what life looked like in Soviet Union."[31] She assumed that "Oswald did want to come to Soviet Union to get education."[32]

In an earlier deposition she had said, "He said when he was staying in Russia as a tourist they did not permit him to stay any longer so he said that he just give up his citizenship in order to stay."[33]

After learning from Marina Oswald's testimony that the tourist Oswald had not planned to defect, that his decision was made on a moment's impulse, it should have been perfectly clear to the House Select Committee on Assassinations that he was not the ardent Marxist he was thought to be and that what had been said about his "possible motives" needed to be corrected. Instead, the committee followed in the footsteps of the first commission: "his political commitment was of paramount importance"; he was prepared to "give up his own life, if necessary, for his political beliefs"; before the assassination he thought of returning to Russia or living in Cuba "to fulfill a political goal."[34]

*After Oswald left the Marine Corps . . . he almost
immediately left for the Soviet Union . . . Oswald
thus committed an act which was the most striking
indication he had yet given of his willingness to act
on his beliefs in quite extraordinary ways.*

Warren Report, 7:390

After buying an airplane ticket in London, some Soviet tourist
vouchers, and paying his hotel bill in Helsinki,[35] Oswald had only
about $100 left. When he arrived in Moscow he could easily foresee
that he would find himself in a hopeless situation if he were not
immediately transferred from his hotel to a university. When his
six-day visa expired, Intourist would put him on a train for Helsinki, where he would be on the street or would be turned over to
the American embassy, assuming he had no return ticket.

He certainly told the Intourist people right from the start that
he wished to study in Russia. But actually establishing at what
precise moment Oswald decided to present himself as a defector
hardly matters. The fundamental point is that he did not leave Fort
Worth with the idea of defecting to the Soviet Union. The young
man who arrived in Moscow on October 16, 1959, was no enthusiastic partisan. He was a pseudostudent who wanted to become a
real student in order to escape from his humble background, and
he saw himself as having been almost forced to defect. The plans
he announced to his fellow marines before leaving the service, his
registration at the college in Switzerland, the intentions indicated
on his passport application, the statements made at the New Orleans steamship office, his exchange of views with his cabin mate
on the freighter, his plan to spend a week in England before con-
tinuing his grand tour, his stopover in London—all this gives us a
coherent picture of what he meant to do. His scheme failed, however, when he found himself short of money, and he was compelled
to look for a solution. He thought he would find it in the Soviet
Union.

In Fort Worth and New Orleans he probably had not yet decided on the length of his stay in Europe. He had told the steamship
office that he would make a two-month trip; in his passport application he said four months. He may have thought that the Swiss
college would accept him in January instead of April without any

difficulty or that he would return to Europe in the spring. In any case, he had a habit of lying, even about the smallest things.

He was out of touch with reality to an extraordinary degree. He had had very little formal education and grew up in an impoverished and uneducated environment. He was not even twenty yet; he had been in the marines for almost three years. Out of this inexperienced, insecure young man who entertained illusions about himself but whose ambitions were of the utmost banality, the commission constructed an exceptional individual, capable of formulating sophisticated ideas and of conceiving the elaborate plans needed to attain preestablished ends.

A few months before being discharged he had explained what the future world would be like to a fellow marine, who recalled the following:

> How did he phrase it—everything was common or something like that. . . . Instead of everybody being an individualist and just a few of them having—if they all got together in one common denominator, if everybody worked with the state owning everything, and everybody worked for the state. . . . He would bring out that the military, there was always one boss, and if he tells everybody to do something, they all do it with no question, and everything runs out smoothly. But in our government, no one person could give that order where the whole populace would obey or act to it. There were a whole bunch of individualists. Some may, some won't, and some would argue about it. That's not the same exact word he used.[36]

In the totalitarian, military state that, in Oswald's mind, the United States would be, he would no longer be one of the crowd; he would exercise authority in a factory, an office, or a newsroom. All he needed was a diploma—so he had learned in the marines.

It was only after his return to the United States that he indulged in the illusion he could advance from success to success, thanks to his accidental defection and the prestige he believed he had acquired. His few short writings, in which he set forth some of his ideas, were a mishmash of pseudo-Trotskyism, national socialism, and infantile anarchism. Did he himself know what he believed in? Between the two world wars, mediocre men, ruled by others and aspiring to rule in their turn, with no understanding whatsoever of political problems, would-be executioners and assassins, men like Oswald, threw away their red shirts one day and put on black or brown shirts.

> *It seems that Oswald immediately attempted suicide, a striking indication of how much he desired to remain in the Soviet Union.*
>
> Warren Report, 7:392

Oswald wrote the story of his stay in the Soviet Union and called it "Historic Diary"; it was composed in Minsk after the incidents described took place. From this diary we know something about his days in Moscow or, to be more precise, his version of what happened there (Oswald's spelling and grammatical errors will always be respected in the quotations):

Oct. 16. Arrive from Helsinki by train: am met by Intourest Repre. . . . Reges. as 'studet' 5 day Lux. tourist. Ticket.) Meet my Intorist guied. . . . I explain to her I wish to appli. for Rus. citizenship. . . . She checks with her boss, main office Intour; then helps me add. a letter to Sup. Sovit asking for citizenship, mean while boss telephons passport & visa office and notifies them about me.

The visit to Moscow began on the seventeenth. On October 21, the expiration date of his tourist visa, Oswald was summoned to the Passports and Visas Department, where he was questioned and then told he had to leave the Soviet Union that very day.

I am shocked!! My dreams! I retire to my room. I have $100 left. I have waited for 2 year to be accepted. . . . 7:00 P.M. I decide to end it. Soak rist in cold water to numb the pain. Then slash my left wrist. Then plaug wrist into bathtub of hot water. I think "when Rimma [Intourist guide] comes at 8. to find me dead it will be a great shock." somewhere, a violin plays, as I wacth my life whirl away. I think to myself, "how easy to die" and "a sweet death, (to violins)."[37]

It was not in the evening and there were no violins. Oswald was found after lunch by the Intourist guide, who had come on a routine visit to give him his last tour of the city.[38]

Oswald was not in the least interested in dying; in fact he probably slashed his wrist when he heard the guide knock on his door, which was locked. The guide, not seeing him downstairs, had checked that his key was not at the desk and had gone up to his room to get him. The ambulance arrived at the hospital at 4:00 P.M. The Warren Commission believed that Oswald had attempted to kill himself, although the hospital records released to the American government indicate that he had stated he inflicted wounds on his forearm "in order to delay his departure,"[39] not because he wanted to die. Oswald had once before suffered self-inflicted wounds, in Japan, when his unit was assigned to be transferred to the Philippines. A loaded revolver had "accidentally" fallen out of his locker.

Oswald told the doctors he was sorry for what he had done and wanted to return to the United States. He then went through a period of indecision. He would not have reacted this way if he had "strongly desired" to become a Soviet citizen, as the commission believed. In the commission's view, "Oswald was discovered in time to thwart his attempt at suicide. . . . It shows how willing he was to act dramatically and decisively when he faced an emotional crisis."[40] Any doubt about his "suicide attempt" vanishes when Marina Oswald's testimony is read; she confessed that one evening, feeling she could no longer put up with his brutality and the misery of her life, she had tried to kill herself. "Only foolish people would do it," he had commented.[41]

The "suicide attempt" drew attention to his case. He could not be allowed to try again. It would be most unfortunate if so soon after Khrushchev's conciliatory gestures toward the United States an American tourist were to be found dead in Moscow. After he left the hospital Oswald was summoned to the Passports and Registration Office, where he expressed, or reiterated, his desire to become a Soviet citizen. He was told that a decision would be made in due course.

Three days later Oswald had not heard anything and was anxiously awaiting a decision which, according to his guide, could quite possibly be a definitive refusal. She had apparently submitted an unfavorable report on him.[42] Without a cent to his name—his last $100 were supposed to cover the costs of extending his stay, and he had been at his hotel for three days at $30 a day[43]—he decided he should try to force the authorities' hand, "to have some sort of showdown." The "showdown" consisted of returning his passport to the American embassy. Without any papers he could not reenter Finland or any other country, nor could he leave the Soviet Union. He convinced himself that the Russians would have to keep him; he wrote in his diary that he was sure the Russians would accept him "after this sign" of his "faith in them."[44]

He presented himself at the embassy by "placing his passport on the receptionist's desk." He informed her that he had come to "dissolve his American citizenship."[45] He then declared to the official who received him that he wanted to renounce his American citizenship and become a Soviet citizen; the consular official refused to accept his renunciation on the pretext that the office operated with only a skeleton crew on Saturdays. The real reason was that he wanted to prevent someone driven by a "sudden quixotic or irrational impulse" from doing something irrevocable.[46] This attitude toward Oswald's action shows that the official did not believe the whole thing had been planned in advance ("sudden impulse"), or even that Oswald was acting in accordance with well-reasoned ideological principles ("quixotic, irrational"). He asked him to come back and fill out the necessary papers on the following Monday.

Oswald did not go back. He realized that he would be a defector in the eyes of the Russians when they learned he had returned his passport and that by leaving things as they were, he would not lose his American citizenship. He wrote to the embassy the next day, November 3, 1959, complaining it had refused to accept his repudiation of his American citizenship, an outright lie. It was common knowledge that all letters sent to the embassy were read by the KGB before being delivered, and he had carefully calculated every word to show the Russians that he wanted to defect at any price.[47]

After Oswald's visit the consular official thought that having him interviewed by press correspondents might make him think the matter over "before taking the final plunge." This was the start of the defector case. It was mentioned in some American newspapers, and Oswald began to take himself seriously. He was astounded at all the attention he received. "I am flabbergasted," he wrote in his "Historic Diary."[48]

After two weeks of utter loneliness in his hotel room, notified at last that he would not be obliged to leave the USSR but that no decision had yet been reached as to what was to be done with him, Oswald agreed to see the press correspondents with whom he had previously refused to meet. He intended telling them what he thought would please the Soviets.

The first correspondent to interview him, Aline Mosby, could not understand what was behind his stay in the Soviet Union. Defectors were "high-level officials who transferred their knowledge to the Soviet side" or "people who wanted to escape personal problems," she said.[49] She justly classified Oswald as a one-man third category.

He talked to her about his convictions. She felt that he was totally disinterested in anything but himself. During the interview he happened to tell her that he was not a real defector. Here are his exact words: "I never thought that I'd be an immigrant from the United States to some other country. Like a German living in America."[50] This was inconsistent with everything else he said on Marxism and the failures of capitalism, which was intended to show him in a good light to the Russian authorities when they read the interview in American newspapers. He did not use the word defector when speaking to Aline Mosby about his situation; he used the word immigrant, and he compared his situation to that of a German citizen living in the United States, who could become, if he or she so wished, an American citizen. He did not understand that an American citizen who defected to Russia was not in the same category as an American citizen who emigrated to Canada or Mexico. That such a fuss was made "flabbergasted" him, since thousands and thousands of Germans had emigrated to the United States without attracting notice.

Everything the Warren Commission had stated about the "defector's commitment to Marxism and Communism" was invalidated by this remark of Oswald's, but its importance went unnoticed. The members of the commission never questioned Wesley Liebeler's conviction that Oswald was an ardent Marxist whose decision to defect had been made long before his discharge from the Marine Corps.

The second press correspondent, Priscilla Johnson, felt there was something more to Oswald's story than he claimed: "I had the impression that unconsciously, he wasn't 100 percent behind what he was doing, that he wanted to get out of it."[51] She was puzzled by his refusal to go back to the embassy. During the interview, Oswald returned again to what he called the embassy's illegal treatment of him. His words were somewhat bitter, but "he was avoiding hearing from them."[52] He was "very anxious as to whether [the Russians] were going to let him stay."[53]

He wondered whether the Russians would believe what he said about, first, wanting to renounce his American citizenship; second, the Americans not allowing him to do so; and third, the reason he gave for not returning to the embassy, namely, that it would be unnecessary. Johnson told the commission: "I wanted, if I could, to help him, warn him subtly that he was going to be trapped. . . . But I assumed that my room was wired, and I couldn't be so obvious about it, and I tried to do it by talking to him about economics."[54]

After Mussolini and Hitler came into power, some of those who believed that the Soviet Union was the promised land emigrated there. If there were any twenty-year-olds among them, they had been militants in their countries, had been exposed to some danger, had not spent the first three years of their adult life in the marines, and had not arrived in Moscow with the intention of going to school.

Priscilla Johnson had no way of knowing that the contradictions in Oswald's statements stemmed from the fact that some of the statements were intended for the Russians. Oswald thought that one way or another, through the tapes or through Johnson's article, he would succeed in getting his own way. Like Aline Mosby, she realized that Oswald was different from the normal defector: "I had never heard of anybody of that age in the first place or that generation, taking an ideological interest to the point where he would defect. His age made him extraordinary."[55]

Johnson came close to finding out what was "behind Oswald's professed reasons," particularly when she found him "notably reticent" about his financial situation: "He bristled on the point, and I assume . . . that there was something there. I just didn't know what it was, and I couldn't get it out of him.[56] . . . It came up almost as a leit motif of this conversation, his anxiety about staying, and his recent reassurance by them that he could remain as a resident alien had not altogether quelled the anxiety."[57]

Oswald's fate was finally decided in December; he was sent

to Minsk. Upon his arrival there he was taken to see the mayor who promised him an apartment that would be "rent-free."[58] His ambition to go to school had not been realized, but recommended by Moscow, he started out as a defector who had to be treated well. He began working a few days after his arrival at an unskilled job in a factory manufacturing radio and television sets.[59]

A few passages from his diary show how removed he was from the image of the devoted Marxist, the Communist eager to work for the good of his fellow men. In January 1960 he wrote, "I'm living big and am very satisfied." He received monthly subsidies from a special agency, curiously called the Red Cross, in addition to his salary. In Russia defectors enjoy preferential treatment in order to encourage desirable defections. Also, the Russians know that living conditions are so much better in the West that foreigners subjected to the Soviet life-style would quickly lose their illusions.

Six months later Oswald wrote that he was becoming "increasingly conscious of just what sort of society" he lived in. He mentioned "mass gymnastics, compulsary after work meeting, usually political information meeting. Complusary attendance at lectures and the sending of the entire shop collective (except me) to pick potatoes on a Sunday, at a State collective farm." In January 1961 he wrote, "I am stating to reconsider my disire about staying. The work is drab the money I get has nowhere to be spent. No nightclubs or bowling alleys no places of recreation acept the trade union dances I have had enough."[60] The following year, when he was preparing what he would say when asked in the United States why he had stayed in the Soviet Union for such a long time, he wrote, "I was living quite comfortably, I had plenty of money, an apartment rent-free lots of girls ect, why should I leave all that?"[61] These considerations, so revealing with respect to Oswald's character, views, and behavior, which form a picture of a strange sort of "committed Marxist," were judged by the Warren Commission as being of no importance.

In February 1961, one year and three months after his arrival in the Soviet Union, Oswald wrote to the American embassy, informing them that he wanted to return to the United States.[62] He met Marina Prusakova in March and married her in April.

In Minsk Oswald began his career as a writer—probably when he made up his mind to try to leave Russia—with a fifty-page text recording his observations of the life around him. He hid the manuscript in his shirt with the "Historic Diary" when he left for the United States. He had the beginning typed. (He paid the typist with $10 borrowed from his mother.) He was able to finish the typing himself later, when he enrolled in an evening course that provided students with typewriters on which to type texts of their own choosing. However, the many ink corrections of spelling mistakes on the manuscript make the final product almost illegible. Exposing his ignorance, Oswald mentioned the popularity of "Alexander Drue, the French author of Count Margo," in the Soviet Union.[63] (In his "Historic Diary" he wrote that Lenin, whose portrait hung on the wall of the factory, kept watch as the workers toiled, and he commented, "Shades of H. G. Wells!!"—meaning Orwell.)[64] He showed the first ten typed pages to George De Mohrenschildt, the person who was closest to him in Dallas, who did not find them of any interest.[65] This was a great disappointment to him. There is nothing in his piece that has not already been said many times, and said better, nor is there much that would contribute to our knowledge of him. There is a uniformity of tone in the countless pieces written by Communists or sympathizers who lost their illusions after getting too close to reality. Oswald's tone was entirely different; he was interested only in what was happening to him.

In January 1962 Oswald was advised by his mother, with whom he had renewed contact, that following his defection the Department of the Navy had changed his honorable discharge and he was excluded from the Marine Corps Reserve. He wrote to the secretary of the navy to protest, saying in his letter that he had "the full sanction of the U.S. Embassy in Moscow."[66] He always convinced himself that people would take his word for what had happened, or, better yet, that his lies had a magical power to change things, to erase what inconvenienced or worried him. Once he had sent off the letter, he imagined he had conclusively established that he had been in the Soviet Union against his will for a year and a half and that he had been struggling in vain to get out.

The *Warren Report* conceded that "he thought he had been unjustly treated." By recognizing that his protest had been made in good faith, the commission undermined its own theory that Oswald had been a Marxist wanting desperately to live in the country of his dreams. It tried to explain why he protested against his treatment: "Probably his complaint was due to the fact that his discharge was not related to anything he had done while on active duty and also because he had not received any notice of the original discharge proceedings, since his whereabouts were not known."[67] This was not the case. In a second letter, in which Oswald made a formal application for a review of his discharge, he said that the board of inquiry did not have the facts, that he had not violated any law, and that his residence abroad was legal.

The Warren Commission's investigators saw Oswald as an idealist who sympathized with the underprivileged, but the truth was that other people did not matter to him. They saw him as a scornful critic of his country's government; actually, it was segregation, the extension of racism, that irritated him. (De Mohrenschildt testified that Oswald discussed only racial problems with him.)[68] They assumed he was a Marxist, a renegade who admired the Soviet regime; in actual fact he was unable to understand Marx and had no liking for communism.

The schoolboy who thought he knew as much as his teachers, the marine who deserved the rank of officer in command, the young worker who did not want to be an unskilled laborer for the rest of his life—Oswald was ensnared in the web of his own illusions and lies: his illusions about the possibility of a brilliant career for a man without education—ineffectively self-taught—and his lies, emerging when he tried to impress people or when he got into difficulties. His adventure was unique. Real defectors disappear into obscurity and are forgotten, or manage to return, shamefaced, to their country, where they try not to attract attention. Oswald was of a different breed. He believed that under the current system, where true talent went unrecognized, he would have difficulty taking his rightful place; this system, however, could not be maintained much longer—Marx and Orwell had made that clear. He was in the lead because he knew the doctrine well. His success was assured. Lying at first to others and, in the end, to himself, he was counting on receiving the recognition he believed he deserved, some time in the future. He left Minsk, full of hope, on May 23, 1962.

5

Misinformation
on Oswald's Motives

> *His commitment to Marxism and Communism appears to have been another important factor in his motivation.*
>
> Warren Report, chap. 7, p. 423

Everything Oswald ever said or wrote shows he did not have even the most elementary understanding of Marxism and that he condemned communism. We know which books had an influence on him by looking at his application to the college in Switzerland. He did not mention Marx, and he listed Charles Darwin, Norman Vincent Peale, and Jack London. In 1955 Jerome Lawrence and Robert E. Lee's play *Inherit the Wind,* which ridiculed the fundamentalists for their position in the Scopes trial, had made the idea of natural selection popular. The first words of Norman Vincent Peale's *The Power of Positive Thinking,* published in 1952, were "Believe in yourself, have faith in your abilities." He who doubts his own capacities, Peale professed, he who accepts defeat too easily, must improve his self-image in order to become a member of the elite, one of those hard-driving individuals of whom one says that they have something. For Peale, high self-esteem is the key to success. According to Jack London, self-taught journalist whose books had enjoyed considerable success and who was always seeking adventure, the revolutionary was a superman in a corrupt world.

Oswald's readings, as well as the ideas he had about the books he had not read, shaped the way he looked at the world and the way he conducted himself: the strong man, the gifted man, is the one who wins in the struggle for life, the one selected to succeed, admired by other men. To attain the standing Jack London had achieved, he would claim he was a Socialist and he would travel.

The Warren Commission ignored this information, provided directly by Oswald himself, about his intellectual background and tastes. Rather, they relied on a statement he had made to Aline Mosby in Moscow: "I became interested about the age of 15. An old lady handed me a pamphlet about saving the Rosenbergs." Oswald was thirteen and a half years old when he read the pamphlet on the Rosenbergs,[1] who were executed in June 1953 for having allegedly given atomic secrets to the Soviet Union. Between the ages of fourteen and fifteen, until June 1955, his only friend was a classmate, Edward Voebel, who testified: "I am sure he had no interest in those things at that time. The only things he would be reading would be comic books and the normal things that kids read."[2]

At the age of sixteen and a half, between January and July 1956, Oswald took *Capital* and *The Communist Manifesto* out of the city library. If he ever even opened the first book, it may be assumed, given his intellectual limitations, that he closed it right away. He read the second, which was probably the extent of his indoctrination. He joined the marines in October 1956 and had only a few months to indoctrinate himself. At the same time, he was learning by heart the Marine Corps manual his brother had given him.[3] It seems highly unlikely that he was able to devote much time to Marx and Marxism.

Oswald thought that a totalitarian regime was more rational than any other regime, but "he was not for the communist way of life," according to a fellow marine.[4] Another marine was "quite surprised" when he learned that Oswald had gone to Russia.[5] Another said, "He wanted to be on the winning side for one thing, and, therefore, the great interest in Communism."[6] "I think he accepted Orwell's premise in this that there was no fighting it. I think this was the central thing that disturbed him and caused many of his other reactions."[7]

The consular official who saw Oswald in Moscow found him "intelligent, articulate, unintellectual, excessively assertive, intense and humorless." Oswald used "no profanity and maintained self-control" during the interview. The overall impression he made on the official was one of "overbearing arrogance and insufferable adolescence."[8]

Priscilla Johnson told the commission what she thought of Oswald's political ideas: "He liked to create the pretense, the impression that he was attracted to abstract discussion and was capable of engaging in it, and was drawn to it. But it was like pricking a balloon. . . . Whatever he was talking about was really Lee Oswald. He seemed to me to have really zero capacity for a sustained abstract discussion on economics or any other subject, and I didn't think he knew anything about economics."[9]

In Minsk Oswald did not attend the courses on Marxism-Leninism given at the factory. Marina Oswald told the Warren Commission that his interest in Marxism was a way of getting attention. She told the committee on assassinations: "Newspaper reporters call him Marxist or Communist. He was neither of those. He maybe was so-called self-proclaimed Marxist because it happened to be maybe he read the book and maybe he agrees with Karl Marx, some of the theories, but as far as belonging to the party or something like that, that is not so. He did not call himself a Marxist or say I believe in that kind of ideas."[10] To appear familiar with Marxism was, in his mind, a sign of competence in political matters.

George De Mohrenschildt was able to give the commission valuable insight into Oswald's "philosophy": "Well, he was not sophisticated, you see. He was a semi-educated hillbilly. And you cannot take such a person seriously. All his opinions were crude, you see. . . . His mind was of a man with a poor background, who read rather advanced books, and did not understand even the words in them. He read complicated economical treatises and just picked up difficult words out of what he has read, and loved to display them."[11]

De Mohrenschildt was described by his friends as eccentric. He himself admitted he had a provocative personality.[12] He was known in Dallas as "the mad Russian."[13] He was high-strung, had horrible headaches, and had been having trouble concentrating for a long time.[14] The kindness he had shown the couple and his easygoing attitude during his testimony were harshly judged by his business contacts. His material situation became difficult. After four suicide attempts, having undergone electroshock therapy, he succeeded in killing himself in 1977.[15] According to some of the conspiracy theorists, like Summers[16] and Buchanan,[17] he killed himself because he could not face the prospect of having to appear before the assassination committee.

On the ship home from the Soviet Union, Oswald wrote an outline of his political views: he stated his opposition to the systems of the "two great represnetve of power in the world" and tried to define "the two monumentle mistakes which Marx and Engles" made. (In Moscow Oswald told Priscilla Johnson that he had read Engels, but he was incapable of naming a single book by him.)[18] He wanted an "allturnative": "To where can I turn? to factional mutants of both systems, to odd-ball Hegelian idealists out of touch with reality religious groups, to revisinist or too absurd anarchism. No!"[19]

A few months later Oswald wrote out a program that is reminiscent of the proclamations made by the first Nazis; his obscure, confused ideas recall those of young Germans who called themselves Marxists when they were sixteen and were cheering Hitler by the time they were twenty. (Marina Oswald said that in Dallas her husband read a biography of Hitler.) Oswald was aware that Lenin and his comrades, as well as Hitler and his cohorts, had waited years before coming to positions of power. Like them, he had to be patient. Here are the highlights of Oswald's platform in which well-written passages were presumably borrowed. (Many political pamphlets were found among his belongings.)

> The Communist Party of the United States has turned himself into the traditional lever of a foreign power to overthrow the Government of the United States . . . in anticipation of Soviet Russia's complete domination of the American continent. . . . The Soviets have committed crimes unsurpassed even by their early day capitalist counterparts, the imprisonment of their own peoples, with the mass extermination so typical of Stalin, and the individual supresstion and regimentation under Kruschev.[20]
>
> . . . It is foreseeable that a coming economic, political or military crisis, internal or external, will bring about the final destruction of the capitalist system, assuming this, we can see how preparation in a special party could safe-

guard an independent course of action after the debacle, an American course.[21]

As one of his fellow marines said, Oswald was not a militant, a fighter; this can be seen in the following paragraph of his program:

We have no interest in violently opposeing the U.S. Government, why should we manifest opposition when there are far greater forces at work, to bring-about the fall of the United States Government, than we could ever Possibly muster. . . .[22] Membership in this organization implies adherence to the principle of simple distribution of information about this movement to others and acceptance of the idea of stoical readiness in regards to practical measures once instituted in the crisis.[23]

What he called a "pure Communist society" was the goal that should be pursued, but he wrote that "nationalization or communizing of private enterprises would be forbidden," thus negating communism.[24]

By the summer of 1963 Oswald had given up his dreams of being a great success in the United States, and his new hope was to resettle in Cuba, with his wife and children joining him later, or to return to Russia where, all things considered, life had not been so bad. He had had a steady job, a nice apartment, good friends. And his reasons for having returned to America had proved illusory.

The list of books he borrowed from the New Orleans library shows that although in June he thought he had a future in politics and was interested in world affairs, by September he was taking out books that were purely recreational. The first three books he took out after arriving in New Orleans were *Portrait of a Revolutionary: Mao Tse Tung, The Berlin Wall,* and *The Huey Long Murder Case*; the last books were a science-fiction novel, *Ben Hur, The Bridge on the River Kwai, Ape and Essence, Brave New World, Goldfinger,* and *Moonraker.*[25] In Russia, according to his wife, he read "some Russian literature just for entertainment . . . maybe some historical books about Russian history," and nothing about communism.[26]

Although in the winter he said he would one day be prime

minister,[27] by the following fall he thought it would be his hoped-for son who would have a great career.[28] Ruth Paine, who had taken in Marina Oswald while Oswald was in Mexico, saw him almost every weekend after his return; she described him as "a man striving, wanting to achieve something, a man without much formal schooling nor much native intelligence, but a striver, trying hard." She added that she had never felt "in any sense during that period that he might be a violent person or apt to break away from mild maladjustment to active violent hostility towards an individual."[29]

Oswald chose to return to the United States because his hope of attending a university or technical school, the reason for going to Moscow, had not been fulfilled, because the food was bad and he was deprived of the material comforts enjoyed by even the least successful Americans. He thought his article on life in Russia would open the publishing houses' doors to him.

On his return Oswald indicated an interest in writing during an interview at the Texas Employment Commission, but he added that he would first have to attend a local college. He had to "postpone carrying out those plans" because of "his immediate financial needs and responsibilities."[30] He did not give up his dreams for many months. A witness testified that he always spoke of going back to school and getting a degree, studying "economics and history and philosophy and things like that."[31] He finally gave up when he realized that he would not be able to advance himself in the United States. This is when he tried to go to Cuba.

It was just before his return to the United States that Oswald convinced himself he could have a political career. In his mind he was somebody in the United States; the Marine Corps' position with respect to him, its refusal to reconsider its view of him as a defector, was proof of his importance. He had become widely known because of the statements he had made in Moscow; even the Washington and New York papers had reported his defection. He had managed to get his way with the American consulate, and the Russians had yielded when he wanted to stay, and later, when he wanted to leave. Back in his own country he would enjoy, he thought, the prestige of those rare people who had taken every risk in their quest for the truth and who were qualified to speak from personal experience of life under two radically opposed political regimes. He would prove to everybody that "he had something"—Norman Vincent Peale's expression—and would impress them with his lucidity and cleverness. The story of his trip, and his condemnation of accepted beliefs, would make him popular, like Jack London. If people persisted in calling him a defector, his defection would be his greatest asset.

Living a lie, Oswald excited interest in his case in Minsk because it was thought that he had fled from America. He aroused curiosity in Dallas because it was believed that after fleeing the United States he had fled the USSR. The misguided "student" who had extricated himself from a very difficult situation by pure chance took full credit for his narrow escape and thought that he could manipulate others as it suited him, that he was the master of his fate. Playing the part of defector and Marxist, he deluded himself into the belief that he could control his destiny and was entitled to a great future. George De Mohrenschildt asked him teasingly one day if he would like to be a commissar of the people in the United States, and Oswald took the question seriously.[32]

Oswald genuinely believed he was capable of working out a program—Marxism-Oswaldism, which was, at best, sheer nonsense and at worst, a kind of nazism—that would someday gain recognition. This heady exhilaration lasted until August or September 1963, when he realized at last that he had been living in a dream world. He then began leading his life in accordance with his real personality—until those two days in November 1963.

Fairly often the investigators asked the people who had met Oswald whether they had ever heard him talk about John Kennedy. The answer invariably was that he had always spoken highly of the president. De Mohrenschildt said, "I thought that Kennedy was doing a very good job with regard to the racial problem, you know. . . . And he also agreed with me: 'Yes, yes, I think he is an excellent President, young, full of energy, full of good ideas.'"[33]

When articles on the Kennedys appeared in popular magazines, Oswald translated them for his wife. She never heard anything bad about Kennedy from him. He spoke admiringly of the Kennedy brothers but felt that they had received all the advantages from their father—wealth, education, and at a young age, important government posts.[34]

Should we be surprised to hear that Oswald never showed the slightest animosity toward John Kennedy? He had a high regard for him, and he had a high regard for himself; Oswald destroyed him and he destroyed himself. His feelings toward the president had nothing whatsoever to do with the decision he made on November 21 or 22, 1963.

> *Long before the assassination he expressed his hatred for American society and acted in protest against it.*
>
> *Warren Report*, chap. 7, p. 423

Like many words, *hate* has both strong and weak connotations—thus, "the forces of darkness, bigotry and hate," and "developed a hate for string quartets."[35] Oswald used expressive words rather loosely. Overstatements often get results; they diminish one's opponent. The Moscow consular official found Oswald "excessively assertive." Oswald told him that he "hated" the United States because he had been brought up to "hate" blacks. He told Priscilla Johnson that he had "hated" to be part of an invasion when his unit had been sent to the Philippines and that he had "hated" participating in what for him amounted to American imperialism.[36] She noted that his "hatred" for the United States seemed "strange," although she "could not fathom the reason."[37] In the draft of a speech he never delivered, he mentioned reasons to "hate" and mistrust communism.

Asked whether Oswald expressed his feelings about the United Sates when he was in the Soviet Union, Marina Oswald answered:

> When I asked him if he liked America, he said that he liked it, but not everything in it; for instance, unemployment, discrimination, the fact that it is very difficult and expensive to get educated, the high cost of doctors when one is ill. But he said very proudly that in America the apartments are prettier and not so crowded, and that the stores have things for every taste provided one had money.
> . . . He said that in America there is more democracy and that every person can say what he wants in the press, on the radio, or on TV.[38]

She also told the commission that he had been homesick in Russia. "He said many good things. He also said that he had good memory of his service in the Army."[39] In her deposition for the House Select Committee on Assassinations, she said every time somebody in Minsk would make an unfair statement about the United States, he would defend it.[40]

After his return to the United States, according to his half-brother, John Pic, the only feeling Oswald expressed toward the United States was his bitterness at his undesirable discharge from the Marine Corps. George De Mohrenschildt said, "Here is a chap who suddenly appears in [the] Dallas area. . . . He had been to Russia, went to Russia, came back, and has no hatred either for Russia or for the United States, and is just a man with no hatred."[41]

All this is a far cry from the "hatred" for the United States mentioned in the *Warren Report* as one of the factors involved in Oswald's motivation for the assassination. Oswald was attached to his country. He thought that the "system" would change, and when he tried to sort out his ideas, he wrote, "It is imature to take the sort of attitude which says 'a curse on both your houses.'"[42]

Before he knew whether or not he would be allowed to stay in Russia, Oswald had sent a letter to his brother Robert on November 3, 1959. It began, "Well, what should we talk about? the weather perhaps?"[43] In his view, the following sentence would please the Russian officials who were studying his case and who would get a copy of his letter from the censors: "I will never return to the United States which is a country I hate."

Oswald was told on November 16 that he would be allowed to live in the Soviet Union but that no decision had been made regarding his future status and residence. Probably after receiving Robert Oswald's answer, he sent him another letter, his first essay in political science. He developed in greater detail the statements he had made earlier to the American press correspondents. Maybe the authorities had not been convinced that he was a worthy Communist by his letter to the American embassy, by the brief sentence in the first letter to his brother, or by the tape of his interview in Priscilla Johnson's room. They would see he had cut his ties with his country of origin and that his love for his dream country was so deep that in the event of war he, as a Russian soldier, would not hesitate to kill his brother Robert Oswald, an American soldier.

"In the event of war, I would kill *any* american who put a uniform on in defence of the american government—any american. . . . I have no attachment's of any kind in the U.S. I want to, and I shall, live a normal happy and peaceful life here in the Soviet Union *for the rest of my life*. . . . My mother and you are . . . *not* objects of affection, but only examples of workers in the U.S."[44] The letter had few spelling mistakes. Oswald spent days and days writing and rewriting it. He did not care what his brother would think; the letters were really written for the Russian censors, regardless of the address on the envelope.

Oswald had not discovered anything new. Astolphe Custine, the author of *La Russie en 1839*,[45] published in 1844, told a friend in a letter probably sent by the embassy's diplomatic pouch: "I shall finish my day by writing to you another letter which I shall send tomorrow through the post-office: everybody, everything I see here will be extravagantly praised in this letter. You will see that I admire this country, everything about it, everything that is done here, without restriction. . . . The pleasant thing is that I am sure that the Russian police and that you yourself will be equally taken in by my feigned enthusiasm and by my commendation without judgment, without restrictions. . . . If you don't hear from me any more, think that I have been carried off to Siberia."

Oswald fooled the Soviet police just as Custine had fooled the Tsarist police. The Warren Commission too was misled: "The extent of Oswald's desire to go to the Soviet Union and of his initial commitment to that country can best be understood, however, in the context of his concomitant hatred of the United States which was most clearly expressed in his November 26, 1959 letter to his brother Robert."[46]

> *Oswald's political activities after his return to the United States center around his interest in Cuba and in the Fair Play for Cuba Committee.*
>
> *Warren Report,* chap. 7, p. 406

This statement is wrong. Oswald returned to the United States in June 1962; he killed the president seventeen months later. His political activities, which ceased totally two and a half months before the assassination, "centered around Cuba" for only five months, from May 1963 to September 1963.[47]

Between June 1962 and April 1963 Oswald believed he could make a name for himself in the United States and tried to become known in the most traditional fashion. He read books he thought would teach him how to rise in the hierarchy of an existing party or how to create a new party; he read *The Rise and Fall of the Third Reich* and biographies of Hitler, Khrushchev, and John F. Kennedy. He read, or tried to read, Marx and Lenin. He got in touch with the two extreme left-wing parties. He subscribed to both *The Worker,* the Communist organ, and *The Militant,* the Trotskyist paper, in August 1962 (Oswald informed the second paper of his change of address on November 14, one week before assassinating the president). He sent both parties requests for their pamphlets and bought some of their publications. He subscribed to Soviet periodicals and to *Time* magazine. In October 1962 he wanted to become a member of the Socialist Workers party, but there was no chapter of this Trotskyist party in Texas. In November 1962 he asked the Socialist Labor party to send him some of its literature. It thus appears that he had not yet decided whether to start his career with the Communist party, the Socialist party, or the Trotskyists. While working for a commercial photography firm, he sent samples of his work to *The Worker* and to a Communist committee; he offered to assist them by preparing posters free of charge: his offers were politely declined.

In January 1963 Oswald paid back the last installment of the loan he had received from the State Department for the return trip to the United States. He also paid back $200 his brother had lent him after his arrival in New York. Relieved of his debts, he felt he had the right to indulge in an expense—the purchase of a revolver. At the age of sixteen Oswald had put the first paychecks he had earned working as an errand boy toward the purchase of a rifle, which he had sold to his brother before going into the marines. He had had a revolver in Japan. Like many good Texans, he thought that the possession of firearms was essential.

On February 17, 1963, Oswald decided he had been on the wrong track and owed it to himself to take action. This was after reading an article in the *Dallas Morning News* that gave the address and schedule of former Major General Edwin A. Walker, whom

Oswald saw as the American Hitler. He shot at him on April 10, 1963, and missed.

Desegregation had begun a few years earlier, but massive resistance from southern congressmen and governors and mob violence had prevented integration in the universities. One of the gravest incidents took place in October 1962: the federal government had to send 3,000 troops to Oxford, Mississippi, to put down rioting led by Edwin Walker. The students wanted to prevent a black from enrolling in the state university. Edwin Walker, who had had to leave the army after being reprimanded for indoctrinating the units under his command with John Birch Society propaganda, was arrested.

The *Dallas Morning News* article quoted General Walker, who was leaving Dallas for a "crusade" from city to city in order "to alert America" before the next election. Right after reading the article on February 17, 1963, Oswald pressured his wife into writing a letter to the Soviet embassy in which she requested permission to return to the Soviet Union with her daughter.

In March Oswald asked Marina to take a picture of him, with revolver and rifle, dressed as a street fighter in a civil war, holding up both *The Militant* and *The Worker.* (He did not see the incongruity of the juxtaposition.) She asked him why he wanted her to take such a silly picture; he replied that he wanted to send it to *The Militant,* and also that thanks to the picture, someday his daughter would remember him. If he could not impress his wife, he would at least impress his daughter.

It was on April 10, 1963, six months after General Walker's name had been in all the newspaper headlines, that Oswald shot at him. The pseudohero wanted to perform some sort of inspired act more than he wanted to kill: a homicidal maniac or a terrorist would not have lost his head after the first shot and would have fired at least twice to be sure he hit his target. Perhaps he thought that dramatic actions were necessary for his biography. His "Historic Diary" would be the first chapter; the killing of General Walker would be the second. In his mind his daring act would not come to light until after the regime had collapsed. He would then be recognized as a man of action, a great revolutionary, a hero. Everybody would know that he had been the one to strike the first blow at the old regime.

Marina Oswald, who was asked by the Warren Commission

what she had observed that made her think Oswald felt he was "different," answered: "His imagination, his fantasy, which was quite unfounded, as to the fact that he was an outstanding man and the fact that he was very much interested, exceedingly so, in autobiographical works of outstanding statesmen of the United States and others. I think that he compared himself to these people whose autobiographies he read."[48]

The commission saw Oswald's attempt on General Walker's life as proof that he was prepared to act violently "in furtherance of his beliefs."[49] But what we know of him, of his ambitions, during those months demonstrates that he was chiefly trying to show his wife, who made fun of his pontificating ("Oh, that crazy lunatic. Again he is talking about politics . . ."),[50] that she had to take him seriously, to recognize his outstanding merit—that she should admire and respect him. She would realize at last that she could not stand in his way. Killing a political enemy would show her he could not only discuss politics but also take action, like all those great men who fought for their beliefs. It would also confirm in his mind that he had a future in politics.

Other misfits have become criminals because they could no longer bear to be despised or rejected. John Hinckley, the perpetrator of the attempt on President Reagan's life in 1981, before going to shoot him, had left in his room a letter addressed to a young actress he wanted to impress: "If you don't love me, I'm going to kill the President."[51] Oswald, however, was not so naive: in the back alley where he positioned himself to shoot, at night, there was no risk of being seen. Unlike Hinckley, he was aware that after such a crime committed in broad daylight, the reactions of the beloved are unimportant, that the life of the perpetrator is destroyed.

Oswald had been at the height of the first phase of his political life—the phase of self-effacement and preparation before dazzling success—on the night of April 10, 1963, when he thought he had killed General Walker. He was no longer the unemployed laborer living in a miserable apartment. Along with Mao Tse-Tung on the Long March, Tito in Bosnia, Castro in the Sierra Maestra, he had gone over to armed insurrection. Yielding to his wife's entreaties, he destroyed the notebook that was a complete account of his preparations. He had left on his desk a list of instructions for her to follow in the unlikely event he got arrested. The list, proof of his bravura, was found in Marina Oswald's cookbook after the assassination. (A technically advanced analysis, performed in 1978, of the bullet that had missed General Walker confirmed the "high probability" that it was fired from a Mannlicher-Carcano.[52] Oswald's rifle was a Mannlicher-Carcano, as previously mentioned.)

When the media said the police had no clues as to who had tried to kill General Walker, Oswald heaped his scorn on them: "They were too stupid." He would remember how stupid they were when he tried to deny assassinating President Kennedy. He thought they would never be able, clever as he was, to prove anything against him.

Those supporters of the conspiracy theory who thought he was a scapegoat had to see him as an ordinary man who would not hurt anybody; as for the Russians and their followers, they never mentioned the attempt on General Walker. Anything that could enlighten their readers, help them to understand what was behind Oswald's crime, had to be ignored. If it was shown that he was not a professional killer, that he had a complex personality, that he could kill for reasons of his own, that he had been after all the master of his destiny, the disinformation campaign would have been less effective.

When Oswald was questioned after assassinating the president, he said that Kennedy's death would not change anything, that Lyndon Johnson, whose views were the same as the late president's, would simply take his place.[53] He thought then that General Walker's death would not have changed anything either, that he too would be replaced by someone else. Oswald's attempt to kill Walker was not a political act; it was supposed to impress his wife and add a striking chapter to his biography. Had Oswald been successful, he would not have been a political assassin. (In his platform Oswald had written: "Refraining from any demonstration of force must be our doctrine."[54]) He probably planned to reveal that he had been the author of the crime when the time was ripe, after the revolution, and would then enjoy the prestige achieved by those willing to sacrifice themselves for the public good. He was paid, not with money like a hired assassin, but with the guarantee that one day he would be greatly admired. It was the central act of his life. When he shot President Kennedy six months later, he was actually accomplishing or completing that first act, as if he had been given a second chance, as if a combination of circumstances offered him another target. He had spent two months planning the attack on General Walker, writing down the smallest details of his preparations, and he had failed; the assassination of President Kennedy had not been premeditated, and he succeeded.

Oswald was not discouraged by the failure of his first act, but it made him think. In any event he would not take direct action again; when such a brilliant plot fails, one does not persist. If he could not prove himself in the United States, it was in Castro's country that he had to seek a solution to his problems. The eleven-month period of political activities, conformist or criminal, ended with the unsuccessful attempt on Walker's life. It was then, and not before, that Oswald began to show an interest in Cuba.

The Warren Commission believed that Oswald wanted to go to Cuba because it was his ideal country; the Russians pretended to believe he was an agent for the CIA, which wanted to post him there. In late April or early May 1963 he planned for an eventual departure and started to put together a dossier that he hoped would impress the Cubans. It would show them he had engaged in activities for their country.

He remembered his conversations with the marine Delgado. He had failed in his hope of going to college when he had decided to go to Russia instead of Switzerland, and also in his hope of becoming a writer, when he had had to face the fact that his chronicle of Russian life would never be published. His third project, living in Cuba, was not going to be easy to carry out. Castro had just come to power when the nineteen-year-old Oswald first thought of working as an instructor in the Cuban army. In those days Americans were allowed to visit Cuba and were encouraged to do so by the Cuban government. Now, when he wished to go there, communications between the two countries were cut off and American citizens were barred from going to Cuba.

The director of the Fair Play for Cuba Committee, a New York-based organization, had managed to go to Cuba illegally and was prosecuted. The example encouraged Oswald, who planned to establish close ties with the director in order to improve his chances when dealing with the Cuban authorities. In Moscow he had learned how to play the part of an ardent Communist sympathizer; in the end it had worked very well. The wise thing to do was to prepare for his departure by playing another part for a few months, the part of an ardent Cuban sympathizer. He felt sure this would guarantee him favorable treatment on his arrival in Cuba.

Oswald wrote to the Fair Play for Cuba Committee and offered to open a branch in New Orleans; he ordered a handbill with the heading "Hands Off Cuba," application forms, and membership cards for the proposed chapter. The director of the committee answered his first letter, indicating his interest. Oswald sent him more letters bragging of real or imagined activities on Cuba's behalf; he never got an answer. Marina Oswald later said, "I only know that his basic desire was to get to Cuba by any means and that all the rest was window dressing for that purpose."[55]

In June a large group of American students, invited by Castro, had managed to go to Cuba; they left the United States to visit Czechoslovakia and returned via Havana. Three of the students stayed in Cuba. Oswald was not sure of being able, like them, to reach Cuba; he also wondered if, succeeding, he would not be disappointed after all. During the first week of July the Soviet embassy in Washington received a letter from Marina Oswald requesting visas for the whole family—Oswald had added a note asking for his "return entrance" to be considered "separtably." Letters were sent to friends in Minsk announcing their imminent arrival. Oswald had told his wife that there was nothing keeping him in the United States, that he had nothing to lose if he left, that he wanted to stay with her, and that the only thing that mattered was to be able to stop worrying about tomorrow.[56]

Marina Oswald said in her testimony he had no intention of going to Russia, that she was to join him in Cuba somehow. He would get in touch with the Soviet embassy in Havana to try to bring her to Cuba or for her to go to Russia. "Sometimes he really wanted to go to Russia and sometimes not. . . . He did not know himself."[57] It did not occur to him that the Russians might not have the slightest wish to see him again. He still believed that the Soviet Union was an open country, just like the United States.

Oswald's hopes of being welcomed in Cuba were encouraged when the idea came to him that he could try making friends with Cuban refugees and thus obtain valuable information about anti-Castro plots, which he would give to the Cuban authorities, increasing his chances of getting into their good graces. At the end of July a ton of dynamite, napalm, and war matériel was seized in a New Orleans house, where it had been stored by Cuban refugees. In order to infiltrate one of the anti-Castro groups, Oswald visited Carlos Bringuier, a politically active refugee, and offered his services as a convinced enemy of Castro. But a few days later he was on the street, in the center of the city, handing out leaflets for the Fair Play for Cuba Committee. Another Cuban saw him, reported it to Bringuier, and both men went to investigate. There was a dispute when Bringuier recognized his visitor; he wanted to hit Oswald who crossed his arms over his chest and said, "O.K., Carlos, if you want to hit me, hit me," and Bringuier realized that Oswald was trying to appear as a martyr and did not hit him.[58] This was the time of non-violence in the struggle for racial integration. Oswald, however, was thinking about his file; if he could give evidence that he had been beaten up by anti-Castro Cubans, he would take his place among Castro's most fervent supporters. He was arrested and spent a night in jail.

Marina Oswald said, "I think that he engaged in this activity primarily for purposes of self-advertising. He wanted to be arrested. I think he wanted to get into the newspaper so that he would be known."[59]

Oswald's arrest led to his being interviewed on a radio program on August 17 and to his being invited to participate in a debate with Bringuier on another program on August 21. His stay in the USSR was brought up by his opponents who had done some research into his background. His pro-Castro activities could no longer be effective. "I think that we finished him on that program," said the moderator.[60] Oswald realized that he was handicapped by his past record and should now "remain in the background."[61]

He started studying Spanish again; his status as a defector would be a stepping stone to a better life only in Cuba—the radio debate had proved it. The idea he had entertained four years earlier of freeing a Caribbean island revived, and he practiced with his rifle almost every evening. His wife made fun of him; Cuba, she told him, would get on perfectly well without him.[62] She thought that after his arrest "he cooled off a little."[63] Actually, if he did not make pro-Cuban propaganda after his arrest it was because there was nothing more he could do to impress the authorities after his hypothetical arrival in Cuba. The only problem was how to reach Havana. He considered hijacking a plane. Marina Oswald said her husband had mentioned hearing stories on the radio about airplane piracy. He would buy a pistol for her. She was to stand up at the back of the airplane at the appointed time and yell "hands up" in English. Marina Oswald managed to talk him out of the plan by explaining that, eight months pregnant, she would look ridiculous, instead of terrifying, brandishing a little gun.

Then he found, he believed, the perfect solution: he would go to Mexico and obtain a visa from the Cuban consulate. He arrived in Mexico City on September 27. He had prepared memoranda containing all the information that could possibly persuade the consular officials to give him a visa. He had letters from the Soviet embassy in Washington and the Communist party in the United States (polite replies to his own letters), newspaper clippings, his Russian work permit, the certificate of his marriage to a Russian girl, and every scrap of evidence he could think of to prove he had worked devotedly for the Fair Play for Cuba Committee.

Nothing went as he expected. He told the Cuban consulate that he wanted to stay two weeks or longer if possible and then go on to Russia. He thought that, once in Havana, by some clever maneuvering he would be allowed to stay and would be offered a position. He was told he would not be given a transit visa for Cuba unless he could show an entry visa for the Soviet Union; at the Soviet embassy he was told there would be a waiting period of four months.[64] In any case, a transit visa would have permitted him only to wait for the Russian plane at the Havana airport. His second attempt to seek better opportunities in a foreign country was as unreasonable as his first. He attributed the failure of his escapade to "a gross breach of regulations" on the part of the Cuban consul.

Once his dossier was complete, Oswald had shown no further interest in the Fair Play for Cuba Committee. In October, having failed to get a visa, he dropped the whole thing and lost interest in Cuba. For three months, until the eve of President Kennedy's assassination, he did not engage in political activity. Back from Mexico, without giving up the idea of returning to Russia, he settled into the role of family breadwinner, working hard, trying hard to be a good husband and father.

The Commission does not believe that the relations between Oswald and his wife caused him to assassinate the President.

Warren Report, chap. 7, p. 423

Nevertheless, a few pages earlier, the commission had said, "The relations between Lee and Marina Oswald are of great importance in any attempt to understand Oswald's motivation."[65]

After the assassination Marina Oswald was under the protection of the FBI and, in fact, cut off from the outside world for a few months. (If another Ruby had been able to find her before she testified before the Warren Commission, it would have been a catastrophe.) After the assassination she was questioned only by the FBI. When she finally appeared before the commission, Chief Justice Warren was very friendly and tried to make her comfortable. (The journalists used to call Marina and the members of the commission Snow White and the Seven Dwarfs.)

Oswald had always complained that the FBI was trying to "inhibit his activities" and prevented him from finding decent jobs. Marina Oswald thus gave the FBI agents as little help as possible. It was discovered that she had not disclosed to them, of her own accord, everything she knew about Oswald's activities—for example, his attempt on General Walker's life. It seemed to the FBI that she was not a totally reliable witness.

She explained how she felt to the House Select Committee on Assassinations. "My husband committed a horrible crime. I did not know if I would be prosecuted for that just as well, being his wife, because I did not know the rules and regulations and law of this country at all. . . . I tried to protect myself. . . . To tell you the truth, I did not like the FBI. I did not like the treatment. I am sorry to say that I was frightened and I sometimes was maybe deliberately difficult in giving information to the FBI."[66] She said, "There was quite mixed emotions."[67]

The attorney of the Warren Commission who had been assigned the task of preparing the general counsel for the examination of Marina Oswald stated that "on balance, Marina Oswald's testimony was less significant by the time [the investigators] were through than might have appeared at the time [they] started [their] investigation."[68] Indeed, she tells us nothing of importance that we would not have learned without her. Everything she says about

Oswald's character and the intimate life of the household is corroborated in the depositions of those who had close contact with Oswald and by Oswald's writings.

Back in his native country the Commander, as Oswald called himself, became tyrannical, even cruel, with his wife. She had contemplated suicide soon after her arrival. She had told an acquaintance that she was quite afraid of him and that she intended "to leave him when she got to know a little more English."[69] People who knew them in Dallas all mentioned Oswald's brutality: "I heard repeatedly from . . . others that Oswald was physically mistreating her."[70] He "slapped her in the face twice" in front of a stranger "because the zipper of her skirt was not completely closed."[71] He forbade her to smoke and once took a cigarette away from her and slapped her in public. She complained that everybody else lived well but that Oswald did not make enough money. Everyone had a car, she said, except them.[72] She had no way of supporting herself. Oswald did not want her to learn English, on the pretext that he would forget his Russian if they spoke English at home. The real reason, probably, was that he was afraid she would leave him if she were able to manage by herself.

In Fort Worth the Texas Employment Commission had referred Oswald to an engineer who spoke Russian; he wanted a certificate indicating his competence in the language, thinking this would enable him to get a job as an interpreter or translator, work for which he felt himself to be qualified.[73] This was how the Russian-speaking community of the Dallas–Fort Worth area learned that a young Soviet woman had just arrived; their curiosity was aroused and they wanted to meet her. Marina Oswald's extreme poverty moved them: "They didn't have nothing."[74] "Marina never had any money, not even pennies."[75] "They was just existing."[76] "Sometimes she call . . . and said she don't have nothing to eat for her kid, if they cannot help."[77] "The Oswald child had no baby crib or bed but was kept on the floor in the bedroom either in a suitcase or between two suitcases."[78]

In Fort Worth, and later in Dallas, the people Marina Oswald met helped her by giving her food or clothes. Oswald resented their concern for her; he wanted his wife to be utterly dependent on him. He knew that they felt sorry for her; he guessed that some of them advised her to get a divorce, and his attitude toward the whole group was hostile. She complained bitterly in front of

George De Mohrenschildt and his wife that Oswald was a poor lover.[79]

After living with him in Dallas for a few days, she left him and took refuge with Mrs. Anna M. Miller, a Russian woman she hardly knew. "She was staying in light blouse and skirt, with baby on her hand, couple diapers and that was all: no coat, no money, nothing."[80] De Mohrenschildt, his wife and another member of the Russian community who wanted to protect her from Oswald's rage accompanied her the following day to help her pick up the baby's bottle and some dresses. "I seem to remember," testified De Mohrenschildt, "that Marina said he will beat her so hard some time that he will kill her. We said, 'Well, let's save that poor woman.'"[81] Oswald managed to find out where she was and made every effort to win her back. Marina Oswald explained: "I saw him cry. . . . He begged me to come back, asked my forgiveness and promised that he would try to improve, if only I would come back." Oswald told her that if she did not return, he did not want to continue living.[82] She gave in.

Only ten days after shooting at General Walker, Oswald, about to leave the house, took his revolver and told his wife that Richard Nixon was coming to Dallas and that he wanted to go and have a look; "If there is a convenient opportunity," he would use the gun.[83] She called him into the bathroom, managed to get out, and to close the door, which she held shut by bracing her foot against the wall. They struggled, and Oswald, after a few minutes, quieted down. He took a book and read for the entire morning.

Richard Nixon was nowhere near Dallas that week. It was a ploy Oswald used to make his point. After putting up with his wife's scorn and persistent complaints for a few days, he had decided to show her once and for all that he expected to be feared and respected. He knew quite well that she would prevent him from leaving the house. He had shown what he was talking about by way of his attempt on General Walker's life, and she still refused to admire him. To punish her for not understanding him, to upset her, was satisfying to him. While one of the reasons for shooting at Walker was his desire to be admired by her, the sole reason for "the Nixon story" was to show her that she should be in awe of him.

When testifying, Marina Oswald recognized that Oswald could have easily opened the door if he had really wanted to leave

85

the bathroom. She realized only then that she had been taken in, that Oswald did not want to get out at all, that he only wanted to "wound" her, to make her "feel bad."[84]

Visiting a friend of the De Mohrenschildts, Marina had met Ruth Paine, a compassionate woman who was studying Russian. The two women stayed in touch after the Oswalds left Dallas for New Orleans. Ruth Paine wrote to Marina, telling her that she would be welcome to come and live in her home in Irving, in the Dallas suburbs. Marina answered that she would accept the invitation if the violent scenes with her husband started up again; she had already stayed at the Paines' home for about two weeks when Oswald had gone on ahead to New Orleans to look for a job and an apartment. When he was ready to leave for Mexico, Ruth Paine went to New Orleans to get her friend and the Oswalds' child. She was told that Oswald was going to Houston or some other city to look for work.

After Oswald returned from his unsuccessful trip to Mexico, he had only his unemployment benefits, which were soon going to run out. Marina Oswald was in her ninth month of pregnancy; she valued the company of the Russian-speaking Ruth Paine. Oswald expected to resume living with his wife after the birth of the child. In the meantime he rented a room in Dallas, and it was agreed that he would spend his weekends in Irving. During the week he called her once or twice a day. At a neighbor's suggestion, Ruth Paine called the Book Depository, where the neighbor's brother worked. There was a job opening and Oswald was hired. On Fridays the brother drove him to Irving.

At the Paines' home Oswald generally left the table before the others had finished eating in order to go back into the living room to read or watch football games on television. On October 25 he went to hear a lecture by General Walker, whose head he had had in his rifle sights a few months earlier. On October 27 he accompanied Ruth Paine's husband to a meeting of the American Civil Liberties Union.

The FBI had interviewed Oswald twice after his return from Russia; they decided that he had not been sent back as a Soviet agent; this was the only thing that interested them, and they did not give him any further attention until they learned of his pro-Cuba activities in New Orleans and of his trip to Mexico. This led to routine visits by James Hosty, an FBI agent, three weeks before the assassination.

On Friday, November 15, when Oswald called his wife at lunch time, she asked him not to visit her that weekend. Ruth Paine was giving a birthday party for her little daughter, and Marina Oswald thought that Oswald was imposing on her hostess by coming too often. On Saturday the sixteenth he went to the Motor Vehicles Bureau to get a driver's license. Ruth Paine had given him driving lessons during his weekend visits. There was a long line, so he decided to return another day. On Sunday the seventeenth he stayed at home and read. The housekeeper at his rooming house said that he always spent his time reading or watching television; there was a set for the guests. He had called his wife twice on the previous day and had been quite affectionate. She felt like calling him. The person who answered the telephone at the rooming house said there was no Oswald living there.

Oswald had had to vacate the room he had rented on his return from Mexico after living there one week. The landlady did not like him. Convinced that the FBI was getting him into trouble with his bosses at work, and now his landlords too, he had registered in the rooming house in which he was now staying as O. H. Lee. When he called his wife on Monday, November 18, she frantically asked for an explanation. He told her that the FBI must not find out where he was living. Besides, everybody knew that Oswald had spent years in the Soviet Union. Marina Oswald complained bitterly: "When will all your foolishness come to an end? All of these comedies. First one thing then another. And now this fictitious name?"[85] She was upset, alarmed. She mistakenly thought that she had erred in believing Oswald had accepted his lot since his return from Mexico. She now feared nothing had changed since General Walker and the rifle, Nixon's "visit" to Dallas and the revolver, Cuba and the hijacking plan: Oswald was planning some new ridiculous scheme. He called several times; she refused to speak to him.

On November 19 the morning paper published the itinerary of the president's motorcade. Oswald learned of the itinerary either that day or the next when he heard people talking about the incoming visit or when he found a newspaper (he avoided buying newspapers). It was by the merest chance that President Kennedy would be in Dallas on November 22 and that the motorcade would drive past the depository at lunchtime, when many workers would be outside to see it as it went by. A space had been cleared on the sixth floor in preparation for the laying of a plywood floor. Heavy cartons of books had been moved in front of a window. They would shield a person standing at the window.

Now that Oswald was familiar with his rifle, the president would be an easy target for a few seconds. On the twenty-first he asked Ruth Paine's neighbor to drive him to Irving after work. If his wife listened to him, he would forget about the motorcade. When she had left him the previous year, he had been eloquent enough, or pitiful enough, to win her back.

The idea of doing something the next day may have already crossed his mind, but when leaving his room that morning, he had not taken his revolver with him. This time he would be very nice to her and try to regain the upper hand; but he sensed that his wife, since she had begun living at Ruth Paine's, had seen that she could survive without him. She had told her friend that she did not know "whether this marriage would last or should."[86]

Oswald kept his rifle in the Paine's garage, with the Oswalds' few possessions. A few days earlier a worker at the Book Depository had shown the other workers a rifle, which they had discussed. Oswald may have decided that the right place for his gun, the proof of his virility, was in his room. He brought paper and tape from the depository so as to be able to carry it to Dallas. He may have planned to take it the next day, regardless of whether he won his wife over or lost her for good; depending on what she decided to do, he would either take it to his room after work, or assemble it in the morning at the Book Depository.

We have all the elements we need to fill in those evening hours. Ruth Paine arrived home from grocery shopping around 5:30. Oswald, she said, was playing on the front lawn with his daughter. She found him friendly. She presumed that his having come without permission was a way of making up for the fight on the telephone. She remembered that Oswald had retired a little earlier than he normally would. She thought that "Marina did not want to discuss the quarrel."[87] Marina Oswald for her part depicted clearly the emotional crisis Oswald went through during the course of the evening: "He said that he was lonely . . . and he wanted to make his peace with me."[88] Later on: "He said that I didn't need him."[89]

And finally: "He stopped talking and sat down and watched television and then went to bed." He hoped to get her back. He had failed.

Marina Oswald told the commission how she treated her husband.

> He tried to talk to me but I would not answer him, and he was very upset. . . .
>
> He tried very hard to please me. He spent quite a bit of time putting away diapers and played with the children on the street. . . .
>
> He tried to start a conversation with me several times, but I would not answer. And he said that he didn't want me to be angry at him because this upsets him. . . .
>
> He said that he was tired of living alone and perhaps the reason for my being so angry was the fact that we were not living together. That if I want to he would rent an apartment in Dallas tomorrow—that he didn't want me to remain with Ruth any longer, but wanted me to live with him in Dallas.
>
> He repeated this not once but several times, but I refused.[90]

She did not say whether he tried to make her change her mind during the night, to get close to her; if he did, she certainly rejected him. She told the investigators that she had only wanted to assert herself, to show that Oswald could not take things for granted with her. But this time she succeeded in convincing him that his suspicions were well founded, that she had definitely decided to walk out on him, that he had lost her and the children for good.

Jeanne, George De Mohrenschildt's wife, said in her testimony: "And then with the baby, he was absolutely fanatical about the child. He loved that child. You should see him looking at the child, he just changed completely. He thought that she was not too good with the child. The child was already spoiled to no end. Every time the child makes a noise, she picked it up. If she is not there in a second to pick the child up, Lee is after her."[91]

Marina Oswald later acknowledged that she had not really been angry with him. She was convinced, she said, that if she had agreed to return to him, the next day would have been a day like any other. "Perhaps (if Lee was planning anything) he staked everything on one card. That is if I agreed to his proposal to go with him to Dallas, he would not do what he had planned, and if I did not, then he would."[92] She did not remember that he had told her the previous year that without her he did not want to continue living. Oswald's decision to act on the twenty-second was made the evening of the twenty-first. The visit to Irving would not have taken place if he had already made up his mind.

> *No one will ever know what passed through Oswald's mind during the week before November 22, 1963.*
>
> *Warren Report*, chap. 7, p. 421

We do know, in fact, what passed through his mind between Friday, November 15, and Monday, November 18, when the row with his wife began over his assumed name; he had become an ordinary working man, and what passed through his mind was what passes through the mind of any man who goes to work in the morning, comes home in the evening, enjoys light reading at night (the Dallas library, unlike the New Orleans library, did not keep a record of the books borrowed), or watches television, and who has a row with his wife now and again.

The couple's last row took place on Monday, November 18. On Tuesday the nineteenth or Wednesday the twentieth, when Oswald learned that the president would pass in front of the depository, the memory of his attempt to shoot General Walker may already have crossed his mind. On Thursday, November 21 he was no longer angry with his wife, and he expected to be able to make up with her. He had a growing sense that everything would be all right with her if she stopped living at Ruth Paine's, where she was rapidly losing her interest in him. But by evening he had convinced himself that she would never come back to him. As to the remaining hours of the week before November 22, we can only try to suggest what passed through the mind of a man we know very well, who thought he had to face the future without his wife and children, who had lost the desire to live.

Oswald lay in bed that night in a half-awake state. (Marina Oswald went to bed two or three hours after him, and it seemed to her that he was not really asleep.[93]) The visions unfolding in the mind of a man on the eve of committing a crime can only be evoked by novelists, not by historians. The visions evoked by the Warren Commission, those of a revolutionary who would show by his act that his world was condemned and that a Marxist, Communist society would replace it; those of a man who would go down in history in full glory—are those the visions that unfolded themselves in Oswald's mind?

A few weeks earlier Oswald had seen two films in a row on television. In the first the character played by Frank Sinatra shot at the president and missed. In the second a character played by John Garfield was plotting to kill a dictator; he failed too, but he had given the signal for the uprising, and the revolution would triumph. Did Oswald imagine himself failing or succeeding?

Did everything he had been thinking before his attempt on General Walker's life come back to him? Was he persuading himself that if killing General Walker was good, killing President Kennedy would be better?

The young boy who had been sent to the Youth House for observation had acknowledged fantasies about "being powerful. . . . He ha[d] dreams . . . entirely pleasant in nature and which [were] usually a fulfillment of fantasies that he might have had when he was awake."[94] Was he indulging in those fantasies as he approached what were to be the last days of his life? The men whose names belong to history had had, one day, the daring that made them leaders of other men—was he thinking he would be like them? Was he thinking that he had almost given up but that now he was his own self again? That if he were captured, there would be an epoch-making trial, he would have a rostrum, he would tell them what the regime he was planning would be like? Perhaps. What is certain is that the image of his wife sleeping peacefully at his side was everpresent with him, even as incoherent thoughts and dreams rushed through his mind.

He had gone to Irving, as if the answer to his fate lay there, and Marina had given him this answer. She made fun of him: "Look at the big shot," she used to say in front of strangers.[95] He would show her that he was the big shot she refused to admire. In the morning he went out through the garage and picked up the rifle he had wrapped up the previous evening while the women were putting the children to bed.

A few hours later, having returned to his senses, the illusions of the night were dispelled, and coming to grips with the hideous reality, he saw clearly that he could not pretend to have been an instrument of history. He swore that he was innocent.

6

The *Warren Report*

The President's Commission on the Assassination of President John F. Kennedy—the Warren Commission—submitted its report to President Johnson on September 24, 1964. *Oswald, Assassin or Fall Guy?,* Joachim Joesten's first book, was reviewed in the September 23, 1964 issue of *New Times*[1] by an "American journalist Victor Perlo"; Victor Perlo, a former employee of the War Production Board, had been the leader of the "Perlo group," accused of espionage during the McCarthy era.

Instigating the writing of this book—or writing it—was the first covert propaganda undertaken by the Russians in their disinformation campaign, which would subsequently evolve at the same time as the mis- and disinformation circulated in the U.S. and Europe.

Joachim Joesten, a member of the German Communist party before the war, traveled to Russia in 1932–33. He came to the United States from Sweden through the Soviet Union in 1941.[2] He was in charge, or took charge of the disinformation campaign in Germany. Two weeks after the tragedy he spent five days "investigating" in Dallas. He and his wife had a date for dinner on the day of his return, December 11, 1963, but his wife found a note when she got home in the evening telling her that he had left for Europe.[3] One cannot help wondering what caused his unexpected and abrupt departure.

He soon submitted an article to *Stern*; they refused to publish it and the article grew into a short book. The translation *Oswald,*

Assassin or Fall Guy (*Die Verschwörung von Dallas*) was published in London by the Merlin Press and New York by Marzani and Munsell before the *Warren Report.*

The beginning of the *New Times* article reads: "Americans await the long-delayed report of the Warren Commission on President Kennedy's assassination. Indications are that it will adhere to the FBI-police version that Kennedy was murdered by a lone operator, Lee Oswald, for no rational reason. Most Europeans, and many politically-oriented Americans, believe otherwise. They suspect Kennedy was the victim of a Rightist political plot."

Tribute to a former member of the Communist party and to a "progressive" followed: "Unofficial investigators have done much research. The Buchanan book attracted much attention in Europe, but was kept from significant circulation in the United States. Attorney Mark Lane, former member of the N.Y. State Legislature, has been the leading advocate of a real investigation."

According to *New Times,* the American publisher of Joesten's manuscript "deserved credit for promoting it." "Thousands of copies" were sold in a short time "despite a blacklist by commercial publishers." (The publisher, Carl Marzani, was convicted in 1947 for making false official statements in denying his membership in the Communist party and was sentenced to one to three years in prison.)[4] Oswald, said *New Times,* "was 'a fall guy,' to use the parlance of the kind of men who must have planned the details of the assassination," chosen because "as a petty, and perhaps discarded agent of the CIA, and later of the FBI, he was an ideal scapegoat."

Joachim Joesten had already published a book in Germany in 1958 about the CIA, *Wie American Geheimdienst arbeitet.* In the eyes of the KGB the CIA is, like itself, above the law and capable of anything. Soviet commentaries and Soviet-inspired commentaries always portray the CIA as having played the biggest role in the conspiracy story.

New Times echoed some of the reasons Joachim Joesten gave to "demonstrate" that the assassination was the work of a "powerful conspiratorial group." The scheduled itinerary of the motorcade was to have passed a block and a half away from the depository and had been changed at the last minute. The final route subjected the president to a cross fire from the depository and from the underpass ahead. (The underpass—the overpass for Thomas

Buchanan—subsequently became "the grassy knoll.") In fact the parade's itinerary was the normal, direct and only permissive route to the site of the luncheon given by business and civic leaders. The initial statement issued by the doctors showed that some of the shots came from in front. (This point is cleared up in chapter 7.) Ruby was a police-station hanger-on and operator of a night club at which the police procured prostitutes. (The only thing that has been uncovered on this point is that a policeman married one of Ruby's former employees.) Such a man, added *New Times,* would not be moved by righteous indignation to avenge the murdered president, and his police pals had conceivably assigned him the job of executing Oswald without trial. The police showed two different guns at different times as being those Oswald was alleged to have used. (This was an invention of Mark Lane's.) A man carrying a rifle was arrested in the railway yard minutes after the assassination and was never identified. (This was a variation on one of Thomas Buchanan's allegations.)

Joachim Joesten, continued *New Times,* was "barred from access to official documents and material exhibits," and he had to rely on press reports supplemented by "his own observations and measurements" in Dallas. This was virtually an acknowledgment on *New Times'* part that his documentation rested on rumors and speculations. The official documents and material exhibits were published ten months after the assassination.

The official theory, explained *New Times,* is probably a police fabrication. Oswald may or may not have participated in the assassination but was not "its sole executor or main arranger."

> There are forces in America who would stop at nothing to achieve their aims of fascistizing the country and initiating nuclear aggression overseas. . . . Seeing the assassination as a job of the ultra-Right, world capitals were alerted against new sorties and provocations from the United States, and rebuffs to aggressive American initiatives became more pronounced. . . . The German and Japanese militarists and fascists made effective use of political assassination in their drive for world conquest. . . . It is only people prepared for any adventure who will risk using such a poisoned weapon. . . . Under some conditions such actions can critically aggravate the danger of thermonuclear war.[5]

The specter of thermonuclear war was judged by the Soviet Union to be of the utmost importance in its campaign to detach Western Europe from its great ally. The charge would be heard again and again in the disinformation campaign, especially in Germany. Germany would be the first victim of the atomic war that, insisted neutralist propaganda, the American militarists wanted.

Two months after it published its review of *Oswald, Assassin or Fall Guy, New Times* pronounced judgment on the *Warren Report* in a few lines:

> The commission upholds the Dallas police version, conceived within minutes of the fatal shooting, that Lee Harvey Oswald alone, acting on his own and without accomplices, was responsible for the crime. . . .
>
> One is inevitably reminded of *Seven Days in May,* the popular [American] novel. . . . In it militarists infuriated by the conclusion of an American-Soviet nuclear disarmament treaty plot to overthrow the government. The president and his closest associates manage to disarm the conspirators on the quiet, without attracting public attention. When at a press conference he is asked whether the dismissed army generals were not plotting to overthrow the government, the president flatly denies it for fear the truth would imperil American prestige as he understands it.
>
> It looks as if the Warren Commission were guided by the same considerations.[6]

The portrait the Warren Commission investigators painted of Oswald was so false that it was impossible to understand his motives for killing John F. Kennedy. Consequently, those who, for a variety of reasons, deceived the public were readily believed.

Although the commission's description of Ruby was accurate, and although the commission had demonstrated that there was no connection between the assassination of President Kennedy and the murder of his assassin, many people continued to believe in Ruby's complicity in the so-called conspiracy. Therefore, even if the commission had painted a more accurate picture of Oswald, its detractors' stories would still have enjoyed a certain amount of credibility, but there would have been, in all likelihood, a rather more healthy skepticism about some of those stories.

The conspiracy theory was kept alive by Communists and fellow travelers who had seized on the opportunity to weaken the United States, as well as by people who were simply taking advantage of the public's interest in sensational stories. There were also those whose belief in the "conspiracy" was genuine. They had adopted a position based on the wild speculations and rumors circulating at the beginning of the investigation, before the *Warren Report* was published, and never reconsidered their position. This third group, sometimes without realizing it, joined in the efforts of the two other groups to persuade Europe that the United States was in a state of decline.

The misinformation given out by the newspapers, Buchanan's book, the numerous lectures and interviews Mark Lane gave prior to the publication of his book, Bertrand Russell's, or rather his secretary's article—all had clouded the issue before the commission's report was published. The *New York Times* described the state of public opinion six months after the assassination. In England, Buchanan received "widespread publicity through lengthy reviews in newspapers of every political opinion and every quality." The illustrated magazine *Review* published a summary of his book. In Russia, the magazine *Za Rubezhom* reproduced it in its entirety; so did *Il Tempo* in Italy. In Spain, *Blanco y Negro* said that unanswered questions deepened the distrust with which the United States was viewed from abroad. In France, "where the affair was deeply felt," the version that Oswald acted alone did not suit "the logical French mind"; there had to be a plot, and because the assassination had occurred in a city with a powerful right- and anti-integrationist wing, the plot had to come from that quarter. Applying its policy of disinformation, the Soviet Union, having originally set the party line, pressed the theme mainly through the Czech media or by reproducing Western speculations on the subject.[7]

Presumably publishers of the translation of the report in foreign countries omitted the appendixes, following the example of the French publishers. Consequently foreign journalists did not know that the report examined 126 commonly heard allegations in support of the conspiracy theory, and demonstrated how frivolous they were.[8] (Another important appendix proved that Oswald never received any money from anyone. His expenses after his return and up until the assassination, established by Internal Revenue Service experts, matched what he had been earning as income from his salary and the unemployment benefits he had collected.[9] The balance was within twenty dollars of the sum he had on the day of the assassination.)

In Western Europe, said the *New York Times,* "the communist and pro-communist press bluntly condemned the Report as a whitewash," and numerous references were made to Bertrand Russell's charges that facts were suppressed.[10] In the United States the conclusions of the report were initially generally accepted. It was only after years had passed that a new wave of "critics" caused a growing segment of the population to doubt the ability or sincerity of the Warren Commission. Whereas only 31 percent of the population still believed in the conspiracy theory after the publication of the report, by early 1967[11] (shortly before Jim Garrison, the New Orleans district attorney, appeared on the scene), the percentage had doubled. When the second investigative commission, the House Select Committee on Assassinations, was established, 80 percent of the population believed the critics of the report.[12]

Immediately following the publication of the report, in England the *Daily Telegraph* affirmed that "every reasonable person must accept the validity of the Commission's unanimous finding," and the *Guardian* described the report as an impressive document whose conclusions were supported by almost overwhelming evidence.[13] However, the French newspaper *Le Figaro* commented:

> No doubt the American authorities, very preoccupied with the criticisms and sarcasms aroused abroad by their previous affirmations, are hoping that the ample collection of documentation . . . will succeed in shaking skeptics' beliefs and silence them. . . . It was essential to prove that Oswald had brought with him the murder weapon. . . . Readers will have some difficulty imagining Oswald assembling the parts of his rifle while he was alone for only a few minutes and had to set up a pile of book cartons. . . . The Report relies on [Marina Oswald's] word for considering valid the identification of the rifle.
>
> [The Report] claims that, despite the implausibility of this, Lee Oswald was the man who shot at General Walker on April 9, 1963.[14]

The reader can see how unfounded these allegations are by

referring to the *Warren Report,* pages 119, 130, 143, 181, 183–5, and 248.

Sometimes, judicious observations could be found in the foreign press. "The value of the Report has been considerably reduced by the Commission's absolute inability to discover Oswald's motives," said Prague Radio. "The phrases 'confused by Marxist ideas' and 'hatred of American society' hardly suffice for a psychological explanation [of Oswald's motives]" observed the *Suddeutsche Zeitung.* [15] On the other hand, *Konsomolskaya Pravda* used the title of Thomas Buchanan's book, *Who Killed Kennedy?,* for a long article. Communist *Neues Deutschland* said that "a dead man was found guilty in order to protect the living murderers." [16]

On the day following its first article, *Le Figaro* echoed the *New York Times.* A columnist had commented that the affair was too serious to be the concern of only the journalist and the historian. He wondered at what he called extravagant coincidences. They caused him to pose questions that had already been answered by the Warren Commission, which indicates he had not read the report carefully, about Oswald's assignment to Minsk, his meeting with his future wife, the loan the State Department had consented to make to him for the trip home. (Answers to these questions were given on pages 696, 702, 752–66, of the report.) An interview with Buchanan was on the same page. "The Commission," he said, "allowed itself to be used as an instrument of foreign policy." [17] The next day *Le Figaro* claimed that it was impossible to fire three shots in five seconds with Oswald's rifle. [18] (According to early rumors, the first shot struck the President in the neck, the second wounded the Governor and the third shattered the President's head, with the time span from the first to the third shot being between five and five and a half seconds. The Commission determined that one shot missed; the time span was seven seconds or more if it was either the first or the third one.) [19]

Earl Warren, chief justice of the United States Supreme Court, served as chairman of the first commission of inquiry. The Warren Commission was composed of two prominent senators, a Republican and a Democrat; the Democratic majority whip of the House; the chairman of the House Republican Conference—future president Gerald Ford—and two professional lawyers who had held high offices in the administrations of Democratic and Republican presidents. The general counsel was a former solicitor general. [20]

To accuse them and their eighty assistants of obstructing justice required believing they were all party to a plot involving the tacit complicity of thousands of people. One had to believe also that they had been able to force witnesses, experts, physicians, FBI, CIA and Secret Service agents, the Dallas police force, Oswald's acquaintances, and Ruby's friends to keep silent or to give false testimony, in which case at least one out of hundreds, out of thousands, would have given himself or herself away or would have retracted testimony given. One also had to believe that in addition to the commission's members, Robert Kennedy, who was still attorney general, and the other cabinet members, who all maintained that there was no evidence of a conspiracy,[21] had participated in a criminal cover-up they knew they could not pull off and which sooner or later would be uncovered, would dishonor them, and would do irreparable harm to their country. (America was dragged through the mud when the commission members were merely accused of having disgraced themselves. What would it have been like if it had actually been proved?) It would be necessary to accept that not a single one of the six thousand journalists in Washington, who all dream of the scoop that will make their career, could find a flaw in a mountain of lies. Furthermore, if the commission had discovered that individuals from the Dallas police or from a federal agency, certain politicians, *mafiosi,* or oil magnates were guilty, it would have had no reason to hush it up; confidence in the United States' governing body would not have been shaken in the least.

To the great satisfaction of its enemies, the image of the United States changed: the America of John F. Kennedy, of Jacqueline Kennedy, was fading away. The worst kind of reactionary politics reigned supreme in America, its enemies proclaimed.

Public opinion tends to see extraordinary events as having a dark and mysterious dimension, and public gullibility is easily exploited. Mark Lane had recognized in the first days following the assassination a situation that could be used to his advantage. His book, *Rush to Judgment,* published two years after the *Warren Report,* in mid-1966, popularized the conspiracy theory. Shortly after the publication of Lane's book, the *New York Times* said that it was to the American people's credit that they had so far refused to be stampeded into imagining a conspiracy, but that in Europe there was a close link between anti-Americanism and conspiratorial themes. The *New York Times* added that conspiracy theories were held intensively, especially in Paris, and that the belief in a conspiracy had not spread in America.[22]

Between 1964 and 1966, preparing for the publication of his book, Mark Lane gave numerous lectures on the university lecture circuit. He claimed that the Dallas police, FBI, CIA, Warren Commission, and United States government were all united in a second conspiracy aimed at a cover-up, that no shot had been fired from the Texas School Book Depository, and that Oswald was innocent.

Lane's *Rush to Judgment* first came out in England. It was at the top of the best-seller list in America for a long time, with more than 100,000 copies sold during the months immediately following publication. A chapter was added to the French edition in which Mark Lane claimed that five shots had been fired. He returned to Paris in March 1967 to promote the book. In an interview with *Le Nouvel Observateur,* he insinuated that President Johnson's role was suspicious: "Johnson would not have been kept as Vice President for Kennedy's second term and was therefore politically finished." He added that the person in charge of the assassination inquiry was Dallas district attorney Henry Wade, "a political friend of Johnson." He also mentioned that Wade's appointment to a federal judgeship had been turned down by Kennedy a few days before the assassination.[23]

His book looked credible because it gave thousands of references, but "close to 90 percent of his footnotes did not check out."[24] His readers were not going to look at his sources. The commission had put out a complete account of its work; it had listened to the most absurd claims. All Mark Lane had to do was to cite some of these claims seriously in order to cloud all the issues. He even wrote that he knew who had pulled the trigger.[25] He produced and distributed a film in which he showed a few of the bystanders whose testimony had been presented to the Warren Commission. The San Francisco magazine *Ramparts* disclosed that these "witnesses" were paid: "Mark Lane had located a witness to the shooting whose brother was mysteriously killed, and arranged to meet him . . . for a filmed interview. Lane offered him $100."[26] These bystanders were not only paid but also prepared: "Trial lawyers usually prepare a witness by discussing his story with him before he testifies."[27] Thus, the people who appeared in Mark Lane's film rehearsed their roles and received a fee. They were not disinterested seekers of the truth; they were just actors.

Mark Lane did not change his technique when he gave a lecture or appeared on television. For example, one of Oswald's coworkers who had seen the package containing the rifle on the morning of the assassination estimated the length of the package at twenty-seven or twenty-eight inches, while the bag Oswald was carrying was actually thirty-eight inches long.[28] This co-worker also said that Oswald had walked from the car to the Book Depository with the package under his arm and resting in the palm of his hand. Lane showed his audience a shoe box, put it under his arm, letting it rest on his hand and asked if it were large enough to contain a rifle. He omitted to quote another statement from the co-worker's deposition: "I was walking along there looking at the railroad cars and watching the men. . . . I didn't pay too much attention on how he carried the package at all."[29]

Mark Lane's film opened in Paris; it was not shown until months later in the United States. The BBC paid $40,000 for a single broadcast and aired it in January 1967. (It had cost $68,000 to produce.)[30] A few days later the BBC returned to what it called the "Warren dispute."[31] Three days before the film's premiere in Paris, French television showed excerpts of interviews with Edward Jay Epstein, the author of *Inquest* (see next chapter); Mark Lane and Léo Sauvage, the French journalist who had established himself as a conspiracy expert during the first few weeks after the assassination with his hastily written articles for *Le Figaro*; and two lawyers from the Warren Commission. The moderator concluded that the truth would probably never be known unless some unknown person were to come forward with a confession. The viewers were influenced by what was then happening in their own country. General de Gaulle had narrowly escaped an assassination attempt. Other attempts had been planned, and his enemies, hoping that one would be successful, looked forward to a coup d'état. Two entirely different situations were compared, and people thought that racists had eliminated John F. Kennedy, anticipating that after his assassination, the orientation of Washington's policy would undergo radical changes.

7

New Times (*Novoe Vremia*)

Pursuing its usual line of conduct, *New Times* gave much attention to the books published in the United States that it believed deserved a large audience. The 1966 books were reviewed in long articles that appeared on September 21, 1966; September 28, 1966; October 26, 1966; and December 21, 1966. The disinformation without political intent in Europe and America and the disinformation spread by the Soviet Union would henceforth reinforce each other.

An American philosophy professor, Richard H. Popkin, had published an article in the *New York Review of Books* that commented at length on two books by the early "critics" of the Warren Commission. In France *Le Nouvel Observateur* reproduced the article in two installments under the title *Oswald n'a pas tué* (Oswald was not the killer) in big red letters, followed by a subtitle, *Trois ans après l'assassinat de Kennedy un document bouleverse les américains* (Three years after Kennedy's assassination Americans shaken by document).[1] Professor Popkin did not produce any document, and Americans were pretty indifferent to his articles.

Here is the text, entitled "New Books on the Kennedy Assassination," that prefaced the first *New Times* article:

> Several books have appeared lately which seriously question the official Warren Commission account of the circumstances of the assassination of President Kennedy. Two such books in the United States are "Whitewash" by

Harold Weisberg and "Inquest" by Edward Jay Epstein; in Switzerland a book by Joachim Joesten is due to come off the press shortly. A number of articles in the periodical press likewise challenge the Warren Commission findings. In a study in the *New York Review of Books* the American journalist Richard Popkin analyzes the new publications on the subject, and his conclusion is that the Kennedy assassination was the outcome of a carefully laid plot in which influential quarters were implicated.

In this and further issues of *New Times* we are printing some excerpts from Mr. Popkin's study.[2]

Harold Weisberg, a newcomer, was an impassioned and sincere critic of the commission who published several books at his own expense.[3] Edward Jay Epstein's *Inquest* was, said *New Times,* "a remarkably effective book" presenting "startling new data about the internal workings of the Warren Commission."

Edward Jay Epstein condemned the *Warren Report* on the basis of mistakes uncovered in some of the materials received by the Warren Commission, although it had corrected them in the course of its work. His plan was to study the procedures and methods of the commission; there had never been a comparable body, and a precedent had been created. When Epstein started out, he was only doing research for a master's thesis. He easily obtained the information he needed from the junior lawyers he met. Some of them mentioned points that had not yet been elucidated. Wesley Liebeler confided in him that he was in disagreement with his colleagues; this was on minor details and not on the main issues. Howard P. Willens, assistant counsel, mentioned "the substantial errors that characterized Mr. Epstein's original work."[4] The *New Times* article opens with the following sentences:

When John F. Kennedy was assassinated, a solution emerged within hours: one lonely alienated man had done the deed all by himself. The investigation by the Dallas police and the FBI then proceeded to buttress this view. The Warren Commission, after many months of supposed labour and search, came out with a conclusion practically the same as that reached by the FBI, except for details as to how it happened. The ready acceptance of this by the press and the public—except for a few critics—sug-

gests that the American public got the kind of explanation
it wanted, and perhaps deserved. Western European critics can only see Kennedy's assassination as part of a subtle
conspiracy, involving perhaps some of the Dallas police,
the FBI, the Right-wing lunatic fringe in Dallas . . .

Before these writings appeared, there were already
strong reasons for doubting that Oswald did the shooting
alone, or at all. The majority of eye- and ear-witnesses
who had clear opinions as to the origins of the shots
thought the first shot was from the knoll or the overpass.[5]

To be exact, twenty out of 178 bystanders had made this
claim,[6] influenced perhaps by the reaction of one of the motorcycle
policemen who had rushed toward the railway underpass—and not
the "knoll" (the grassy bank)—where he had seen an agitated
group of people.

New Times continued:

Now the material presented by Epstein and Weisberg un-
dermines the Commission's case in two ways. First, they
closely examine both the sequence of the shots and the
available medical evidence in order to demonstrate that
all three shots could not have been fired by Oswald. Sec-
ondly, they show that the Commission's theory is in conflict with the FBI's on a number of crucial points: indeed,
one can only conclude either that both theories, considered together, are impossible, or that they establish that
more than one assassin was firing at the President.[7]

Inquest was addressed to a more demanding audience than
Rush to Judgment, and Edward Jay Epstein bears much of the
responsibility for the spreading of the conspiracy theory and the
tales of a cover-up. It is essential, therefore, to clear up the dis-
crepancy between the FBI's early report and the commission's conclusions.

The president had been rushed to the hospital. His life needed
to be prolonged just enough for the last rites to be performed; a
cannula was placed in a small wound on his neck for a tracheotomy.
He was declared dead at 1:00 P.M., and the doctors were besieged
by the press; the whole world was eager to learn how the president
had been killed. The doctors were not supposed to examine the

president's body; they mentioned the small wound on the front of the neck. It was actually the point of exit of the first bullet, but at that moment it was assumed to be a point of entry. It then seemed to everyone that the bullet had entered there and had shattered the skull, and this was the news that was broadcast. The doctors had not turned the body over, so they did not yet know that two bullets had hit John Kennedy, one at the back of the lower neck, the other at the base of the skull. The newscasters gave credibility to the hypothesis that the sniper had fired from the grassy bank or from the railroad bridge over the underpass toward which the motorcade was heading.

An autopsy was performed in Washington that evening after X-ray and conventional photographs had been taken. Many people attended it, including two FBI agents who left during the night, before it had been completed. The bullet that had killed the president was the one that had entered at the base of the skull. The chief autopsy surgeon, Dr. James J. Humes, presumed at first that the bullet that entered at the back of the lower neck had remained in the body, that external heart massage was administered in Dallas, the bullet falling out through the entry wound at that time,[8] when the bullet had actually exited through the front part of the neck. The wound there was the site of the incision made in order to perform the tracheotomy. This point was clarified the following morning after a telephone call to Dallas: the wound made by the exiting bullet had been masked by the incision. The bullet had continued its course.[9]

Nothing had been said about the details of the autopsy to the Dallas doctors who now knew from the media that three cartridge cases had been found near a window in the Texas School Book Depository and, consequently, that three shots had been fired. The next time they were interviewed, they said that the first bullet had entered the president's throat, its point of exit being through the head, that the second bullet had critically wounded Governor Connally, sitting in front of the president, and that the president had been hit a second time, by the third bullet, in the head.[10]

Dr. Humes finished his report in the night, using copies of the blood-stained notes he had taken during the autopsy, notes which he then destroyed.[11] (In the conspiracy legend this was interpreted as the destruction of the original report, replaced, on someone's orders, with another one.) The final typed report, to which was appended the preliminary handwritten draft, was given to the authorities. It was not passed on immediately to the commission, which was then in the organizing stage. No one thought of giving a copy to the FBI or of telling the two agents who had been present for only part of the autopsy that the final conclusions had not been reached until the following day. Therefore, the FBI continued to believe that the bullet that had caused the wound to the base of the neck had fallen out, whereas it had exited and also hit and seriously wounded Governor Connally. The FBI's first report, sent out in December 1963, and its supplement, issued in January 1964, were not immediately made public. Both the report and the supplement, which Wesley Liebeler had mentioned to Edward Epstein,[12] contain the error concerning the bullet.

Dr. Humes's drawings on the autopsy report showed a crudely drawn body, full-face and back view. The wound was located approximately 5½ inches below the tip of the right mastoid process. Dr. Humes put it too low; he indicated, however, the reference points in the margin of the drawings. This should have prevented any confusion: 5½ inches below the tip of the mastoid process is definitely not a point on the back. Overlooking these specifications, Epstein thought that the bullet that had entered through "the back" could not have come out through the neck, and that the wound to the neck might thus have been caused by a second bullet, shot from a spot in front of the car. He kept calling for the publication of the autopsy, photographs and X-rays, hinting that if these were not exhibited, it was because they proved the commission had ratified the doctor's lies.

Chief Justice Warren thought the photographs and X-rays did not add anything to Dr. Humes's testimony; he had decided not to have them produced during the physicians' hearings in order to avoid the necessity of publishing them as part of the commission's exhibits. Their publication would have been mandatory had they been produced as evidence during the hearings. He and several of his colleagues merely glanced at them. One of the junior assistant counsels, who had the responsibility of "determining the basic facts of the assassination," objected that it was "indispensable" that the commission obtain them; he was overruled.[13] Earl Warren wanted to keep the pictures out of sensationalist magazines in order to spare Jacqueline Kennedy and her children.[14]

After his book was published, Edward Jay Epstein recognized

in a magazine article that if the autopsy photographs showed "the wound to be in the back of the neck," [there could be] "no further doubt as to the accuracy and authenticity of the autopsy report."[15]

The commission's detractors kept going back to the questions asked in Epstein's book. For years it was claimed that the autopsy report had been falsified, that the doctors had been ordered to lie, and that the photographs and X-rays had been destroyed because they proved it, because they established that the fatal bullet had not been shot from the Book Depository. To put an end to these claims, it was finally decided that the photographs and X-rays would be deposited in the National Archives but that they would not be available to the public for several years, and then only to "qualified persons." This was a big mistake: during that entire period, and even later, when they were made public, people who had not read Edward Epstein's magazine article kept referring to his book.

The qualified persons who had been allowed to see the photographs and X-rays at the archives did not publish their conclusions, or if they did succeed in publishing them, were not read or believed. A panel of four medical experts published their conclusions as early as January 17, 1969, as the "Report of the Panel of Forensic Pathologists on the Autopsy Findings, Photographs and X-rays [of President Kennedy]," in *The New York Times*. On the panel were Dr. William H. Carnes, Dr. Russell S. Fisher, Dr. Russell H. Morgan, and Dr. Allen R. Moritz. There was, in theory, no objection to the materials being shown to qualified persons. This writer arranged an appointment for Professor L. Derobert, head of the Institut de Médecine légale, Place Mazas, Paris, by contacting Professor Burke Marshall, who was in charge of the documents. Professor Marshall wrote on March 13, 1974 that this writer should tell Professor Derobert to inform Dr. James B. Rhodes, Chief Archivist, that Professor Derobert had been granted permission to inspect the materials in April 1974.

Tass characterized the fact that the photographs and X-rays were kept almost secret as an attempt to hide clues to the mystery of the assassination.[16] (They were published in 1979 by the House Committee on Assassinations.) *New Times* expatiated on the single bullet in the third article of 1966, examining a new book by Joachim Joesten, *Oswald: The Truth*.[17]

The second series of allegations to which *New Times* gave a great deal of attention was related to the fable of the "second Oswald." "Numbers of strange episodes were reported" that the commission "dismissed" despite the fact that the sources "seemed reliable." The incidents in question, said *New Times,* seemed to involve Oswald, and the commission "considered itself satisfied" when it was able to prove that he could not have been where he was said to have been seen and that the person described could thus not have been Oswald. For example, Oswald did not know how to drive and one episode put him at the wheel of a car. His rifle had come equipped with a telescopic sight; a gunsmith said that Oswald had left his rifle with him in order to make holes for a scope. These incidents, said *New Times,* had been interpreted very early on by Léo Sauvage, the correspondent for *Le Figaro,* in an article published by *Commentary,* the American magazine, six months after the assassination.[18] For Sauvage, the incidents in question involved someone who wanted to pass himself off as Oswald.

The following passage, taken from the beginning of the chapter "Questions of Evidence" in Sauvage's book *The Oswald Affair,* shows plainly the author's illogical reasoning: "I admit the authorities proved [Oswald] owned a rifle. So what? For Oswald it apparently was enough to hold the rifle or pose for photographs with it so that he could feel like a revolutionary hero. . . . The order . . . did not include any cartridges. Thus, contrary to what had been thought, the investigators did not even prove that Oswald owned the 'lethal weapon'; an unloaded rifle is not a lethal weapon."[19]

The investigators found that "the cartridge [was] readily available for purchase from mail-order houses as well as a few gun shops; some 2 million rounds ha[d] been placed on sale in the United States."[20] Sauvage criticized the commission for not having tried to find out where Oswald had bought the cartridges.

Léo Sauvage signed a contract for the American edition of his book in March 1964, and then another contract with a French publisher. After publication of the *Warren Report* on September 27, 1964, the American publisher canceled Sauvage's contract and wrote him that "any book which attempts to question Oswald's guilt would be out of touch with reality and could not be taken seriously by responsible critics."[21]

Another American publisher, the World Publishing Company,

was found in 1965. The printing of the French edition was completed on February 20, 1965; the Warren Commission's hearings and exhibits had been published in November 1964. This did not allow Sauvage much time to revise the book, which was chiefly a compilation of articles he had written for *Le Figaro* and various magazines—all based on rumor, personal impressions, or supposed leaks from the commission—before the publication of the *Warren Report.* Sauvage did not suppress the main text of his manuscript, which did not make much sense when all the details of the investigation were made public. (Nevertheless, the subtitle of *L'Affaire Oswald* was *Réponse au rapport Warren.*) This explains the existence of chapters bearing intriguing titles such as "The Mystery of the Chicken Bones," "The Mystery of the Italian Rifle," "The Mystery of the Irving Gunsmith," "The Mystery of the Oak Cliff Agent," "The Mystery of the Texas Theater," "The Mystery of the Clipboard," mysteries that had all been cleared up by the Warren Commission in November 1964 but which were to remain in the minds of Léo Sauvage's readers.

Sauvage set forth with the utmost sincerity three conspiracies: one to assassinate the president, planned by an organization of notables from the South; another to eliminate Oswald, organized by the authorities in charge of the investigation, "primarily the [Dallas] Police Department and District Attorney's office"; and the last a cover-up by the Warren Commission. Here is his explanation of the second "conspiracy":

> For [the authorities] a trial ending in acquittal of Oswald would have amounted to a personal disaster, if nothing worse, they would be compromised morally and scorned professionally. In certain cases where clearly illegal acts had been committed in the probe, administrative penalties or even court proceedings appeared inevitable. For those who were guilty of such acts and who risked at least the end of their careers, the instinct for survival would dictate that the trial be prevented—in other words that the defendant be done away with.[22]

Why would the Dallas police department have preferred being suspected of, accused of, and finally condemned for killing Oswald over being laughed at for its obligingness toward the journalists, its negligence in taking appropriate precautions, its rash and fool-hardy statements?

The last conspiracy, said Sauvage, was conceived to protect the guilty party, and he gave as an argument the *raison d'état*: "[It] is even possible to see in it the foundation of a third plot, not unlike the second, but which fortunately required no victims: a conspiracy of silence."[23] The Warren Commission would have had to do more than remain silent. It would have had to suppress documents, influence witnesses, use threats, if not worse, in order to hide the truth. (The expression *raison d'état* is connected in French minds with the Dreyfus affair, which was evoked in the title of Sauvage's book, *The Oswald Affair.* In the Dreyfus affair the military men and statesmen who conspired to block the reopening of the case for reasons of state believed the army was being attacked by the enemies of the establishment and by anarchists, and even that there was a threat to peace.)

As the New York correspondent for *Le Figaro,* a respectable conservative newspaper, in France Léo Sauvage was considered the expert on American affairs. *L'Express* said that his book picked out the weak points in the testimony with the skill of a virtuoso, and *Le Monde* called it an indictment which demanded a response.[24] Consequently, the French were—and still are—convinced that Oswald was innocent, that there had been a conspiracy, that America was in a state of decay. The articles Sauvage wrote for *Le Figaro* and a few American magazines had already, directly or indirectly, influenced many people. Although he denounced the Lanes and the Buchanans, his book merely confirmed their erroneous views.

The Richard Popkin articles were chiefly elaborations on the theory of the second Oswald, which rapidly became popular. His articles and the book that followed[25] were a godsend for the theoreticians of the "conspiracy." The conspirators, according to Richard Popkin, found a double with a perfect resemblance to Oswald, whose role was to be at the center of various incidents that when recalled, as they would be after Oswald's arrest, would compromise him.[26] (Marina Oswald, who had some difficulty seeing the point, commented that if there had been two Oswalds, she would surely have noticed.)[27] When a dangerous criminal is wanted, it is expected there will be people everywhere who will claim to have seen him. Something similar happened when Oswald's picture was flashed all around the world. The FBI reported that "people from one end of the country to the other called their local FBI office to report seeing Oswald in their neighborhood in the preceding weeks."[28] The Warren Commission had closely examined, among the reports concerning the second Oswald, those claims that seemed to have some validity. Each time, it was obvious that Oswald could not have been where he was supposed to have been spotted. In its investigation of these reports, the commission had drawn up a list of the places and times the second Oswald was "seen."

New Times gave several columns to this second Oswald. Oswald could not drive but "Oswald" told a car salesman that he would come into a lot of money in a couple of weeks. "Oswald," Marina Oswald, and Oswald's daughter—doubles of the whole family—visited the manager of a radio station. "Oswald" and Marina Oswald, with, this time, two children, looked in a furniture store for part of a gun. A grocer reported that "Oswald" came several times to his store, and a barber said that "Oswald" came into his shop with a fourteen-year-old boy and that they both made leftist remarks. "Oswald" appeared at a rifle range and did a number of things to attract attention. "Oswald" was seen running down from the Book Depository a few minutes after the assassination, getting into a station wagon, and driving off.[29]

One of those who testified they had seen Oswald somewhere he could not have been finally commented to the FBI agent who visited him that young men with a face like Oswald's and a build like his were legion in this part of Texas.

Another "striking" incident involved a Cuban refugee who was then living in Dallas, Sylvia Odio. Professor Popkin explained that Sylvia Odio and her sister were visited by two Latins and one "Leon Oswald," who claimed they had come from New Orleans, were about to leave on a trip, and wanted backing for some violent activities. In a phone call the next day, Mrs. Odio was told more about Leon Oswald by one of the Latins called Leopoldo.[30] Professor Popkin then quoted a part of Sylvia Odio's testimony: "The next day Leopoldo called me . . . then he said, 'What do you think of the American?' And I said, 'I didn't think anything.' And he said, 'You know, our idea is to introduce him to the underground in Cuba because he is great, he is kind of nuts. . . . He told us we don't have any guts . . . because President Kennedy should have been assassinated after the Bay of Pigs, and some Cubans should have done that. . . . And he said, 'It is so easy to do it.'"[31] Professor Popkin picked up the thread again. She was also told that Oswald had been in the Marine Corps and was an excellent shot. When Mrs. Odio heard of the assassination, she was sure these men were involved. When she saw Oswald's picture, she knew! The Commission made sporadic attempts to discount Mrs. Odio's story, but kept finding that Mrs. Odio was a quite reliable person, sure of what she had reported.[32]

Sylvia Odio was an important figure in the anti-Castro movement. The visitors told her they had come to enlist her assistance in preparing a letter in English that they wanted to address to prominent Americans who might be willing to help the organization known as JURE (Junta Revolucionaria Cubana). Odio had attended JURE meetings[33] and was probably a prominent member. They claimed to be friends of her father, who was in a Cuban jail at the time and about whom they had remarkably detailed information. They told her that since she was active in the underground anti-Castro movement—which she denied—they wanted her to meet the American who was with them. The Warren Commission asked the FBI to uncover the identities of the three visitors; the commission was given the names of people who later on denied having visited Sylvia Odio, and the investigation did not go any further.

One would have to wonder why Oswald had gone to Dallas from New Orleans when he was leaving for Mexico and hoping to settle in Cuba. What had been said to Sylvia Odio about "the American" could as easily have been said in his absence. It is also puzzling why two anti-Castro militants would go from New Orleans to Dallas to ask a person they did not know help them draft a letter. JURE was considered a left-wing organization that supported a kind of "Castroism without Castro" and was denounced by many in the anti-Castro movement. Six months earlier the State Department had agreed to support JURE, along with other Cuban organizations controlled by the CIA, on certain conditions, one of them being that its operations would be carried out only by Cubans and outside the United States.[34] Sylvia Odio stated that she doubted her visitors belonged to JURE. It would thus seem that the object of the visit was to make her show interest in an American willing to work for JURE and to compromise both her and the group.

If Odio was not mistaken about the identity of the American, the only possible explanation would be that Oswald, in his attempts to infiltrate anti-Castro organizations, came across Cubans hostile to JURE or across CIA undercover agents he approached the way he had approached Carlos Bringuier, the Cuban militant mentioned earlier. The CIA had an interest in knowing whether JURE was engaging in secret activities or was respecting its commitments. The fact that the FBI investigation of the identity of Sylvia Odio's visitors was left in abeyance supports the hypothesis that they were CIA agents.

New Times had announced on page thirty of the September 21, 1966 issue that excerpts of "Popkin's study" would be printed in the future, but nothing appeared in the following issues. *New Times* appears to have backed Popkin's theory until they realized its absurdity. Here is what Popkin said on the subject of Tippit:

> One very suggestive sign of a second Oswald is a report by a waitress that he had come into the Dobbs House restaurant on North Beckley on November 20 at 10 A.M. (when the real Oswald was at work) and had become very nasty about the way his order of eggs was prepared. At this time, Officer J. D. Tippit was there, "as was his habit" each morning at this hour, and glowered at Oswald. The FBI, in this report, rather than being excited at this sign that Oswald and Tippit had encountered each other before November 22, merely commented that Oswald was reported to have worked from 8 until 4:45 on November 20.[35]

Indeed, Professor Popkin offered a curious explanation of police officer Tippit's murder. Oswald was a stooge; the killer was the second Oswald, who had called attention to himself on purpose before the assassination in order to get the police to pursue the real Oswald when the time came, overlooking all other leads, all other suspects. (There were never any other leads or suspects.) Driving slowly by in his car, Tippit saw Oswald, whom he believed to be the man who had complained about his eggs. He stopped him to remark upon his behavior at the coffee shop. Oswald's getaway car supposedly was a secondhand police car, and Oswald thought Officer Tippit was the driver of the getaway car. "A monumental misunderstanding occurs"; Oswald suddenly feared the police officer "realized what had been going on"—hence, the shooting of Officer Tippit.[36]

Professor Popkin believed that the X-ray and conventional photographs of the autopsy had disappeared. He also claimed that almost all of the medical experts were in agreement on the impossibility of a single bullet having caused the president's first wound and Governor Connally's wounds, an untrue statement.[37] He said that Oswald spent the morning of November 22 normally, and that he was seen working on different floors.[38] (Only one employee saw him, at 11:45 A.M.)[39] He suggested that President Johnson might have participated in the conspiracy.[40] He asserted that Professor Liebeler disagreed with his colleagues and was starting a new inquiry, assisted by a team of students.[41] Here is, however, a passage from a letter this writer received from Liebeler in May 1967:

> As far as my own personal view is concerned, I have not in any way questioned the basic conclusions of the Report. At the same time I have certain reservations about some of the procedures that the Commission followed and the way in which some of its former members and representatives have responded to the flood of criticism which followed the publication of the Report.
>
> The notion that the work that we are doing here now—which we presume to regard as an objective consideration of the problems involved—is being done for the purposes of questioning the conclusions of the Warren Report is absolutely false.

The allegation that Liebeler was reconsidering the whole question may have been the basis for a successful French film produced ten years later (see below).

One week after the publication of Professor Popkin's article in *Le Nouvel Observateur,* another article written by Professor Hugh Trevor-Roper, the author of the preface to Mark Lane's book, was published in *L'Express,* giving a further exposition of the critics' claims.[42] Professor John H. A. Sparrow, warden of All Souls College in Oxford, had demonstrated in the *Sunday Times,* in December 1964 and January 1965, that an earlier article by his fellow Oxonian was a misrepresentation; in December 1967, in a piece in the London *Times,* he demolished the position of Trevor-Roper, "Mr. Lane's disciple," as he called him.[43]

Joachim Joesten came back to the subject in 1966 with a book published in Switzerland and Holland and translated into English with the title *Oswald: The Truth. (New Times* had announced on September 21 that the book would come off the press shortly.) In 1967 he published *The Garrison Inquiry* and *Marina Oswald* in London and *The Case against Lyndon B. Johnson in the Assassination of President Kennedy* in Germany. In 1968 he published *How Kennedy Was Killed* and *The Dark Side of Lyndon B. Johnson* in London. Between 1968 and 1970 he wrote revisions or supplements to previous books: *The Biggest Lie Ever Told* in four volumes and *Trilogy of Murder* in five volumes, which included a new study, *Murder Marches On,* all published at his own expense in Germany. In 1972 he published *Cuba, Vietnam, Oil—Three Reasons Why President Kennedy Had to Die.*[44]

Just prior to the Kremlin ban of the translation of the *Warren Report,* in September 1966, *Izvestia* and *Trud* were quoting Joachim Joesten, who accused President Johnson of having seized power and having maneuvered to cover up an ultraright-wing plot. Everything Joachim Joesten said, *Izvestia* assured its readers, had been taken almost entirely from the *Warren Report*—then unobtainable—and the hearings.[45]

New Times reviewed Joesten's second book, *Die Warheit über den Kennedy-Mord; Wie und Warum der Warren Report lügt* (The Truth about the Kennedy Murder; How and Why the Warren Report Is Lying) in October 1966.[46] This book, like its predecessor, was to all appearances sponsored by the KGB.

Tribute was again paid to Harold Weisberg and to Edward Jay Epstein who, according to *New Times,* had virtually disproved the official theory. Joachim Joesten's life, the reader learns, had been difficult. After his first book was published, he had thought it prudent to leave the United States and had settled in Switzerland, where he was "kept under close surveillance by those who wanted to stifle the truth." (Given the close relationship between Joesten and *New Times,* this writer will quote only passages cited by *New Times* and never refer to Joesten's book. Joesten's assertions will be those *New Times* dictated to him or found in his book; they will be reproduced from the *New Times* article.) "American secret services" had obtained the cooperation of Swiss authorities in taking him out of circulation; arrested in Zurich, he was committed to a "psychiatric hospital" and had great difficulty getting himself released. His notes and documents "had been confiscated."

The reason for Joesten's harassment was to prevent him from demonstrating that Oswald had not gone to live in Russia because of his Marxist ideas, that Oswald had not returned to the United States because he had become disillusioned. The real facts, Joesten affirmed, were that Oswald, a secret agent for the United States, had been unmasked and, no longer able to accomplish his mission, had been ordered by the CIA to return to the United States. The CIA tried to use him again in "subversive activities against Cuba."[47] Finally, Joesten concluded, following a new failure Oswald found himself once again in the United States in the position of a "discredited agent." It was then that the right-wingers who were trying to figure out how to get rid of John F. Kennedy stumbled onto Oswald. He was exactly what the conspirators wanted; he could easily pass, in the eyes of the public, as half-mad. The Warren Commission, said *New Times,* still quoting Joachim Joesten, "concealed . . . that Kennedy had enemies in his own camp . . . the oil tycoons of Texas . . . whose tax privileges he was planning to cut: the retired generals whose military wings he had cut . . . the ulti-Right secret John Birch Society . . . the fanatical racists of the South . . . influential elements of the CIA who hated him."

The *New York World Telegram and Sun* was quoted; it had criticized the *Warren Report* for not taking into account the climate in Dallas.[48] In this city "the rich did inherit the earth" and they ruled it "with guns, money and the whip of hate."

Elaborating on Edward Jay Epstein's book, Joesten claimed that the Warren Commission had considered only the testimony that suited it from among the testimony given by all the witnesses questioned. A bullet "zigzagging in the most amazing fashion" could not have passed through the body of the president and then the governor's body. He asserted that the Dallas doctors had "operated on Kennedy," whereas they had only opened his shirt collar to perform a tracheotomy. More falsehoods followed: They had been "unanimous" in affirming that the wound in the neck was caused by the entry of the bullet, which had then lodged itself in the lungs. Alleging that it was "contrary to the laws of the United

States and to custom in all civilized countries" to move a body without first performing an autopsy, Joesten assured his readers that "the experts in forensic medicine" had protested against taking the body to Washington. He said that the autopsy had been performed too late, in a navy hospital, and that the doctors who had performed it were bound by "military discipline" and kept silent, the implication being that this made possible all the machinations deemed necessary.

Joachim Joesten also claimed that the president had been "stripped to the waist" in Dallas and that doctors and nurses "had not seen holes" in his jacket, vest, or shirt, holes "which they would certainly have seen" if he had been shot by a bullet fired from behind him. He quoted a doctor who had not seen President Kennedy, Dr. Shaw, who had, according to Joesten, declared that the first bullet had hit the president in the trachea and had been removed from the lung during the autopsy in Washington.[49] The fact is that Dr. Robert Roeder Shaw, chief of thoracic surgery, had been assigned to take care of Governor Connally and completed his operation on the governor long after the president's body had been removed. He knew nothing of what his colleagues had seen or done; what he believed for a short time was only what he had heard. Whatever declarations he allegedly made to journalists after the assassination were soon shown to have been wrong. Quoting them three years later, Joesten concluded that a bullet that had been removed from the president's lung could not have wounded Governor Connally and that there had been four shots.

Joesten then attacked Ruth Paine, accused of belonging to the CIA; he asserted that she had played a suspicious role in helping Oswald get hired at the Book Depository.[50] (The Warren Commission had thoroughly investigated the backgrounds of Ruth Paine and her husband; their relationship with the Oswalds is examined closely on several occasions in the report.)

The allegations concerning the "insufficient time" Oswald had "to barricade himself and to assemble the rifle," those about the "second Oswald," and the alleged last-minute change in the motorcade's itinerary were repeated. "Joesten presents interesting data about how the question of going to Dallas arose," continued *New Times*. Originally, the president's trip "did not include Dallas." (Several pages in the *Warren Report*, however, explain how the Texas trip was planned. The basic decision was made in June.

The initial plan was for only a "whirlwind" visit to Dallas, Fort Worth, San Antonio, and Houston. In September the trip was extended and the decision was made that a motorcade would drive through Dallas.) Here is what *New Times* said:

> The *Dallas Morning News* reported on November 23, 1963, leaders of the Democratic Party urged the President to drive through Fort Worth and Dallas so as to give a greater number of voters the chance to see him. . . . Kennedy consented. "Unfortunately," writes Joesten, "the Warren Commission did not enquire what 'leaders of the Democratic Party' persuaded President Kennedy to ride in a slow-moving motorcade through the inner streets of the ultra-reactionary cities of Fort Worth and Dallas. . . . Joesten draws the conclusion that the attack on Kennedy was thoroughly planned out beforehand: the ambush was laid in accordance with the strategy and tactic of guerilla warfare, in which the high-ranking military specialists party to the conspiracy were peculiarly experienced.[51]

It was thus not only the ultraright that instigated the assassination; now leaders of the Democratic Party were also in it.

Articles "published in the *Midlothian Mirror* [a Texas newspaper], unknown to the broad public, that named people who were killed because they knew too much," were briefly mentioned. More pages were devoted to "the murdered witnesses" in the next article, published two months later, in December 1966, under the title "Echo of Dallas."[52]

The first assertion was that the administration made a big sum available for press coverage of the *Warren Report*. Then the works that "challenged the official version" were quoted, namely, the books of Joachim Joesten, Mark Lane, Thomas Buchanan, Harold Weisberg, Léo Sauvage. *France Presse*'s observations on the development of the controversy in public opinion were also quoted. This controversy, commented *New Times*, was as lively in Europe as in the United States. *New Times* also referred to a "documentary" that "challenge[d]" the Warren Commission's conclusions and that had been shown "privately" in Paris and London. This "documentary" was Mark Lane's film, discussed above, which had been televised by the BBC and shown in a movie theater in Paris.

The assistant counsel on the Warren Commission who had

been the first to think of the possibility of a "single bullet" had become, *New Times* informed its readers, the district attorney of a large city, the implication being that the post was the reward for a useful suggestion.[53] The former assistant counsel, Arlen Specter, explained to the assassinations committee why this conclusion had forced itself on the commission: "The most persuasive evidence was the alignment of the president, the trajectory of the bullet," which, not having struck the car, necessarily hit someone in the car. The fact that the bullet was yawing on entering the governor's back and lost velocity in tumbling through his body was consistent with the single-bullet conclusion.[54] Moreover, in his opinion, if the single-bullet theory was not valid, there could still have been only one sniper. As there was enough time, the president and the governor could have been hit by two bullets. He did not think, however, that was the way it happened.[55]

New Times gave considerable attention to an article published in *Life* magazine that quoted the governor, who thought he had started to turn to his right upon hearing the first shot and was then hit.[56] A delay in sensory perception is not uncommon: "We have all had experience in which persons have been seriously injured and have not known they were injured for a few minutes," said Dr. Michael Baden, the chief medical examiner for the city of New York.[57] The fragments of metal found in the body of the president and the body of the governor "were very likely fragments from Mannlicher-Carcano bullets," and "there was evidence of only two bullets among all the specimens tested," which included those found in the car and the so-called magic bullet.[58]

New Times reproduced a cartoon from the Stockholm newspaper *Aftonbladet* showing a pathologist opening the door, to what was supposedly a morgue, for two orderlies carrying a corpse on a stretcher. "What?" said the doctor, "another witness?" Here is the explanation *New Times* gave of the cartoon: "People connected in one or another way with the Dallas mystery have had a curious way of vanishing from the scene. On the third anniversary of the assassination, UPI recorded sixteen such deaths, and gave details about most of them."[59]

New Times then gave the names of the "murdered witnesses" with alleged reasons for their deaths, and commented that there had been a high mortality rate among those who knew too much. On the evening of Oswald's murder a reporter for the *Dallas Times-*

Herald, Jim Koethe, and another journalist, Bill Hunter, had met Tom Howard, Ruby's lawyer before the event, at Ruby's apartment. All were dead. "They had discovered something of some importance," asserted *New Times.* A fourth victim was the well-known columnist Dorothy Kilgallen: "she had covered the Ruby trial." Striptease dancers were disappearing like newsmen. Mentioned were Nancy Mooney, a performer at Ruby's club who had hanged herself in her jail cell after being arrested for taking part in a brawl, and Karen Carlin, "the last person" to have spoken with Ruby before he killed Oswald. The husband of one of the Carousel's (Ruby's nightclub) employees, Hank Killam, had been knifed to death. William Whaley, the driver of the taxi Oswald had taken after the president's assassination, was the eighth victim. Lee Bowers, a railroad employee, and Earlene Roberts, Oswald's landlady, had also died. "And so the list goes on," affirmed *New Times.* The background of the murdered witnesses story is as follows.

The founder and editor of *Ramparts,* a California-based Catholic publication, had ruined himself trying to keep the magazine going. Warren Hinckle, who was in charge of advertising, proposed a radical change in the magazine's orientation. He left for New York where, he said in his memoirs, there were "pink fortunes." He raised "left-wing gold"—no names were given, either of individuals or foundations—and *Ramparts* became an antiestablishment organ. Warren Hinckle launched, in the spring of 1965, the story of the "murdered witnesses," which was widely accepted in Europe. It was, he said, "an overnight sensation"; he stressed that European newspapers ran scare headlines.[60]

Hinckle had always been antiestablishment himself; he disclosed that he was sympathetic to Eldridge Cleaver and the Black Panthers.[61] After its transformation, *Ramparts* carried partisan articles on the student protests at Berkeley, the medieval views of the Catholic Church, Black culture, and so on, with advertisements for posters of Castro, Marx, Trotsky, Stalin, Lenin, and Mao. In one year circulation jumped from 25,000 to 150,000. The magazine's success was due to its metamorphosis into a big-money left-wing professional publishing operation, as Warren Hinckle himself described it.[62] Reproducing the story about the "murdered witnesses" was one of the magazine's promotional operations.

Warren Hinckle had picked up the story in the weekly paper of a small Texas community (population: 1,521), the *Midlothian*

Mirror, which was then publishing—instead of the local news—
excerpts from the *Warren Report* accompanied by commentaries
written by its publisher-printer, Penn Jones, who became famous
when the world press learned through *Ramparts* that he had uncovered mysterious deaths connected with the assassination. He
was "doing the job that the Commission flubbed." In fact none of
these "murdered witnesses" had witnessed anything, and only one
had been murdered. The list got longer, depending on the whim of
journalists: the victims became fifteen or twenty or more; names
were rarely given. When names were given, they were invariably
of people who had as little connection with the Dallas event as
Penn Jones's first "murdered witnesses." *Ramparts* published a
ninety-six page collection of articles on "the assassination and its
aftermath." It contained "the story of a Texas editor's brave search
for the truth about the assassination, and the incredible weave of
circumstances and intrigue he uncovered, including mysterious
deaths of the persons connected with the tragedy."[63] *New Times*
omitted one name only from the *Ramparts* list: the name of the
brother of someone who had seen a man running with a revolver
in his hand after Tippit's murder.

Jim Koethe, the first on the list, was killed in his own home;
"robbery appeared to be the motive for the crime," *Ramparts* admitted,[64] explaining that an ex-convict had been arrested while
trying to sell some of Koethe's personal belongings. Bill Hunter
was killed by a stray bullet in California while some officers at the
police station were playing with their guns. Tom Howard died in
March 1965 of a heart attack. (Curiosity might have led several
people to go and look at Ruby's apartment or to search for his
roommate after Ruby killed Oswald; it was perfectly normal for
Koethe and Hunter, newsmen, or for Howard, Ruby's lawyer, to
do the same.)

Dorothy Kilgallen died after combining alcohol with an over-
dose of sleeping pills. (*Ramparts* felt compelled to state: "We know
of no serious person who really believes that the death of Dorothy
Kilgallen was related to the Kennedy assassination.")[65] Nancy Mooney had attempted suicide twice during the weeks preceding the
final attempt. The rumor spread that she had worked at Ruby's
nightclub; the investigation, however, showed that it was without
foundation. Karen Carlin died of gunshot wounds in Houston, according to Penn Jones. (She testified to a commission lawyer after

the reported date of her death;[66] *Ramparts* deleted her name from the list.) Hank Killam had died in a freak accident in Florida. The store window in front of which he was found was shattered; a shard of glass had severed his jugular. Hank Killam, according to Penn Jones, had two connections with the Dallas events: his wife had been one of the cigarette girls at Ruby's nightclub and a fellow house painter had lived in a furnished room in the same house as Oswald. (Thomas Buchanan wrote in *Le Nouvel Observateur* that Hank Killam had been found with his throat slit, without mentioning that it had been slit by the broken glass from a store window.) William Whaley and Lee E. Bowers died in automobile accidents. At the time of the assassination, Lee Bowers was in a railroad tower from which he could see the parking lot behind the grassy bank; he testified that he had not noticed anything suspicious. Earlene Roberts died of a heart attack; she was a half-blind elderly woman whose health had been deteriorating for some time. Whaley, Bowers, and Roberts had given testimony two years earlier.

Thus, only three of these "witnesses" to the assassination were vaguely connected with the investigation: William Whaley and Lee Bowers, who were killed in automobile accidents, and Earlene Roberts, who died naturally. Karen Carlin, Hank Killam, Nancy Mooney, and Tom Howard had no more connection with the assassination than any other inhabitant of Dallas. Jim Koethe, Bill Hunter, and Dorothy Kilgallen were journalists whose interest in the affair was professional.

Penn Jones thought that President Kennedy had been killed by the federal government "with the connivance of the FBI and CIA and at least tacit approval of Lyndon Johnson." Ten years after the *Ramparts* article appeared, he proclaimed that he had a list of seventy-two suspicious deaths.[67] His expert knowledge had won him a major role in Mark Lane's film. Warren Hinckle described *The Midlothian Mirror* as the only antiestablishment newspaper in the proximity of Dallas.

The House Select Committee on Assassinations added to the *Ramparts* list the names of "murdered witnesses" found in the writings of the *Warren Report*'s critics. For good measure it supplemented these with the names of two mafiosi, Sam Giancana and John Roselli—both killed many years after the Dallas assassination, a normal end for Mafia bosses—because some CIA agents had contacted them in 1963, when the assassination of Castro was being considered. After having inquired, the House committee reported that "the available evidence" did not establish anything "which would indicate that the deaths were . . . caused by the assassination of President Kennedy or by any aspect of the subsequent investigation."[68] A rumor due to "a careless journalistic mistake"[69] had held the attention of the committee; the careless journalist had written that the odds against the 15 witnesses supposedly victims of mysterious deaths being dead by February 1967 were one hundred thousand trillion to one."[70] The figure was used for the promotion of a movie "based on Mark Lane's novel [*sic*] *Rush to Judgment*," according to the member of the staff in charge of the research; in fact, it was used for the promotion of the movie based on the novel *Executive Action*.[71]

Ruby in his prison cell, concluded *New Times,* seemed to be pretty safe: "But now we hear that [he] is a very sick man, he is supposed to have a diagnosis of cancer, and it looks as if soon the man who silenced Oswald will himself be silenced for all time."[72] Ruby died the following year of a blood clot in the lungs; the autopsy showed terminal cancer of the lungs and tumors in the brain. Thomas Buchanan wrote in *Le Nouvel Observateur,* "As foreseen" (foreseen by *New Times*)—"the name of Ruby is added to the list of the murdered witnesses."[73]

In 1967 Joachim Joesten published *La Vérité sur le cas de Jack Ruby* (The Truth about the Jack Ruby Case) in Paris.[74] Readers were told that Ruby had been in prison eight times and that his history was littered with corpses. Joesten also "disinformed" the readers of a popular French magazine: Oswald was innocent, but he had been done away with because he knew too much. The death of President Kennedy, who had been able to win the confidence of Soviet leaders, could profit neither international Communism nor the extreme left in the United States[75]—this statement was intended for those who persisted in accusing the Soviet Union of having used an American Communist to assassinate President Kennedy.

At that time several foreign publishing houses bought the rights to a parody of *Macbeth* entitled *MacBird*—written by a "veteran of the Berkeley student wars"—which had been produced in California, New York, and London. In translation, *MacBird,* whose chief merit lay in its author's thorough knowledge of Shakespearean English, lost its flavor. All that remained was a murder accusation leveled at Lyndon Johnson. Interviewed in *Le Nouvel Observateur*, the student acknowledged that the accusation was gratuitous; but if the president had really had John Kennedy killed, she added, it would be the least of his crimes.

Two years after the publication of the *Warren Report*, the Paris bureau of the *New York Times* wired, "France has been, and continues to be, more agitated about the assassination than probably any other foreign country, and perhaps more than the United States itself."[76]

Five years after the assassination of John Kennedy, killed by a despairing man simply because he was the president, Kennedy's brother Robert was killed by an Arab for having made pro-Israeli statements. For some of those who played on the credulity of their readers or listeners, the conspirators, whose hatred, they said, was relentlessly pursuing all the Kennedys, had shown themselves again. Thus, the conspiracy myth served the ambitions, doubtless legitimate, of Edward Kennedy, who in taking his brothers' places seemed to be braving death. In January 1977 *New Times* published this item about him:

> More than four years ago, at the time of the 1972 election campaign, Democratic Party leaders worked hard to induce Edward Kennedy to accept the Democratic presidential nomination, but he refused, pleading "personal family responsibilities." . . . The press at the time indeed made it plain that Edward Kennedy was bound to be killed if he decided to contest the election. . . . It was revealed that at the time of the 1972 presidential campaign [Howard Hunt] had been plotting against Edward Kennedy. Pinned down by the facts, Hunt admitted that he had persuaded General Lansdale and Commander Conein, both of the CIA, to join in the projected secret operation. . . . The new plot was abandoned because Edward Kennedy publicly announced that he would not run for President.[77]

Howard Hunt, known for his participation in the Watergate break-in, was presumably a former CIA agent. If there had been the slightest bit of truth in this allegation, the repercussions in the United States would have been tragic. The technique of Soviet disinformation is to use false information already circulating and which has taken root—or even information that is true—and add outrageous falsehoods that profit from proximity to allegations that have been accepted or to reliable testimony. A similar approach was used in the American film *Executive Action*. An actor playing a television newscaster in what appeared to be, down to the smallest details, a real newsroom read false news. These shots were skillfully interspersed with authentic newsreels from the period; thus the newsroom scenes appeared to be authentic.

The conviction that the way in which the Warren Commission had conducted its investigation had been scandalous was reinforced when it was announced that the New Orleans district attorney, Jim Garrison, had solved the assassination and knew who the conspirators were. Jim Garrison had been released from active duty in the army years before for "a severe and disabling psychoneurosis of long duration."[78]

Since Oswald had lived in New Orleans, Jim Garrison could take legal action against any individual living in the city whom he would accuse of having been Oswald's accomplice. For months he had tried, in vain, to build a case against David Ferrie, an anti-Castro activist whose name had been mentioned in connection with the assassination in 1964. A break came when Jim Garrison received a letter from an insurance salesman who said he had known Ferrie and could give some information about him. The newcomer talked about a plot for the first time while he was in a "deep hypnotic trance" and while being asked a series of leading questions.[79] He said that one evening, at Ferrie's home, he had heard him say "We'll get him," meaning John F. Kennedy, in the presence of Oswald, a bearded, unkempt man who was living with Ferrie.[80] Oswald never had a beard and was living with his wife on the date of this alleged gathering; moreover, David Ferrie's bearded, unkempt friend was later identified. Jim Garrison accused a retired businessman, Clay Shaw, of having been Ferrie's accomplice in the conspiracy. What followed showed that there had been no real reason to choose Shaw over any other resident of New Orleans other than the fact that he was, like Ferrie, a homosexual.

The district attorney's statements were broadcast the world over; Mark Lane, Richard Popkin, and Harold Weisberg rushed to New Orleans to give Garrison the benefit of their deep knowledge of the affair. The result was that he soon announced that his investigation was going to lead to a considerable number of arrests and that the country would be shaken to its very foundations. He could demonstrate that sixteen assassins had been positioned in five different places. He declared, "I assume that the President of the United States is not involved; but wouldn't it be nice to know it?"[81]

In the many interviews Garrison gave—one, in particular, to *New Times,* which devoted several columns to him in 1977—Garrison said he had been slandered by the New York papers. The European press did not mention or hardly mentioned the daily disclosures of his irregular doings. In March 1967 Mark Lane wrote in *Paris-Match* that Jim Garrison had become the most important man in the United States.

Members of Garrison's staff, in trying to strengthen the case against Clay Shaw, had threatened or bribed potential witnesses or subjected them to harassment. They had tried to get an experienced burglar to agree to plant compromising documents in Mr. Shaw's apartment.[82] Jim Garrison himself told one of his chosen witnesses that "people that helped him he took care of."[83]

David Ferrie died of a cerebral hemorrhage and Clay Shaw was acquitted. The New Orleans Crime Commission said that twenty-two allegations of criminal wrongdoing had been brought against Garrison and his staff, and that it was "essential to look into the allegations."[84] (They involved such instances of wrongdoing as criminal conspiracy, attempt to intimidate and bribe witnesses, inciting to such felonies as perjury, battery or conspiracy to commit battery, criminal defamation and public bribery.)

In October 1975, when the assassination was once again in the news, Jim Garrison was invited to a meeting chaired by Mark Lane at the University of Hartford, in Connecticut. The object of the meeting was to demand a new investigation. Attendance ranged from three hundred to two thousand persons. Jim Garrison claimed that the CIA, with the help of the FBI, had plotted and carried out the assassination. He was given a standing ovation.[85] He knew, like all public relations experts, that when something has been said with enough insistence, whether it be good or bad, only blurred memories remain in people's minds. In the end the name of the person or product, the title of the film or book, is all they remember. Those who applauded Jim Garrison remembered him as having unsuccessfully attacked the commission, and they saw him as a victim of the establishment. Just as the name "Garrison" was all that had remained in the memory of newspaper readers of that period, who did not remember exactly to what he owed his distinction, the word *conspiracy* was what had remained in their memory in connection with the assassination.

Of all the statements made later by the House Select Committee on Assassinations, which tore to shreds the arguments of the Warren Commission's critics, people remembered only the "discovery" of the fourth shot erroneously said to have been fired from the grassy bank; and the National Academy of Sciences demonstrated, in vain, that there had been only three shots, [all fired by Oswald]. (The story of the "fourth shot" is examined in chapter 8.) What stuck in the minds of those who steadfastly believed in the "conspiracy" was a given formula—the "murdered witnesses" or the "magic bullet," or some statement that had impressed them for some reason. Even those able to see that the *Warren Report* was solid nevertheless thought that if there had been so much talk about the assassination, something questionable must have happened, that where there is smoke, there is fire.

The legend had thus finally spread in the United States. The "critics" were invited to talk on radio and television, and they helped each other out: Jim Garrison wrote a preface to one of Harold Weisberg's books. Richard Popkin wrote the preface to Mark Lane's second book, and Joachim Joesten dedicated one of his books to Mark Lane. Léo Sauvage wrote an introduction to a book by Sylvia Meagher, a "critic" who added five murdered witnesses to *Rampart*'s list and who specified their alleged connections with the case and the cause of death. They were a man "who had helped the FBI trace the revolver used to shoot Tippit" and who "had died of natural causes"; an operator of a strip joint "who had employed some of Ruby's entertainers" and who "had died of natural causes"; a bystander "who had witnessed the escape of Tippit's killer" and "who was killed in a brawl in a bar"; an eyewitness to the assassination "who was victim of a motor vehicle accident"; a man who believed he had information about a Ruby-Oswald link and "who had a heart attack."[86]

The list of newspaper and magazine articles, books, and statements made on radio and television that poisoned public opinion is endless. The last bibliography, published in 1980, lists 2,400 books and more or less important articles. Another of the many sources from which *New Times* quoted was the French newspaper,

L'Aurore. According to *L'Aurore,* a former member of the French foreign legion, whom it called Romero, had been supposed to kill President Kennedy while the president was on an official visit to France in 1961. A photograph of the alleged killer was reprinted from the German magazine *Stern.*

> "Two and a half years before John Kennedy was killed by Lee Harvey Oswald, I was asked by Americans to liquidate the President. I was to shoot him in Paris on May 31, 1961, during his state visit to France. The details of the killing would have looked like an abortive attempt on the life of President de Gaulle. For this I was promised 200 million old francs, half of which was paid to me in advance."
>
> . . . when Paris was welcoming John Kennedy, an agent awaiting Romero handed him the assassination plan on which three possible sites for the ambush were marked: a house on the Rue de Rivoli the President was to pass on his way to the Louvre, the Place de l'Etoile or the Arc de Triomphe. Romero was informed where and how he would get the key to a chest containing a Remington-280 carbine with an infra-red sighting device. He was assured that everything had been arranged for an escape after the killing: several cars would be parked in different places to take him out of the country.[87]

After the two Joesten books written for the German and the British markets, the KGB sponsored or fabricated another one for the French market, *L'Amérique brûle* (American burns);[88] the publishing house had never published and never would publish another book. The English version, *Farewell America,* printed in Belgium for a company that had been incorporated in Liechtenstein, was available to any interested distributor (one was never found). Thirty thousand copies were printed. The French edition enjoyed immediate success; by the end of the year sixty thousand copies had been sold.[89] The key to the story behind the book was revealed by Warren Hinckle of *Ramparts.*

Farewell America's author, James Hepburn, said he was an American with a degree from the London School of Economics, "a friend of Mrs. Kennedy before her marriage."[90] (Mark Lane had presented himself in Europe as a friend of John Kennedy.) He recounted that the president's death sentence had come from a committee of prominent citizens in Texas and Louisiana. The killers were professionals who had received direct assistance from the Dallas police and "the entire American power structure."[91]

Warren Hinckle threw some light on what had been just an "active measure" in the disinformation campaign. The correspondent *Ramparts* had sent to Jim Garrison had suggested that "it would be nice to learn what the Russians knew" about the assassination.[92] He probably did not know they had released some documents to the Warren Commission investigators, letting the investigation think there was no other information concerning Oswald in the USSR. They were routine papers, mainly from the Moscow hospital. To have believed it was possible to obtain other documents seems naive.

Warren Hinckle sent an emissary to Mexico whose mission was to explain to the Soviet embassy that information from the KGB concerning "Oswald and others" would be helpful to Jim Garrison.[93] The embassy's response was that compliance was possible, the only condition being that the source of the information would never be revealed. Soon afterward the manuscript of the English version—*Farewell America*—was in Jim Garrison's hands. It contained names and addresses connected with the CIA's clandestine operations, the location of secret CIA schools of sabotage; it gave details about CIA-owned newspapers, radio stations, and publishing houses. Similar details—favorable ones—were disclosed about the KGB.[94]

Hinckle sent to Paris a volunteer who had been working with Mark Lane. He interviewed the publisher of the book, who told him that "James Hepburn" was the pseudonym of a group of European and American researchers,[95] that the publisher had chosen the name because Katherine Hepburn was his favorite movie actress; "James" was for the French *j'aime*. The book was serialized in *Bild,* Germany's popular daily newspaper. It was thought that *Ramparts* could publish it in the United States. Warren Hinckle said that he temporized and ended up doing nothing because he hoped he would get a last chapter that, added to the manuscript Jim Garrison had forwarded to him, would contain the names of the conspirators. He would then have published the whole manuscript with a "terrific cover" and the title "Who Killed Kennedy, by the KGB."[96]

Even if Warren Hinckle sensationalized the story, even if some details are hardly believable (for instance, the publisher taking *Ramparts*' investigator to the Elysée Palace), it is apparent that the publication of *L'Amérique brûle*—and the printing of *Farewell America*—was a KGB scheme. Warren Hinckle asserted that neutralists in the French Intelligence Department, who may have been double agents, had been party to it.[97] The authors of *L'Amérique brûle* also made a film that, although announced in Paris with the title *Mort d'un Président* (Death of a President), was never shown. A number of prominent Americans were accused either directly or by implication of having had knowledge of the plot to kill John F. Kennedy. Fear of a libel suit was the reason the film was not distributed to French theaters.[98] It was shown in the United States only on the campus of the University of California at Los Angeles, in November 1968.

Executive Action, the film adaptation of a book Mark Lane had collaborated on, followed very much the same lines as *L'Amérique brûle*. The screenwriter was Dalton Trumbo, one of the ten alleged Communists blacklisted in the Hollywood of the McCarthy era. The film portrayed the assassination as having been organized by some right wingers who accused President Kennedy of wanting to pull out of Vietnam and of supporting a "rapprochement" between the United States and the Soviet Union. In the film an "extremely wealthy oilman" supplied the funds after coming to believe that if Kennedy were not eliminated, blacks would achieve an unacceptable level of power and influence. Ruby, "a procurer," patiently awaited his big moment.[99] The film was very successful; in 1975 it had already grossed $15 million. It is now available on video cassette and is still shown on television.

Among other such films a Cuban movie, *L.B.J.*, portrayed President Johnson in January 1969 as being responsible not only for the death of John Kennedy but also for the deaths of Senator Robert Kennedy and the Reverend Martin Luther King. Another film, whose distribution assured its success, was made in France, inspired, according to the producer, by the "events in Dallas"; the assassination of witnesses, the guilt of the CIA director, the blind obedience of the Warren Commission to orders from higher up—except for the hero, played by Yves Montand—the signal given with an umbrella to the killer, were all for the producer real historical events. And shown on French television was an American television film, an adaptation of an unsuccessful play, *The Trial of Lee Harvey Oswald,* followed by a debate focusing on the "official murderer" and the "riddles" of the assassination.

There was a resurgence of interest in the assassination in 1975, when, as a result of the Freedom of Information Act, researchers could consult documents kept in the National Archives, those the Warren Commission had considered too unimportant to be published or those whose disclosure had seemed inopportune at the time. As far as the president's assassination is concerned, no one has ever been able to get anything out of these documents that would require changes in the *Warren Report.*

The complete story of a Soviet defector, Yuri Nosenko, a KGB officer, came to light in 1975 or 1976. Assigned to the Foreigner Surveillance Unit, Yuri Nosenko said he had had access to Oswald's file in Moscow. He declared that the KGB had never given much attention to Oswald. The CIA wondered if Yuri Nosenko was not a KGB agent. He was kept in solitary confinement and subjected to harsh treatment for three years before the CIA finally believed him. It is difficult to see the importance of Yuri Nosenko's story where Oswald was concerned. If he had not told the truth, if he was a KGB agent, if he was saying what the Russians wanted the United States to believe—which did not necessarily mean that it was not true—the situation was simply the same as before his defection.

The "revelation," along with the rumor that the CIA had tried to have Castro assassinated, provided the elements for a best-seller. The title was *Legend: The Secret World of Lee Harvey Oswald.*[100] *Legend* was financed by the Reader's Digest press and released in the supermarkets.[101]

Every novel produced for the mass market is required to have its share of pretty women, so Marina Oswald is "an extraordinarily beautiful woman."[102] Epstein also produced an "exquisitely beautiful Japanese woman,"[103] and an "exceedingly beautiful young Cuban woman."[104] But our attention is really drawn to the one hundred or so "strikingly beautiful"[105] hostesses at Tokyo's Queen Bee nightclub. We are told that "according to one source, Navy intelligence was also interested in the possibility that hostesses from the Queen Bee were being used at the time to gather intelligence and . . . Oswald was receiving money from someone at the Queen Bee."[106] Nothing further is said about the "source," and no reference is given. We read about a marine who had seen Oswald with a Japanese woman who, he supposed, was one of the hostesses at the nightclub.[107] Another marine had seen Oswald with a "good-looking Japanese girl," while a third had noticed him with a Eurasian "much too good-looking for him."[108] All this established that the eighteen-year-old Oswald was working for the Russians and that the KGB had arranged the defection of a Marine Corps private as carefully as it would have arranged that of some atomic scientist or prominent official.

That the *Reader's Digest* had emphasized the sensational character of the book emerges from the preface: Edward Jay Epstein expresses his gratitude to several people, one for "his substantial contribution to the text," another for "his sage editorial advice"; a third is "a perceptive editor"; a fourth is thanked "for his deeply perceptive editing of the manuscript."[109] Epstein's reputation, built on his book *Inquest,* was such that *Legend* was successful. Written, published, and advertised at the same time the House Select Committee on Assassinations was conducting its inquiry, the new book helped to gain credence for the committee when it ventured to say that a second sniper had probably fired from the grassy bank. With respect to a second sniper, here is another excerpt from *Legend*: "Even if it were determined that all the bullets fired came from the same rifle—and microballistic analyses of the fragments recovered indicated they were fired from Oswald's weapon—it would still be at least theoretically conceivable that the rifle was passed from the hands of one sniper to another between the shots."[110]

Millions of pages have been written about "the conspiracy"; not a single one contains any valid information. In contrast, not a single sentence in the *Warren Report* concerning the major points—Oswald's guilt, the total absence of any evidence of a conspiracy, and Ruby's role—needs to be altered.

Right from the beginning, the Soviet Union had been able to rely on foreign fellow travelers. Publishers seeking a best-seller or well-intentioned people who may or may not have been manipulated also served the goals of the Kremlin—unwittingly, Thomas Buchanan, Mark Lane, Richard Popkin, and a few others had paved the way; future "critics" would cause mistrust of the commission to become permanently entrenched in the minds of their many readers. As an illustration of the fact that mistrust of Washington was slowly increasing, let us mention that from 1965 to 1973 the percentage of West Germans who wanted their country to adopt a policy of neutrality rose from 37 to 42 percent.[111] Some of the increase can be attributed to the propagation of various anti-American disinformation, one of them being the disinformation on the assassination of President Kennedy.

The Dallas tragedy had become another false historical puzzle, whose alleged mystery fascinated almost everyone. The interest of the Soviet Union in the *Warren Report* received a strong stimulus, in the mid-1970s, with the establishment of the second investigative commission, the House Select Committee on Assassinations.

8

New Commissions of Investigation and *New Times*

In 1975 it came to light that the CIA had at times interfered in matters that fell within the jurisdiction of the FBI; in particular, it had infiltrated dissident groups and eavesdropped on private telephone calls. A commission was formed, with Nelson Rockefeller as its chairman, to investigate these abuses.

A civil rights activist, Dick Gregory—the author of a book on Martin Luther King written in collaboration with Mark Lane—demanded to be heard. He was the spokesman for those who claimed that two individuals visible in a photograph taken at the scene immediately after the assassination were two former CIA agents, Howard Hunt and Frank Sturgis, who had recently been compromised in the Watergate affair.[1] The individuals in the photograph were two tramps known in the neighborhood. The Assassination Information Committee, a small group set up after one of Mark Lane's lectures and which later repudiated him and declared itself to be a Trotskyist organization, used these photographs in a propaganda effort limited to posting them around some college campuses, with an accompanying text notable for its vehemence. Meanwhile, Dick Gregory's allegations led the Rockefeller Commission to examine closely the accusation brought against the CIA of possible complicity in the assassination of the president.

France-Soir carried the news item in an article having nothing to do with what its title seemed to promise: "The Role of the CIA in the Murder of Kennedy. The U.S. Senate Investigates." Here are quotations from the article: "New suggestions crop up at regular intervals. They all collapse, lacking a solid foundation. . . . The French especially are unable to imagine the murder of a statesman without a conspiracy. . . . There will always be . . . new theories explaining that Kennedy was the victim of a plot that no one can logically explain."[2] But rather than these excellent observations, the reader would remember other passages from the article: Oswald was a deserter who had left for the USSR while serving in the Marine Corps; he was under strict supervision by the CIA, if not actually working for it; the deaths, some of them "strange," of "numerous witnesses," were disturbing. Back in the United States the Rockefeller Commission's conclusions, published in June 1975, supported the *Warren Report.*

The CIA was under discussion again several months later, when it was revealed that some CIA agents had had conversations in 1963 with an important Cuban official who wanted to assassinate Castro. When Castro came to power, the CIA had already communicated with former owners of gambling houses or houses of prostitution who thought that everything would go back to normal if Castro were to disappear. Cuba was then accused in some quarters of having been involved in the Kennedy assassination. The reason behind this was curious. If the Americans wished to get rid of Castro, then, logically, the Cubans wanted to get rid of Kennedy; if America wanted Castro assassinated so that Cuba would cease to be Communist, logically Cuba wanted Kennedy assassinated so that Cuba would remain Communist; if the midget is told that the giant is thinking of beating him up, he will take him on first to teach him a lesson.

A new commission of investigation was appointed. The chairman of the subcommittee in charge of examining CIA operations in connection with the investigation of the assassination was Senator Richard S. Schweiker, who had written the preface to the book by Sylvia Meagher already mentioned. Senator Schweiker announced, before any investigation had even begun, that the *Warren Report* was "like a house of cards; it's going to collapse."[3] The house of cards did not collapse; six months later the *Schweiker Report* stated, "The committee emphasizes that it has not uncovered any evidence sufficient to justify a conclusion that there was a conspiracy to assassinate President Kennedy."[4]

During Lyndon Johnson's presidency the war in Vietnam discredited the establishment, and a growing percentage of the population was prepared to believe anything. Similarly, the slander campaign could be successfully revived when President Nixon and close associates of his were shown to have been involved in the Watergate scandal. The media convinced almost everybody that there had been illegal goings-on during the Kennedy assassination inquiry. The problem was agreeing on the identity of the guilty parties. In Europe, and particularly in France, where something still remains of the concept of the two hundred all-powerful families, it was not necessary to be pro-Soviet to point the finger at the Texas oil elite. In America, where powerful business people are seen in a different light, random accusations were made against the CIA, the Mafia, Cuba, and the Soviet Union. The Soviet Union, which wanted from the very beginning to gain some political advantage from the event (or, rather, strategic advantage, by stirring up controversy among America's allies about the value of the Atlantic Alliance) was thinking of the impact its inventions would have in Europe. It was not uninterested, however, in the fact that a certain number of Americans were no longer convinced that their country was the land of law and morality. During the years of war in Vietnam, draft dodgers and deserters felt perhaps they were justified when they read interviews with Jim Garrison in *Playboy*.[5]

Fifteen years after the assassination, in step with the times, the guilty parties were denounced in the Soviet Union, but only for the edification of the Soviet population. The assassins had to be none other than Zionists for those Russians listening to a lecture at Moscow University. Another Soviet view expressed in the magazine *Ogonyok* held that Oswald was a Chinese agent.[6]

New information in the United States had given rise to strong feelings among the admirers of Martin Luther King: from some of the FBI documents published following the passage of the Freedom of Information Act, it was learned that J. Edgar Hoover, director of the FBI, had employed every possible means to discredit the Reverend King.

Mark Lane, who was the defense lawyer for Martin Luther King's murderer, persuaded Coretta Scott King, the reverend's widow, that his client had thought it was to his advantage to plead guilty, but that he was innocent.[7] A great deal was said at that time about the alleged Memphis conspiracy, and this had the effect of reviving the Dallas "conspiracy." Several members of Congress were convinced that the names of the conspirators should and would be found.

They were told that the president, filmed by a bystander, was thrown backwards for a fraction of a second by the mortal bullet.[8] They deduced from this that it had been fired from in front of him by a sniper posted on the grassy bank, which was on the motorcade's route. (The bullet would not have had enough momentum to cause the president's reaction. The backward movement had been caused by a neuromuscular reaction and gave no clue as to the sniper's position. The same sort of reaction is observed, experts explained, when a jackrabbit shot in the head leaps upward as a result of the contraction of powerful muscles in its hind legs.)[9]

Early on, the grassy bank became a "grassy knoll," the inexact and confusing term suggesting that a sniper would not have been in plain view; a sniper would not have been able to hide, either, if he or she had been behind the fence that separates the bank— referred to as "the embankment" in the *Warren Report*—from a parking lot where cars were coming and going and where the conspiracy theorists sometimes placed the sniper.

Mark Lane was the force behind the establishment in 1977 of the House Select Committee on Assassinations, which the Black Caucus had demanded in order to clear up the circumstances of Martin Luther King's assassination. This committee would also examine those of President Kennedy's assassination.[10] The position of chief counsel and staff director was offered to Mark Lane. He turned it down.[11]

Two years earlier Mark Lane had already appeared during a televised hearing of a subcommittee investigating the facts about a note Oswald had addressed to the FBI agent, James Hosty. Mark Lane was close to the chairman of this subcommittee, "silently assisting him."[12] After James Hosty's visit to Irving, Texas, Oswald had hand-delivered to FBI headquarters a note in which he told the agent that he was not to bother his wife again; if the agent persisted, he would take the necessary measures and address himself to the proper authorities. The receptionist at the FBI offices, however, claimed that the note said something entirely different, that it had been a "warning," and that Oswald threatened to "blow up the FBI and the Dallas Police Department."[13] The note was foolishly destroyed by the FBI agent and his immediate superior. They feared J. Edgar Hoover's wrath if he learned that a note from the assassin was being kept in the files of the FBI's Dallas office. James Hosty certainly quoted it correctly. Oswald used the same arrogant tone with other officials, for example, the consular official in Moscow.[14] He was not a man given to making wild threats and the receptionist probably confused his note with an anonymous one, of the kind the police all over the world frequently receive.

During the ten months in which the Warren Commission carried out its mission, it was able to examine the arguments advanced at that time in support of the conspiracy theory and disprove them. Years after the commission had been dissolved, it might have seemed appropriate to assign to another committee the task of showing that allegations subsequently made by the critics of the *Warren Report* could not be substantiated. Among the congresspeople who voted for the Select Committee on Assassinations' preliminary funding and subsequent increases—the vote was always close—some knew that nothing had ever been found to undermine the *Warren Report*; they thought, however, that it was important to demonstrate this fact as definitely as possible once and for all. Other representatives actually belonged to the sizeable segment of the public that believed the fantasies of an imaginative Western European newsperson or of a Soviet agent.

The new chief counsel and staff director, Professor G. Robert Blakey, was an expert on Mafia matters. He chose as his assistants a lawyer who had served with the Organized Crime Strike Force in Kansas City and a former associate editor of *Life* who had written a series of articles on the Mafia.[15] Professor Blakey and his colleagues were convinced before they started that the Mafia had assassinated the president. The subtitle of Blakey's book, *The Plot to Kill the President,* published after his investigation, was *Organized Crime Assassinated JFK*; in his bibliography, he listed more books on the Mafia than on the assassination; his list of sources included forty-three files dealing with the Mafia and only three dealing with the assassination. After the committee published its conclusions, Professor Blakey explained that the committee had not agreed with him, but that there was only one theory that had any weight: "the mob" had killed the president.[16]

One year later, without any new facts, Blakey stated on a television program that he was "open to the possibility of foreign intelligence," that he was "perfectly willing to concede that [he] could have been wrong . . . that maybe the Mafia didn't do it, that maybe it was either the Soviets or the Cubans." He did not, however, destroy the manuscript in which he had established the "unquestionable guilt" of the Mafia; the book was in the bookstores the following year. On the same program he also said, "I am inclined to think that we've focused too long on Lee Harvey Oswald, that . . . the key to the assassination [is] in Jack Ruby's personality, not in Lee Harvey Oswald."[17] Conceding that the guilty parties might have been the Soviets, while still believing that Ruby was the key to the assassination, he was now making Ruby out to be a Soviet agent.

As for Oswald, Professor Blakey established that his mother, before he was born, had worked for many years in the office of a lawyer who became an assistant district attorney "during the period in which that office was later proven to be highly corrupt";[18] that when Oswald was sixteen, she lived in an area "notorious for illicit activities";[19] that at the time, Oswald was persuaded by a schoolmate to go to meetings of the Civil Air Patrol where David Ferrie was an instructor. ("I think that Ferrie was there when Oswald attended one of these meetings, but I am not sure," said the former schoolmate.[20]) Ferrie and Oswald, according to Blakey, may have met at the Civil Air Patrol, and Ferrie was employed in 1963 by an attorney who had a mafioso as a client. Marina Oswald had known a police officer who also worked as a chauffeur and bodyguard for another mafioso. Oswald's uncle had a role in underworld gambling activities in New Orleans and had close associations with a racketeer.[21] This was not much to go on in trying to establish a link between Oswald and the Mafia; nevertheless, Professor Blakey declared, on December 16, 1978, at the close of the committee's work, that in light of the presumptive evidence concerning Oswald's activities and his ties with members of the New Orleans Mafia, the Mafia had been behind him,[22] and still maintained seven months later that elements of organized crime were guilty.[23]

Blakey explained in his report how his investigation was "structured": "Prior to December 31, 1977, the committee undertook to master the critical literature that had been written on the issues. The exploratory phase was also used for the purpose of deciding what specific subjects were worthy of further investigation."[24] The committee "focused its attention on Jack Ruby, his family and his associates."[25] In his book Professor Blakey outlined for the reader the first steps taken by his committee:

> We recognized that the implications of the murder of Oswald were crucial to an understanding of the assassination of the President. We were able to reduce the credible alternatives to just a few. Oswald was one of two or more conspirators, *which we knew to be the case* [emphasis added] and he was killed by Ruby, also a conspirator . . . because other conspirators wanted Oswald silenced. A second possibility was that Ruby . . . was brought in after the fact, still to silence Oswald. Third . . . Ruby acted alone . . . out of personal anger and grief.[26]

Thus, Professor Blakey let slip that before beginning the investigation, after having just "mastered the critical literature," he "knew" that Oswald had accomplices, acknowledging that he had made up his mind before the fact-finding phase of the inquiry.

Contrary to its expectations, the committee had to acknowledge that Ruby was not a member of organized crime. It stated, however, that the evidence indicated he had direct and indirect contact with underworld figures and had numerous associations with criminal elements in Dallas. The fact was that Ruby had grown up in a poor neighborhood in Chicago and that some of his playmates had come to no good. Some of the people he had met during the week preceding his crime, some of those he had called, were far from being respectable, but the committee recognized that as he had said, he was seeking assistance from all quarters in his disputes with the Guild of Variety Artists.[27]

There was a glimmer of hope for Blakey and his staff when someone mentioned that the police communications center had a record of the sounds at the scene of the assassination. Carelessly, a motorcycle officer had left his receiver on. Graphic translations of the sounds were made and compared to impulses obtained after the recording of shots fired from the Book Depository and from the grassy embankment, the committee's expectation being that it would be able to demonstrate that another sniper had fired from that spot. After some complicated analyses had been performed, the expert said that there might have been a fourth shot in addition to the three fired by Oswald. Seventeen public sessions, televised in their entirety, were held. Sixteen established that the Warren

Commission's conclusions were unassailable. The only session expected to contest the commission's conclusions was the last one, the one that analyzed "scientific acoustical evidence." However, contrary to the assassinations committee's expectations, the expert was no longer convinced a fourth shot had been fired. There had been, he explained, a number of undetected "false alarms" still lurking in the data he presented.[28] He admitted, "It is about equally likely that there were three shots."[29] Taking into account the expert's inability to reach a definite conclusion, it was stated that there was insufficient acoustic evidence to conclude there had been accomplices.[30]

The chairman of the subcommittee investigating the Kennedy assassination, Rep. Richard Prayer, was interviewed on September 24, 1978 (another subcommittee was investigating Martin Luther King's assassination). He told one of the interviewers: "The polls right now of course show that 80 percent of the people don't believe the Warren Commission Report. The Warren Commission may have been right, but they were not persuasive; they didn't hold any public hearing."[31] What his committee was aiming at, he added, was convincing the public.

The draft of the "final" report of the committee, dated December 13, stated: "The shots which struck President Kennedy were fired from the 6th floor window of the Texas School Book Depository Building."[32] Interviewd later on, however, the chairman of the assassinations committee, Rep. Louis Stokes, said that there was other evidence suggesting that the president was the victim of a conspiracy.[33] (The two acousticians who had assisted the first expert had told the committee that after reviewing all the data, they could show that the probability of a fourth shot was not 50 percent but 95 percent.) An extra session was held on December 29, two months after the "final" session of the series of seventeen. The original expert was present. He "somewhat inexplicably drastically modified his earlier testimony," as one of the committee members put it.[34] So, at the last minute the committee reversed its conclusion: "The acoustics testimony shows that two armed men very probably fired at President Kennedy . . . probably the victim of a conspiracy."

The committee ambiguously stated that its investigations of Oswald and Ruby showed "a variety of relationship that may have matured into an assassination conspiracy,"[35] thus insinuating, although it did not dare to come right out and say so, that the two had been in the conspiracy together.

It was subsequently learned that Professor Blakey had neglected to inform the committee of the opinions of other acoustical experts, opinions radically different from the ones presented to the members of the committee. He had also failed to take into account the fact that the police officer responsible for radio liaison with his colleagues on duty in Dallas at the time of the assassination had expressed doubts that the tapes could reveal anything.[36]

In this type of parliamentary investigation, the work, important or not, is carried out by the chief counsel and his assistants. This was a large group: researchers, editors, employees of all kinds. In the months of peak activity 118 people were involved in the investigation. Their salaries added up to over four million dollars.[37] They were convinced beforehand that they were going to uncover all the details of a conspiracy. They worked in close contact for nearly two years, animated by team spirit and inspired by the chief counsel. It was probably difficult to accept the idea that they had wasted all that money and effort.

The Warren Commission had been composed of distinguished public figures whose names guaranteed that each important line of the report would be checked; their assistants, involved with the actual investigation, had been selected for their competence. In contrast, the committee on assassinations was made up for the most part of little-known congresspeople; although they proved to be attentive, well informed, and often made intelligent comments during depositions, they could not help but be influenced by Professor Blakey and his staff.

Obviously, the committee was aware that the unexpected reversal of its conclusions was disconcerting. The chairman declared that the Justice Department ought to look at the acoustical evidence, and if they felt that additional study was necessary, they ought "to pursue it." He pointed out, as the chairman of the subcommittee on the assassination of John F. Kennedy had done, that 80 percent of the American people believed that Oswald was not guilty.[38] The respect these elected congresspeople had for the majority's opinion is probably an occupational disease. At the end of the closing session the vote in favor of revising the conclusions was carried five to two. Five members out of twelve were absent. To a reporter who asked if there were any serious differences of opinion, the chairman replied, "Not really."[39] The dissenting views held by several members of the committee were, however, published in the committee's report. One of them said that the decision of the majority was "supposition upon supposition upon supposition."[40] Three weeks before the first televised hearing, the *Washington Post* published an article entitled "House Assassinations Committee, Circus or Catharsis?"[41]

In January 1977, when it was announced that a new committee of inquiry would be formed, *New Times* gave its own version of the facts in a series of articles entitled "On the Trail of a President's Killer."[42] The *New Times* correspondent had interviewed a congressman, Thomas Downing. Thirty columns were given to the "conspiracy" in order to add new accusations to the congressman's assertions—which would subsequently be disproved by the committee formed, he was pleased to stress, at his insistence. Jim Garrison was quoted: interviewed by the *New Times* correspondent,[43] he said that Oswald was instructing terrorists opposed to the Castro government in the summer of 1963 and that the assassination was essentially a camouflaged coup d'état. With the interviews of the congressman, the district attorney, and other ill-advised Americans, both currents of disinformation—the one from Buchanan to Penn Jones, the other from Joesten to "James Hepburn"—seem to have converged—unless, of course, *New Times* distorted their statements.

The name of the new body on assassinations intrigued the *New Times* correspondent. He said it should have dealt with the plans for Castro's assassination: "If you think it proposes to go into the recently revealed sensational CIA conspiracies against foreign political leaders, you are mistaken."[44] He claimed that whatever had been disclosed had been "pigeonholed." (The report of the Select Committee to Study Governmental Operations with Respect to Intelligence Activities, with which Senator Schweiker's name was connected, mentioned that it had forwarded all the files pertaining to the investigation of the CIA operations involving plots against Castro to its successor, the permanent Senate committee overseeing intelligence operations.) The Cuban government informed the new body, the assassinations committee, that the Cuban official who had planned to assassinate Castro with the CIA's help had been arrested and was serving a life sentence.

Thomas Downing, the congressman *New Times* had interviewed, had sponsored the resolution leading to the establishment of the assassinations committee. The congressman had been convinced for years, he said, that there had been a conspiracy. "It is practically impossible," he insisted, "to fire three shots from one rifle in such rapid succession." It certainly appears that he had not read the *Warren Report* attentively, since the report discusses this point at great length. The commission had explained that the version of three bullets hitting the limousine with one of them hitting Governor Connally was false and had demonstrated that the same bullet had wounded both the president and the governor. Congressman Downing added that on this point, he was relying on the opinion of firearms experts; the Warren Commission, more than ten years earlier, had done exactly that. (The assassinations committee used as a point of departure "the critical literature."[45] It had decided to ignore the Warren Commission's work "based largely on the work of the FBI"[46] which had "failed to conduct an adequate investigation into the possibility of a conspiracy in key areas,"[47] implicitly the Mafia area.)

New Times claimed it admired the congressman's courage, "the first to challenge openly these all-powerful quarters who have resisted public pressure for a thorough investigation of the Dallas tragedy for more than ten years."[48] There was no demand for a new investigation until 1975, when past activities of some CIA agents who had thought that the "Cuban problem" would have been solved if Castro were assassinated were brought to light. The preliminary funding and successive increases for the new investigative commission had been voted for in the House of Representatives without pressure against it from anyone. Congress's hesitations were due to the enormous sums of money requested and the lack of seriousness of some of those who had participated in the initial work of the committee. The committee had been established in September 1976 but did not begin its investigation until June 1977, after the resignation of its first chief counsel and staff director. Those who had been involved in the Warren Commission's work did not object at all to a new investigation; they knew that it would render justice to their own work.

Outright lies succeed one another in the article: "There is documentary proof that shortly before the assassination Oswald met with FBI agents and handed them three confidential letters." Also, "the CIA was in possession of taped statements by Oswald," who had "secret connections with CIA hirelings who were plotting to assassinate Cuban leaders." Ruby was an "FBI informer" and "a stooge" for two Mafia bosses.[49] *New Times* interviewed the editor of *Labor Today,* who said that "it [was] not safe to dig into the doings of the Mafia" and that "Intelligence too [was] involved." Alluding to the "fact" that "those who could help bring out the truth had died in suspicious circumstances," the assassinations committee had taken measures to protect those who would help it. Congressman Downing told the *New Times* correspondent that the CIA and the FBI had deliberately deceived and misled the Warren Commission and that, in consequence, these two agencies would be barred from participating in the investigation.[50]

The reasons given in earlier years as explanations for the assassination were taken up again. The president had ordered the CIA to abandon its plan to have Castro assassinated, he had demanded the arrest of the Mafia bosses, he wanted to withdraw American troops from Vietnam, and he was seeking rapprochement with the Soviet Union. The entire military-industrial complex joined forces in order to get rid of him. Generals, politicians, monopolies were all in it together.[51]

Many pages were given to the two Mafia bosses Giancana and Roselli. Ruby, whose real name was Rubenstein, *New Times* emphasized, was no longer just a stooge for Giancana and Roselli. The Chicago Mafia had become powerful enough to set up branches in other big cities: Giancana had succeeded Al Capone in Chicago, Roselli took Las Vegas, and Rubenstein set himself up in Dallas. Ruby had been, in his childhood, a homeless waif and had joined one of Al Capone's gangs in his teens.[52]

The Senate Select Committee on Intelligence wanted Giancana to testify about the CIA-Mafia plot to kill Castro. Giancana was killed in July 1975, before he could appear. *New Times* affirmed that like Roselli, who was killed the following year, he had to die because he had revealed his connection with the CIA to the committee.

Professor Blakey never mentioned Giancana and Roselli in connection with Ruby. In his committee's report, published two years after the *New Times* articles, he mentioned that his committee had found that "it was possible that an individual organized crime leader might have participated in a conspiracy to assassinate President Kennedy." And he added that if such had been the case, the participants would have been Carlos Marcello and Santos Trafficante.[53]

For *New Times*, however, Giancana and Roselli were the Mafia bosses involved with Oswald. "On the eve of the assassination in Dallas" an anonymous counterintelligence agent brought together "in a basement room of the Carousel nightclub" the conspirators and the "puppets." Among the doomed men were "Giancana, Roselli and Lee Harvey Oswald."

The Carousel, Ruby's nightclub, was described as an illegal gambling den where "the unsuspecting were cleaned out at the gaming tables" and where "a brisk trade went on in drugs and prostitution." In passing, *New Times* said that the president's assassination had "set off like a chain reaction an epidemic of deaths of Carousel habitués."[54]

New Times quoted the New York *Daily News,* according to which Roselli had hinted to associates that he knew who had arranged President Kennedy's assassination: Oswald might have shot Kennedy or have acted as a decoy while others ambushed the president at closer range. When Oswald was picked up, Roselli suggested, the underworld conspirators feared he would crack and disclose information that might lead to them, "which would have brought a massive crackdown on the Mafia." So Jack Ruby "was ordered to eliminate Oswald."[55]

There had already been rumors on this subject. Since 1973 Roselli had been in contact with a well-known columnist, Jack Anderson, to whom he had said that the assassination was the work of Cubans connected to Santo Trafficante, that Oswald had been recruited as a decoy, and that Castro was behind the assassination.[56]

The assassinations committee dismissed those statements. It was known that Roselli had confided to a friend that he had invented the story. Blakey tried, however, to find some elements of truth in it. The committee did not go along with him; its report did not mention anything about Roselli's alleged role in the assassination of President Kennedy.

New Times did not forget the grassy bank. Most of the witnesses, it asserted, did not look at the windows of the Book Depository, but at the "knoll" where "gunfire had been heard and the smoke from a gunshot had been seen."[57] This was a distortion of a statement made by a bystander, S. M. Holland, who had modified, for Mark Lane's film, his previous statement to the FBI. *New Times* embellished further: "People at the foot of the hillock dropped to the ground for fear of being hit. And one woman cried: 'They're shooting at the President from the bushes!'"

The last article in the series concluded by quoting some statements made by Bernard Fensterwald, Jr., the founder of an unofficial "Committee to Investigate the Assassination," to whom Congressman Downing had offered the position of chief counsel and staff director.[58] On the subject of Edward Kennedy seeking the presidency, he told the *New Times* correspondent:

> He'd be a fool if he did. For he would surely risk sharing the fate of John and Robert. After all, the killers of the Kennedy brothers, the men who hired the assassins and their omnipotent backers have not been exposed. . . . In the past 15 years or so political assassination has unfortunately become an established tradition in this country. Nowadays national political leaders are being killed, and moreover with impunity. That is why it is essential, even after a delay of 13 years, to find the killers of President Kennedy. This must be done if such things are not to happen again.[59]

"Will there be an end to this violence and terrorism?" concluded the *New Times* correspondent.[60]

It is essential to emphasize once again that *New Times*' articles, Tass's dispatches, or Radio Moscow's broadcasts were fabricated primarily to influence the members of the Atlantic Alliance. Lurid details of the discovery of the corpses of Roselli and Giancana were developed to demonstrate the horror of what the Mafia, working with the CIA, could get away with, with total impunity.

When the committee on assassinations stated that the presence of a second killer was quite possible, the media felt that the conspiracy had been proved beyond all doubt. They did not say that everything advanced in refutation of the Warren Commission's findings had been thoroughly disproved, that the new "fact" was the appearance of a tape recording, the importance of which was immediately questioned, that several members of the committee had refused to accept its new conclusions.

The *New York Times* published a letter to the editor praising "those persistent critics, Mark Lane, for example, who have so tenaciously argued their case over the years." His name was re-membered, but the fact that he had stoutly maintained that Oswald was innocent, although his guilt had been definitely confirmed, had been entirely forgotten.[61] The *New York Herald Tribune,* European edition, published another letter saying that Mark Lane's "lucid book" should be reread as he had said "way back in the early sixties" what the assassinations committee had later concluded after its investigation.[62] Neither of the newspapers mentioned that all of Mark Lane's allegations in support of the conspiracy thesis had been conclusively refuted, and they paid tribute to him when they published these letters.

One of the French television networks also spoke at great length of the Mafia, but later, in September 1981. The producer said that he had been "threatened with death three times" while he was studying "The Kennedy Affair," and that Giancana, the mafioso to whom *New Times* attributed an important role in the assassination, had employed Ruby as one of his lieutenants;[63] he could have read it in *New Times.* French television had already shown a series of three programs on the assassination in April 1978, which were rerun in September 1983.[64] The first images to flash on the screen were of Mark Lane, "Oswald's mother's law-yer," and Penn Jones, the discoverer of the murdered witnesses. The producer said the FBI had erased two gunmen from the film of the assassination that had been made at the scene by a bystander. According to the French political writer Jean-François Revel, this television channel is or was controlled by the Communist party.[65]

Soviet television got into the act in 1978. It sent a camera crew to Dallas. The commentator spoke from the window where Oswald had stood and gave the following account of the events. The snipers might have been hiding behind a fence or on top of the railway overpass or in a covered water hatchway. They escaped along an underground route. The first bullet hit the president "in the throat." Oswald was assigned to play the "part of the fall guy." Only "extremely important" persons could have planned the as-sassination with absolute confidence that everything would go smoothly. Texas multimillionaire H. L. Hunt was linked to the conspiracy. Agents from the CIA and FBI had had a hand in the crime. The explanation may have been "an invisible economic war" between "old moneyed interests in the Northeast" and "oil barons of the Southwest."[66] (Fourteen years earlier, in 1964, the headline

149

of the last Buchanan article in *L'Express* was "Struggle to Death Between Wall Street and Texas.")

The National Research Council established the Committee on Ballistic Acoustics in the fall of 1980. Its report was published by the National Academy Press in Washington, D.C. in 1982 and became available to the public in May 1982. The extensive study undertaken was assisted by funds put at the disposition of the National Research Council by the National Science Foundation. A commission composed of twelve leading acousticians criticized the "subjective" methods of the assassination committee's experts and demonstrated why their calculations had been wrong. They found that the recording contained cross talk from a second police channel. The signals that were interfering with the alleged shots had not been recognized by the committee on assassinations' experts; they were sentences of a message broadcast a full minute after the president was killed. There were no shots on the tape: the sounds were unidentifiable noises; there was no acoustic evidence of a second gunman on the grassy knoll.

Here are some excerpts from the report published by the National Research Council:[67]

> Since the recorded acoustic impulses are similar to static, efforts to attribute them to gunshots have depended on echo analyses; but in these analyses desirable control tests were omitted, some of the analyses depended on subjective selection of data, serious errors were made in some of the statistical calculations, incorrect statistical conclusions were drawn and the analysis methods used were novel in some aspects and were untested at such high levels of background noise.[68]

> The original report claimed a 50% probability of there being an additional shot from the grassy knoll. Even this seemingly modest claim is based on both questionable assumptions and on incorrect computations. This claim was used as a justification for the later more detailed studies.[69]

> Furthermore, some of the recorded background sounds, such as the delay in the sounds of police sirens, are not what one would expect if the open microphone had been in the motorcade.[70]

On the day of the assassination, Channel I was primarily used for normal police activities and Channel II was used for the presidential motorcade.[71] . . . [t]here are clear instances in which phrases recorded on the Channel II tape were distinctly audible on the Channel I tape as well. This is quite naturally explained by assuming that the motorcycle with the open microphone (Channel I) was near another police radio receiving a transmission from Channel II, so that transmissions over Channel II would issue from its loud speaker and be picked up by the open microphone and rebroadcast on Channel I. In addition there are simultaneous broadcasts by the dispatcher onto Channels I and II. Both kinds of cross talk are perfectly clear in many cases. The existence of such identical portions of speech on both channels would allow one to establish precise time synchronizations between specific portions of the two recordings.[72]

. . . a 4-second fragment of speech . . . overlaps the conjectured 3rd and 4th shots on Channel I[;][73] . . . on Channel II, that communication is part of a clear sequence of emergency communications that followed the shooting and occurred approximately one minute after the assassination. It is, in fact, part of Sheriff Decker's instructions to his men in response to the assassination.

. . . arrangements were made to obtain sound spectograms ("voiceprints") of the relevant communications on Channels I and II[74]. . . . The sound spectrograms show conclusively that the portion of the Channel I recording with the acoustic impulses also contains a weak recording on Channel I of cross talk from Channel II of a message broadcast approximately one minute after the assassination.

For these reasons and for others given in detail in the report, the National Research Council Committee on Ballistic Acoustics unanimously concludes that: the acoustic analyses do not demonstrate that there was a grassy knoll shot, and in particular there is no acoustic basis for the claim of 95% probability of such a shot; the acoustic impulses attributed to gunshots were recorded about one minute after the President had been shot and the motorcade had been instructed to go to the hospital; therefore, reliable acoustic data do not support a conclusion that there was a second gunman.[75]

Two years elapsed before the report of the National Research Council was published. It went completely unnoticed in Europe and was hardly mentioned in the United States, whereas the last session of the committee on assassinations had been widely written up. Journalists preferred not to acknowledge that they had been spouting nonsense for fifteen years. They managed to convince themselves that it would be useless to come forward after all that time, that the debate about "the conspiracy" was still going strong on both sides, and that it would be endless. The short article in the *New York Times* giving the news of the report was entitled "New Study on Slaying of Kennedy *Doubts* 2nd Gunman Was Involved" [emphasis added],[76] and it is not listed in "The New York Times Index, 1982."

The public is therefore left with the conclusions of the committee on assassinations, which, as they were understood, confirmed everything that had been said by America's enemies about the deterioration of the country's moral climate and the corruption of its government.

9

Disinformation
and Amateur Detectives

The House Commission on Assassinations established that the *Warren Report*'s critics either had not read the report or were telling barefaced lies, but to no avail. All that people remembered was that the committee had demonstrated the existence of a second sniper, and they ignored, or chose to ignore, the reservations, the disagreements, the fact that the committee itself had requested a third acoustical analysis. They were quite sure that the conspiracy had been officially acknowledged.

As soon as the possibility of a second investigation was mentioned, in 1975, newcomers entertained hopes that they would be able to write best-sellers, like the first batch of critics. This author's purpose in writing the present book is not to expose those who created the myth. Nevertheless, new books on the subject will be briefly examined in order to show how the myth became entrenched in the public's mind.

Someone discovered in the Warren Commission's files at the National Archives a note the FBI had sent to the State Department in June 1960; it said that an imposter might use Oswald's identity papers. The reason behind the note was that Oswald's mother, questioned by the FBI, had said that her son had taken his birth certificate with him and that three letters she had sent him had been returned unopened from Russia. The *New York Times* published a five-column article on this note,[1] and Michael Eddowes's book appeared in 1977, *The Oswald File,*[2] which purported to unravel how the KGB got rid of Oswald upon his arrival in Moscow and how a Russian resembling him had been substituted for him and had later been sent to Dallas with the mission of killing President Kennedy when the chance presented itself. (Strangely enough, Oswald's mother and brother had not noticed the switch.) The author of *The Oswald File* had discovered that Oswald's height was different in some of the documents giving a description of him[3] (experts explained to the committee on assassinations that this is not unusual and gave the reasons for current discrepancies in official documents, particularly military ones.)

The Oswald File was published simultaneously in Canada and the United States, and there was a British edition entitled *Nov. 22.* The U.S. television station CBS produced a program based on the book a year after its publication. Only people who had read it, however, could know the extent of the author's revelations: the cover-up had immediately been decided on by President Johnson and war was thus avoided;[4] Ruby had met Oswald in September 1959 for the purpose of giving him money to finance his trip to the Soviet Union;[5] De Mohrenschildt had been instructed to arrange the attack on General Walker.[6] If the fingerprints of the real Oswald matched those of the impostor, it was because the KGB had been able to change the cards in the FBI's files.[7] When sales of his book began to drop, Eddowes succeeded in getting an order to exhume Oswald's body to check the size of the skeleton. The "Dallas mystery" was once again in all the papers.

The author of *They've Killed the President,*[8] Robert Sam Anson, told how Oswald had had ties with the CIA long before the assassination: the CIA had asked him to disappear some time in 1959 so that it could send a secret agent to the Soviet Union using his papers. The CIA had given them back to him when the false Oswald returned to America, the Russian wife submitting docilely to this exchange of husbands. The committee on assassinations felt it had to ask experts to verify that every document signed "Lee H. Oswald," all notes and letters in Oswald's handwriting, from before, during, and after his stay in Russia had been signed or written by the same person.[9]

The authors of these two books were not writing for sophisticated readers, and their inventions were soon forgotten. But at the time, the books were talked about.

The *New York Review of Books* published a long review of another book, *Conspiracy*,[10] available in 1980, "an important piece of work, both for what it shows about the assassination and for the lucidity that [Anthony] Summers, a British television producer, has brought to the subject."[11] The author of the article had been particularly struck by the "discovery" that Ruby got his start as a "tough street-smart kid . . . running errands for Al Capone."[12] The story behind this is as follows. Even friends from Ruby's adolescence whom he had not seen for years had been questioned by the FBI. One of them, Barney Ross, told the investigator that Al Capone, who lived near him, would sometimes give one of the young boys in the neighborhood a letter to deliver for him: "[I] believe," said Ruby's former neighbor, "that these envelopes, which were sealed, did not contain any message or anything of value. [I] believe that Capone did this in order to make them think they were earning a dollar and in order to keep them from hanging around the streets."[13]

Conspiracy represented the application by an expert of the methods used by the first wave of critics. For the unattentive reader, suppositions, insinuations, and even the most ridiculous fantasies become established truths when the writer skillfully repeats them while appearing to discount them. Everything the inventors of fables had been able to dream up was revived and presented as proved, probable, or possible: "An alarming fact" was that Oswald's uncle had worked for years for an underworld gambling syndicate affiliated with a "crime family"; the committee on assassinations "thought it probable that Moscow had some intelligence connection with Oswald";[14] "this book will look carefully at allegations that Fidel Castro had a hand in killing the President"; according to "a respectable conspiracy theory," the left-wing Oswald was "a perfect patsy" for "the anti-Castro militants . . . inextricably linked with elements of both the CIA and the Mafia"; "eminent and qualified observers" were convinced that Oswald was really "a low-level agent of American intelligence."[15]

Anthony Summers habitually introduced an indefensible claim by preceding it with a formula such as "for some," or "some believe," "some suspect," "some would say," except when he felt he had to elaborate. However, when the absurdity of a given claim was too flagrant, he appeared to concede the point but with a few cleverly chosen words, allowed some doubt to linger in the mind of the reader. "Expert testimony . . . [has] seemed persuasive evidence that this was so. For all that . . . [the claim that it was not so] continues to find supporters."[16] Or in another instance: "When the Assassinations Committee investigated his story, it found no corroborating evidence in the record; I would hesitate, however, to reject [this] account."[17] And further on: "Ferrie's misconduct with youths in the Air Patrol led to scandal. . . . [T]here is not yet any evidence that Oswald was involved in such goings-on, but at the age of sixteen and on the threshold of an adult sexual life, he was certainly vulnerable to the likes of Ferrie."[18] Or: "Nothing . . . suggests . . . indeed the very contrary is true. Yet[19] . . ." And: "The concept is so bizarre that I wanted to reject it. Yet . . ."[20] Again: "The fact that [the witness] was lying made him no less relevant to the inquiry."[21]

Among some of the misinformation scattered through the book, we find that Oswald, as a marine, had served as a radar operator "at a top-secret base" for American espionage operations.[22] (The radar crew engaged primarily in normal aircraft surveillance.[23]) "In his own notes . . . he says he started work in Minsk in June 1960."[24] (He started a few days after his arrival in January 1960.)[25] His fellow workers at the Book Depository "left the sixth floor at about 11:45; they left behind them an Oswald vocally impatient to come down and join them."[26] (They left him at 11:55, and what he actually said to them was that he was not going down to the lunchroom.)[27] The Warren Commission "showed little interest in a full investigation of the Tippit shooting."[28] (The investigation was thorough and left no stone unturned.)[29] By his "own account" Oswald's first Soviet contacts were his Intourist guides and interpreters "who then, as now, are known to be KGB agents or informers."[30] (Tourists were all taken in charge by Intourist.)

In May 1960 the Russians were finally able to strike at a U-2 reconnaissance plane, bringing it down, and put the pilot, Gary Powers, in prison. The author comments, "It is tempting to speculate that Oswald was one of those who secretly watched and listened" through a peephole during Power's incarceration in Lubianka Prison.[31]

The *New York Review of Books* concluded the article: "We may never know who fired the fatal bullet, but we are closing in on why the deed was done."[32]

Anthony Summers was asked to give his views on American

Public Television in 1980; Professor Blakey was invited.[33] A staff investigator of the committee on assassinations had interviewed an anti-Castro activist, Antonio Veciana, who said he had spotted Oswald in the lobby of an office building in Dallas having a conversation with an important CIA agent, with whom Veciana himself had an appointment. An interview Veciana gave to Anthony Summers was filmed. Part of the reel was projected in the middle of the program. Professor Blakey remarked: "How could Veciana remember Oswald? He couldn't even remember the building."[34] Oswald was in New Orleans at the time, and the committee on assassinations had concluded that it could not credit Veciana's testimony.[35]

A *New York Times* article observed: "*Conspiracy* serves to dramatize, as no previous book has done, the superficiality of the Warren Commission's investigation and report[;] . . . it discourages any expectation that the complete truth behind the assassination in Dallas will some day be known."[36]

Time magazine ran an article, six columns long, on Michael L. Kurtz's *Best Evidence,* a "meticulously researched" book published shortly afterwards: "The author has turned up intriguing new evidence of some strange doings with Kennedy's body. . . . There is no factual claim . . . that is not supported by the public record or his own interviews." *Best Evidence* was concocted out of a different set of ingredients; the author did not use anything from previous theories and constructed his scenario around a personal idea. "Somebody removed the body from the casket,[37] hid it somewhere on board the presidential plane," which was flying it to Washington; Jacqueline Kennedy, the new president, and their closest associates took the same plane. The body was "disguised as luggage"; it was slipped out on arrival and transferred to an army helicopter that took it to a military hospital,[38] while the empty casket was ceremoniously transported to the navy hospital where the autopsy was to be performed. The body was "secretly altered." In order to cover up basic facts about the shooting, bullets and bullet fragments were removed from the skull; the bullet's trajectory was changed by surgery on the wounds.[39] A back wound could have been added[40] to introduce a set of false clues, to fabricate evidence against Oswald.[41] The body was then returned to the casket. Two bullet fragments could have been planted[42] in the Kennedy limousine and a bullet could have been placed on a stretcher in the

Dallas hospital.[43] The plot "involved the Executive branch of the Government and the Secret Service."[44] After reading the book, the brigadier general who was then the Air Force aide to the president felt compelled to write to *Time* magazine to say he had been with the coffin the entire time.[45]

Whoever reviewed these books for *Time* magazine, the *New York Times,* and the *New York Review of Books* belonged to the 80 percent of the population conditioned by the disinformation campaign.[46]

Crime of the Century, the Kennedy Assassination from a Historian's Perspective, by Michael Kurtz,[47] came out two years later. This work is mentioned here because its publisher, a university press, reprinted it only one month after it first appeared in bookstores, and because *The Economist,* which rarely reviews works outside the field of finance and economics, devoted almost a full page of commentary to it.[48]

Professor Kurtz adopted the conclusions of the committee on assassinations. The findings of the National Academy of Sciences, although foreseeable, had not yet been published. Nonetheless, in order to respond to objections immediately raised, he made a few changes. First, it hardly seemed credible that an assassin firing from the grassy bank, fifty yards from the motorcade, could not even hit the limousine, while another one firing from the depository, eighty yards away, hit his target. The second objection was that between two alleged shots on the tape there would have been 1.66 seconds, while the rifle could not be refired in less than 2.25 seconds. Kurtz then decided that the gunman on the grassy bank had not missed; he added a third gunman shooting from a lower floor in the depository.[49] According to him, the gunman on the lower floor hit Kennedy in the upper back; the bullet of the gunman on the sixth floor "slammed into Governor Connally's back," and this gunman fired the final shot "in a carefully planned cross fire"; this shot exploded out of the "huge hole"[50] in the president's skull caused by the shot from the "grassy knoll." Thus, this "reconstruction" of events simply ignored everything that had been established long before.

A testimony Professor Kurtz considered valuable was from Garrison's hypnotized witness; others were depositions before the Warren Commission by two witnesses, S. M. Holland and Lee E. Bowers, Jr., that had been altered for Mark Lane's film. A good example of the way disinformation distorts recollections of an event can be seen by comparing pages 118 and 182 of the book. On page 118 the author reports that an employee of the book depository, Carolyn Arnold, "thought she caught a fleeting glimpse of Lee Harvey Oswald standing . . . on the first floor . . . a few minutes before 12:15 p.m." (This was probably Billy Nolan Lovelady, a co-worker who resembled Oswald.) On page 182 "she asserted that she saw Oswald in the second floor lunchroom at 12:15." The first statement was given to the FBI in 1964, the second to the author of *Conspiracy* in 1978.

Future historians will have to be on their guard only when it comes to dealing with works genuinely groping for the truth, like *Kennedy and Lincoln,* produced during the same period as the books discussed above. The author, Dr. John K. Lattimer, is a well-known physician. His meticulously detailed research, the care he gave to verifying what had been said previously by the official experts, his precise descriptions of everything concerning the gunshots and the wounds received by President Kennedy are impressive. His readers may assume his conclusions concerning Oswald—"an enemy sympathizer"—are accurate.[51] One error is his attribution to Marina Oswald of an observation she never made, namely, that when Oswald urged her to return to him, he did so "in a way calculated to permit her to refuse."[52] If this had been the case, Oswald's motivation would still be questionable. Dr. Lattimer probably misinterpreted a conjecture advanced by Priscilla Johnson McMillan. "It seems a fair guess that Lee still on November 21 knew how to obtain the answer yes."[53]

Another error concerns Marina Oswald's account of an incident mentioned previously: In Dallas Oswald led his wife to think that he was going out to kill Richard Nixon—who was not in Dallas at the time—in order to look formidable in her eyes and also to upset her, but Dr. Lattimer wrote that that incident involved a "national figure who was visiting Dallas."[54] When Richard Nixon, who was not in Dallas, is replaced by a "national figure" who "was" in Dallas, Oswald's little game appears to have been a real plan that was aborted at the last minute.

Dr. Lattimer presumed that after killing the president, Oswald, "in all probability, was heading across town to add the assassination of General Walker . . . to his list of newsworthy achievements on behalf of world Communism."[55] Even if Oswald had been a fervent Marxist, this would be giving him too much credit. His attempt on General Walker's life had been, in his mind, a show of courage and power, planned to impress his wife as well as himself. The assassination of John F. Kennedy was an impulsive act, the execution of a man who had everything by a man who had nothing. An assistant counsel member made an interesting suggestion: Oswald might have been heading for an airport with the idea of hijacking a plane to Cuba.[56] We have seen that he had considered doing that two months earlier.

To stay on the right track, one merely had to take a good look at a life punctuated by a series of grotesque incidents. Dr. Lattimer lumped together communists and terrorists, and took Oswald for a fanatic who had immolated himself for his cause. To attribute convictions to the self-centered Oswald has no more basis than to believe that Oswald was, to whatever degree, unbalanced. Had he been an impassioned partisan or a mental defective, observing and analyzing him would be a futile undertaking. With his egocentricity, his absurdities, and his faults, exacerbated by his dyslexia and tending toward extremes, Oswald was still in relatively good mental health, like the majority of assassins. Granted, he had delusions of grandeur—or, more exactly, of grandeur still to come—but only during a relatively short period of his life. He had lost them months before he committed his crime.

In 1982 Princeton University Press published a carefully researched book, *American Assassins: The Darker Side of Politics,* by Professor James W. Clarke.[57] Unfortunately, Clarke relied on chapter 7 of the *Warren Report.* Moreover, his analysis of Oswald's personality was weakened by errors propagated by the investigators' detractors, which, having taken root, were difficult to check. These errors, of varying importance, added up to an incorrect view of Oswald's "motives" and, consequently, of the event.

"There is little doubt," Professor Clarke wrote, "that Lee Harvey Oswald killed President Kennedy," and, he added, "two related major questions remain unanswered. Why did he do it? and did he act alone?"[58] He wanted supporting evidence to surface, evidence other than that furnished by the acoustical analysis, "the only significant evidence of a conspiracy."[59] He stressed that Oswald's motives were "personal and compensatory rather than political";[60] he assumed, however, that Oswald had assassinated President Kennedy partly because the president was "the chief architect of the nation's hostile Cuban policy."[61] As for General Walker, he was "an appropriate target at which to strike a blow for Cuba."[62] Professor Clarke had seen that Oswald "sought to resolve his frustrations by proving his value to himself and the significant others in his life,"[63] but he erroneously added that Oswald wanted to be appreciated by Castro, who was his "hero."[64] He believed Oswald had really meant to kill himself in 1959, "shattered by the cold indifference and skepticism which had greeted him" in "the nation he had elevated to the level of an ideal."[65]

Clarke also stated that President Johnson put pressure on the Warren Commission "to conclude its investigation quickly with a lone assassin explanation even though President Johnson himself believed otherwise."[66] Like General de Gaulle and 80 percent of Johnson's fellow Americans, Lyndon Johnson came to wonder what had really happened: "I don't think [the Warren Commission], or me, or anyone else is always absolutely sure of everything that might have motivated Oswald or others that might have been involved."[67] John P. Roche, special consultant to Lyndon Johnson, and the so-called intellectual in residence at the White House, had, however, dismissed as "marginal paranoids" the proponents of conspiracy theories in a letter he had sent to the *London Times Literary Supplement* in 1968.[68]

As for the "pressure" on the Warren Commission, Lyndon Johnson intervened a few days after the assassination when Earl Warren, who had at first refused to serve as chairman of a presidential commission of inquiry, needed solid arguments to change his mind. Acting Attorney General Nicholas deB. Katzenbach— and not President Johnson—was generally accused of having given instructions to the commission. A sentence from a letter Katzenbach sent to the White House immediately after Oswald's death was always quoted out of context: "The public must be satisfied that Oswald was the assassin; that he did not have confederates who are still at large; and that the evidence was such that he would have been convicted at trial." Other passages from Katzenbach's letter shed some light on what he meant:

> We should have some basis for rebutting thought that
> this was a Communist conspiracy or (as the Iron Curtain
> press is saying) a right-wing conspiracy to blame it on the
> Communists. . . . The Dallas police have put out state-

ments on the Communist conspiracy theory, and it was they who were in charge when [Oswald] was shot and thus silenced. . . . Facts have been mixed with rumor and speculation. We can scarcely let the world see us totally in the image of the Dallas police. . . . I think this objective may be satisfied by making public as soon as possible a complete and thorough FBI report on Oswald and the assassination. . . . I think . . . that a statement that all the facts will be made public . . . in an orderly and responsible way should be made now. We need something to head off public speculation or Congressional hearings of the wrong sort.[69]

The myth of pressure from high places was conclusively disproved on September 21, 1978, during the televised session of the committee on assassinations, which ended with Katzenbach's deposition:

I knew then already that Oswald had been in Russia. Oswald had been in Mexico. Now, if you are going to conclude, as the Bureau was concluding, that this was not part of a conspiracy, that there were no confederates, then you had to make that case with all the facts, absolutely persuasive. . . . [I]f you were persuaded Oswald was a lone killer, you had better put all the facts out . . . and you better say now all the facts are going to be made public. . . . That was the advice I was giving the President and that was the motivation for the Warren Commission. . . . Perhaps you have never written anything that you would like to write better afterwards . . . but I have. . . . I was saying . . . you have got a lot of awkward facts that you are going to have to explain and you had better explain them satsifactorily.[70]

The only pressure exerted on the commission was the pressure of the calendar: "President Johnson, among others in his administration, was anxious to have the investigation completed in advance of the 1964 Presidential Convention, out of concern that the assassination could become a political issue."[71] The committee on assassinations was forced to acknowledge that "the competence of the [Warren] Commission was all the more impressive . . . in view of the substantial pressure to elicit findings in only 9 months."[72]

Professor Clarke knew that Oswald's spelling was erratic, but he did not see that dyslexia was at the root of Oswald's problems. He believed that Oswald's "seventh-grade classmates ridiculed his rural-looking clothes, peculiar mannerisms and southern accent,"[73] whereas he was ridiculed for not possessing the basic writing or counting skills of the average child. It is not true that Oswald compiled a "surprisingly good" academic record, as Clarke believed; he always got Ds in spelling and arithmetic.[74] Reference was made to some evidence Jim Garrison had presented as valuable: Oswald, it was claimed, had been seen in a little city, Clinton, Louisiana, accompanied by David Ferrie and Clay Shaw.[75] The committee on assassinations examined the testimony and concluded that the witnesses were telling the truth "as they knew it"[76]—a nice way of saying they were wrong.

Oswald had not started learning Russian "at seventeen," at the time of his enlistment in the marines;[77] the three marines who testified on this point were in the unit he joined in California the year of his discharge. He did not speak of "joining the Castro guerilla forces in the Sierra Maestra";[78] this was also in 1959; Castro was in power. The two marines, Oswald and Delgado, talked to each other about how they could become officers in the Cuban army.

American Assassins, like *Kennedy and Lincoln,* was rightly read with great interest. The other books mentioned here, bad as they were, were judged worthy of attention, even of praise, by the press. They each played a part in the creation of the myth. And there were worse. In *The Assassination of John F. Kennedy,* a 240-page bibliography, outrageous books are mentioned; one was written by "a certified witch"; the authors of another were seeking an explanation "in ancient Egypt." It is worth noting that the compilers of this bibliography state in the preface: "The books by the early writers, Thomas Buchanan, Joachim Joesten, and Léo Sauvage, remain substantially sound within the context of pre–*Warren Report* materials. . . . each is based on painstaking research and analytical argument. . . . they are essential reading."[79]

The *New York Times* carried a piece on the Kennedy assassination on November 19, 1983. Here are some of the more important passages:

As the 20th anniversary approached, the controversy seemed to have gone full circle and was swinging back to the explanation that . . . Lee Harvey Oswald, an admirer of Fidel Castro of Cuba acted alone. . . . A commission headed by Earl Warren left so many questions unanswered it invited other theories.

In 1979 a House Select Committee on Assassinations concluded that circumstantial evidence pointed to a conspiracy to kill the President, "probably" involving elements of organized crime. It also decided on the basis of disputed evidence that a second gunman had fired a shot from a grassy knoll at the Kennedy motorcade. All the conspiracy theories remained unproved. . . . The most recent conclusion that there was no conspiracy is reflected in a new book, *Oswald's Game,* by Jean Davison. . . . She concluded that Oswald . . . took it on himself to kill the President because the Central Intelligence Agency had tried on several occasions to assassinate Mr. Castro. . . . Yet, as the novelist Norman Mailer said in a preface to the book, neither he nor other conspiracy theorists can be satisfied by the new reasoning. To him the Kennedy assassination will remain "the great American mystery," thus serving as a frequent reminder of the life and death of Kennedy. . . . In Dallas . . . Marina Oswald Porter . . . says . . . at first, she accepted the Warren Commission's findings; but now she has doubts.[80]

The *New York Times* thus feels that Oswald killed John Kennedy because the CIA tried to kill Castro, that there are still "many unanswered questions," that the possibility of a fourth shot having been fired by a second gunman is "disputed" (whereas it was torn to shreds by the National Academy of Sciences), that *Oswald's Game* is the only book worth mentioning because it reflects "the most recent conclusion." The *New York Times* was ill-informed in 1983, influenced by all the nonsense that had been propagated. Believing itself to be impartial, it was joining the ranks of those who created disquiet in the minds of the public. Its readers would now accept the position of the author of *Oswald's Game,* whose reasons for not believing the conspiracy theory are the wrong ones, or of Norman Mailer who beleives there was a conspiracy, or of

Marina Oswald Porter who is wondering whether she should believe the conspiracy theory or not.

Since the *New York Times* intended to give the latest information on the issue by examining Jean Davison's book, her theory should be given full attention. Let us note first of all that she was not sure of herself: she said that if Oswald had accomplices, "which seems doubtful"—only doubtful—she would nominate "the unknown men who helped him try to gull Sylvia Odio."[81] Her book has not dispelled the false ideas of Norman Mailer who still belongs "to the Summers School of conspiracy."[82] Davison, who attributes great importance to Oswald's "hang up on Marxism,"[83] stated that he was "converted" to Marxism,[84] but Oswald was a Marxist in name only. Had he been a true Marxist he would not have been a killer. True Marxists are disciplined; they are not anarchists or nihilists. There has never been a true Marxist who has taken it upon himself or herself to kill for the cause; those who killed for the cause had taken sides in a civil war. Karl Marx wrote, regarding a conspiracy or would-be conspiracy to assassinate Napoleon III, that it was "the greatest stupidity imaginable."[85]

The theory Jean Davison elaborated—it had been suggested in a book written by Daniel Schorr[86]—was that Castro's denunciations of the United States' attempts to eliminate him inspired Oswald to assassinate the president. In order to believe that, one has to be unfamiliar with Oswald's feelings toward Castro. Marina Oswald reported that Oswald considered him only "a very smart statesman, very useful for his government and very active."[87] George De Mohrenschildt could say only that Oswald had "admiration for Castro for opposing such a big power as the United States." It came as "a complete surprise" to De Mohrenschildt and his wife to learn that Oswald "was actually involved in doing something for Castro, selling leaflets or something, in New Orleans."[88] Interviewed after the dispute with anti-Castro Cubans in New Orleans, Oswald declared that the organization he claimed to represent did not support "Castro, the individual," but that it supported "the idea of an independent revolution in the Western hemisphere, free from American intervention"; he specified that "if the Cuban people destroy[ed] Castro . . . that [would] not have any bearing upon the Fair Play for Cuba Committee," that Castro was "an experimentator," a person "trying to find the best way for his country."[89] During his questioning by the police, he said that he was "not going to discuss the merits or demerits of Castro," that he was "primarily concerned with the poor people of Cuba."[90]

During the debate on New Orleans radio that had followed Oswald's arrest, Kennedy's name was mentioned in connection with a speech by Castro who charged the United States with not having respected the conditions governing the release of prisoners taken during the abortive Bay of Pigs invasion. Oswald declared that "the United States had made monumental mistakes in its relations with Cuba," but added that those mistakes were attributable to certain agencies, "mainly the State Department and the CIA."[91] Jean Davison herself recognized that he "seemed to put most of the blame for America's policy toward Cuba on conservative elements, not on Kennedy himself."[92] In recognizing this, she destroyed her own theory. During the same debate Oswald replied affirmatively when he was asked if he knew that Castro was a Leninist-Communist. How could he have immolated himself to pay homage to Castro, the Communist? We have many proofs of his hostile feelings toward communism.

There is no doubt that Oswald thought Castro was a great man, but according to Marina Oswald, he wanted "to go and live in Cuba because that [was] something that he [had] not [tried]."[93] This is a far cry from depicting him as a man sacrificing his life for Cuba and for Castro; he was not interested in anything that did not affect him personally.

The New Orleans *Times-Picayune* reported on September 9, 1963, remarks attributed to Castro—he denied having made them—on assassination plans made "by the United States leaders": "Cuba was prepared to answer in kind." If Oswald read it, which is questionable, it would have left him indifferent. At the time, he had lost all illusions of being able to engage in political activity in the United States, as is proved by the titles of the books he was then reading.[94] On September 5 he had returned two science-fiction books to the library. On September 9—the day the newspaper article affected him, according to Davison, to the point of making him want to kill—he took out three books: a science-fiction novel, *Ben Hur,* and *The Bridge on the River Kwai,* which he read between September 9 and September 23. (He returned the books to the library on the twenty-third.) During this period he had decided, if he did not succeed in going to Cuba or returning to Russia, to settle "in the Baltimore-Washington area."[95] His wife would have an easier time becoming assimilated in a city on the North Atlantic coast, Ruth Paine had one day remarked; she had also suggested that Marina Oswald might even find work there. (Oswald changed his mind after the birth of his second child.) At the end of September, after his failure at the Cuban consulate in Mexico, Oswald gave no further thought to Cuba or Castro.

Jean Davison stated that "Oswald's perception of the plots against Castro had led him to threaten President Kennedy's life on two occasions."[96] She found the first one in Sylvia Odio's testimony. Even if this testimony stuck entirely to the facts, which is hard to believe, if Oswald had said to anyone at that time that the Cubans should have assassinated Kennedy after the Bay of Pigs invasion, it would prove only that he was doing his best to make a good impression while trying to ingratiate himself with anti-Castro Cubans.

According to Davison, the second time Oswald indicated he was thinking about assassinating John Kennedy was during his visits to the Cuban consulate in Mexico City to apply for a visa. In 1977 it was reported that Castro had confided in an American Communist, who turned out to be an FBI agent, that Oswald had then made threats.[97] When Castro received a visit in 1978 from members of the committee on assassinations, he told them that the rumor was absurd, that his moral duty would have been to alert the United States.[98] Despite his denials, it is possible that Oswald uttered threats like the one that has been quoted: "Someone ought to shoot that President Kennedy, maybe I'll try to do it."[99] It has always been known that Oswald's visits to the consulate ended on this statement by the Cuban consul: "A person like you in place of aiding the Cuban Revolution is doing it harm."[100]

None of the papers Oswald had shown the consul about his pro-Cuba activities justified this reaction. Oswald, out of arguments, disappointed, irritated, might have imagined that if he showed his feelings toward Cuba were so strong that he would be willing to kill, he would make the consul relent. Let us remember that when he was trying to gather as much evidence in his favor as possible in order to get permission to stay in Russia, he had written to his brother, for the KGB's benefit, that he would go so far as killing him for love of the Soviet Union; the remark at the Cuban consulate would have been along the same lines.

According to *Oswald's Game*, Marina Oswald told nothing but

lies during her 1964 deposition. As evidence, two or three ambig-
uous answers she gave the assassinations committee in 1978 about
Oswald's last visit to her are quoted. However, she had repeated
many times before giving her answers "I don't remember," and had
said later, "I am sorry; it is very hard for me to remember right
now details whatever." Marina Oswald understandably wished to
forget the events of that week and had succeeded in doing so.
Davison did not quote her final answer to this series of questions:
"Well, since I was angry at him, you know, previous week-end, I
didn't want him to just—I mean I don't want to make up that
easily. I want to, you know, to teach him a lesson, not to do this
anymore."[101] She had told MacMillan, "I was like a stubborn little
mule."[102]

In carrying the examination of Davison's book the *New York
Times* helped to perpetuate the belief in the "conspiracy." Eight
years before, the *New York Times* discredited the authors of "irresponsible polemics" about the *Warren Report* in a long article.[103]
This shows how difficult it is not to be influenced by expert propagandists. The public library in a town where this writer spends
his summers has on its shelves a score of books by the "critics,"
and the copy of the *Warren Report*—a "concise compendium" in
paperback—is relegated to the basement.

A small number of students at Columbia University were in-
formally surveyed in 1983, a few months before the twentieth anniversary of the assassination and thus before the media had begun
talking about John F. Kennedy again at great length. Some of them
knew hardly anything about the assassination. Among the others,
two-thirds were convinced there had been a conspiracy, one-third
thought that Oswald, and he alone, was guilty; only 2 percent had
understood that he had simply given way to despair. A few of these
students knew that Mark Lane had been active in the conspiracy
story campaign, but none of them knew of his "progressive" political position.

The correspondent for *Le Figaro,* Léo Sauvage, came back to
the subject of the assassination in 1983 in his book *Les Américains,*
in which he affirmed: "The conclusions of the Warren Report had
been decided in advance, *ten months in advance,* by the Justice
Department,"[104] after quoting out of context the sentence from
Nicholas Katzenbach's letter dated November 25, 1963.

The success obtained in Europe by the Soviet departments in

charge of disinformation—the IID (Internal Information Department) and the KGB (Commission for State Security) one who only disinforms, the other who employs all sorts of active measures, including disinformation—is easily gauged by the comments of the French press upon the twentieth anniversary of the assassination. In *Le Matin* the sentence Léo Sauvage quoted became "We must conclude as quickly as possible that this was the isolated act of a madman"; the Warren Commission was described as rushing and botching its work and constructing Oswald's guilt. The single bullet turned into an enchanted bullet whose trajectory was shown between "zigs, yaws and zags" in a drawing. (The drawing was found in the L.A. Free Press, special Report Number one, an American magazine whose editor was Larry Flint and one of the senior executive editors Mark Lane.) According to *Le Matin,* it was two acoustics experts from the National Academy of Sciences who established that four shots had been fired, with the result that the probability of a conspiracy became the new official theory. This is the only time, it seems, that the National Academy of Sciences has been mentioned in the French press in connection with the affair, but the mention served only to establish once and for all the prejudices of readers who will forever ignore the fact that the academy's findings reduced to naught those of the committee.[105]

Le Monde, on November 20, 1983, acknowledged that the American authorities did not participate in a conspiracy whose goal would have been to make John Kennedy disappear and did not help to cover up the truth. Very good. *Le Monde,* however, wondered: "Was Oswald an agent in the pay of Soviet secret services? Or a typical unstable personality of which we see so many in America? The question still stands today. But along with how many others!" The author of the article knew nothing about Oswald: "His hostility toward the American system was the cause of intense friction with Marina and led to the couple's separation. . . . Marina was then taken in by a family living in a Dallas suburb." It seems he thought that Oswald had disappeared a few months before the assassination: "Oswald was spotted in New Orleans distributing pamphlets for a 'Fair Play for Cuba Committee.'"[106]

Le Quotidien raised questions that had been answered in 1964 in the twenty-seven volumes giving the account of the Warren Commission's inquiry and answered again in 1979 in the thirteen volumes published by the Select Committee on Assassinations (how could the "famous" bullet, found "almost intact," have simultaneously wounded the president and the governor? Why did Oswald kill Tippit? Were the Dallas police involved in the conspiracy? and so forth). *Le Quotidien* concluded: "What is bewildering . . . is when Oswald goes home, safe and sound, at 13:00, and stays about ten minutes. . . . What pressing needs pushed him to go out again? . . . It is in this departure . . . that the key to the Kennedy mystery must lie."[107] *Le Quotidien*'s writer had not read *Le Monde,* which two days earlier had said: "Almost immediately, suspicion fell upon [Oswald] who had left the building two or three minutes after the assassination. . . . Oswald's description was broadcast over the police radio. . . . He [owned] the rifle found on the fifth floor of the Depository."[108] It so happens that when Oswald was brought in at 2:15 P.M., after killing Tippit, the police captain was on the point of sending out other officers to arrest him at home.[109]

For *Le Figaro Magazine,* the assassination was "the most mysterious crime of the century." It spoke at length of the Warren Commission, but ignored the existence of the committee on assassinations, as well as the findings of the National Academy of Sciences. Thus, it stated that "the exact number of shots fired was never known." It listed the "one thousand and one versions" of the conspiracy that had been proposed and commented, "Perhaps one of these corresponds to the truth."[110]

These four newspapers form public opinion in France; it is thus not surprising that all students questioned at the Sorbonne in 1983, as opposed to only two-thirds in the United States, were convinced that President Kennedy had died as the result of a conspiracy.

France was fertile ground for sensational accusations. In contrast with the French press, the British newspapers showed admirable restraint. During the week of the anniversary *The Times* published an article on the rise and fall of the Kennedy clan, and another on the gathering of the family at a memorial service in Washington, and nothing on the assassination. *The Guardian* published three short articles on the family gathering and on "the glamorous image which surrounded" John F. Kennedy. The only allusion to the assassination was a sentence in one of the *Guardian* articles: "No proof has been dug up . . . to establish the conspiracy allegedly behind his . . . death."[111]

As for Germany, in November 1983 *Der Spiegel* devoted six

pages to the assassination. The title of the article was "Who Killed John F. Kennedy?" and the subtitle, "Was Lee Harvey Oswald the only sniper? Was another marksman involved? Did the Mafia, the CIA, or Fidel Castro want to do away with the President of the United States? Twenty years after his death should the same doubts remain?" Ten photographs illustrated the text. One of them showed Penn Jones looking at a manhole similar to the one where, according to Jim Garrison and Soviet television, the snipers were ambushed. Every conspiracy theory was granted space, even the most absurd that had never taken root. *Der Spiegel,* however, re-deemed itself by mentioning the investigation conducted by the National Academy of Sciences and by adding this commentary: "Will it be shown after all that the Warren Report gave the right answer to the enigma of the century?"[112]

In the United States, a long time after finding a publisher in Holland for a book he had written on the "murdered witnesses," Thomas Buchanan succeeded in getting another book, *Big Brother: Ma vie, revue et corrigée par le FBI* (My life, reviewed and corrected by the FBI)[113] published in 1984, this time only in France. It was the story of his alleged persecution at the hands of the FBI, fol-lowed by new disinformation on the assassination of President Ken-nedy.

Contrary to what might have been surmised, what emerges from this book is that Buchanan had not been blacklisted after losing his job in 1948, when a colleague told their boss that Bu-chanan belonged to the Communist party. His dismissal became a bit of a "cause célèbre": it violated the freedom of opinion guar-anteed by the Constitution.[114] Buchanan claims that after his dis-missal, he was able to find only jobs with little potential for advancement. For a while he lived off his *"winnings at the race track*—a lot of money" [emphasis added].[115] He was under sur-veillance by the FBI, which followed him and eventually contacted him, hoping to "extort from [him] the names of people [he] met at Party meetings."[116] During the McCarthy era, at the height of the Cold War, the FBI believed that some American Communists would pledge their allegiance to Moscow and would form a fifth column in the event of war. Its concern at the time was to have an up-to-date list of party members. Its "persecution" of Buchanan was limited to a few conversations "in a cordial atmosphere."[117] The FBI emptied his trashcans, Buchanan claims; if this is true, it may have been in the hope of finding names of Communist correspondents.[118] Buchanan stopped attending party meetings in 1955 or 1956. The FBI stopped contacting him, but his file was not closed.[119]

Buchanan concedes in his book *Big Brother* that his 1964 articles for *L'Express,* which were examined above in chapter 2, were an attempt "to analyse the version of the assassination offered by the Dallas district attorney . . . an attempt to draw logical conclusions from the facts put forth by this *authorized source* [emphasis added] and by the police who had investigated the assassination *in the earliest hours*" [emphasis added].[120] Thus, Buchanan's readers, "practically the world over,"[121] took the contradictory remarks made by police officers, or the irresponsible statements made by the district attorney in the earliest hours, to be irrefutable proof of the existence of a conspiracy.

The American publisher Putnam waited for publication of the *Warren Report* before printing Buchanan's book; he wanted to release "a *new* book," which would have, however, the same title as the British edition, "for commercial reasons." The book would appear on the anniversary of the assassination. The author was given "*one week*" [emphasis added] to study the report, evaluate it, and compose his reply to it.[122] The difference between the British and the American editions of *Who Killed Kennedy?* was the elimination of some particularly extravagant passages.

Big Brother returns, after a lapse of twenty years, to the long-discredited "discoveries" of other storytellers bearing on such matters as "the burned autopsy notes"; the autopsy report, "which will not be divulged during our lifetime";[123] the alleged absence of an exit wound for one of the bullets;[124] the alleged refusal by the surgeons who operated on Connally to accept the possibility of the single bullet.[125] The author adds new "revelations" accompanied by references to the report. When the reader checks Buchanan's references, he finds that for the most part the passages cited are not to be found in the report, or that Buchanan has quoted a passage that says the opposite of what he claims: Oswald "had asked his fellow marine Delgado" whether he was "ready to desert to go to Cuba"[126] and "had spoken to him at length" of his forthcoming trip to Russia;[127] he bragged about being a "potential enemy" of the United States;[128] the embassy in Moscow, not knowing that he was there "on a mission," had not answered his "frantic calls";[129] he "cooperated"[130] with the FBI and had frequent contacts with its agents;[131] he acknowledged that he had "sold" himself[132] (he was alluding to the "Red Cross" stipend he received in Minsk); a police officer had found "the murder weapon," "a Mauser," on the railway tracks;[133] upon Oswald's death, "the affair" had been "closed" at Hoover's request;[134] the Dallas district attorney had warned the Dallas chief of police: "They say that you're holding the wrong man . . . and that you were moving him with the intention of having him killed."[135] (The meaning of this quotation when taken out of context is entirely changed.) Buchanan also insinuates that the Dallas police planted bullets in Oswald's pockets.[136]

As for Ruby, his stamp of approval was "necessary" in order for anyone to "deal in drugs or open a gambling house in Dallas." He begged to be taken to Washington "because he could not tell the truth in Dallas."[137] (Ruby dreamed of going to Washington "to get truth tests," to which his lawyers were opposed; the reason was that he was not happy with the defense they were preparing for his appeal. Lie detector tests would give him an opportunity to speak on his own behalf.) De Mohrenschildt "had prepared the Bay of Pigs invasion"[138] and had "stolen" his wife from Oswald.[139] (This assertion is a good example of the worthlessness of Buchanan's book. Buchanan refers the reader to page 282 of the *Warren Report*, which says merely "De Mohrenschildt helped Marina Oswald leave her husband for a period in November of 1962." Chapter 5 above explains that Marina Oswald had taken refuge with a Russian friend and that De Mohrenschildt, Jeanne De Mohrenschildt and another member of the Russian community wanted to protect her from Oswald's violence. They accompanied her when she returned home to pick up her clothes the next day.) "All the facts set forth in my book," Buchanan had announced, "were taken from the testimony compiled by the Warren Commission."[140]

Thomas Buchanan explains in his book how he got his articles published in *L'Express*. He was a municipal employee in Paris at the time of the assassination.[141] During the following two months he wrote comments on what he called "the official version," a collection of all the inconsistencies and contradictions that had been put forth by the Dallas police.[142] (His on-site investigation consisted of reading newspapers in his Paris apartment.) A friend of his who was a journalist brought Buchanan's comments about the assassination to the attention of his bosses at *L'Express*. They were found sensational and were published as a series of articles. *L'Express* then proposed that Buchanan follow Ruby's trial.[143]

In the eyes of the French, Thomas Buchanan was a great journalist who had proved the existence of a conspiracy. After the publication of *Big Brother*, he was invited to appear on "Apostrophes," the famous French television program whose renown is so great that it is broadcast every week on the City University of New York's channel. But the host's assistant who was responsible for reading Buchanan's book appeared to have satisfied himself with reading the publisher's blurbs: "Why, in 1961 [*sic*], was Thomas G. Buchanan, who . . . was investigating the murder for *L'Express* . . . being once again pursued, denounced, forbidden to publish? . . . a pursuit that was sometimes laughable, sometimes frightening . . . *1984*: the year of Orwell. The year of Buchanan."

The following is the beginning of the dialogue, as transcribed from the broadcast, between the host of the show and Buchanan, who has become, for the occasion, a great international journalist, a figure regarded by the American Establishment with considerable fear. The story of his short connection with *L'Express* has been altered beyond recognition:

> —One might think that the FBI has given up on you, but, not at all, because there was the Kennedy assassination, and then the European newspapers, in particular *L'Express,* sent you to the United States to investigate. And, at that moment, the FBI starts a movement in France and all countries in Europe to discredit you. This is what happened?
> —Yes. In my book I mention the fact that there was a summit meeting [it was simply a regular session of the Warren Commission] attended by the Chief Justice of the Supreme Court, the Chairman of the Warren Commission [these were the same person], the Director of the CIA [who could not possibly have attended and did not attend], the former Director of the CIA [one of the seven members of the Warren Commission], someone from the FBI representing Hoover, and several members of the Warren Commission.
> —All that for you?
> —All that for me. Amazing, but true.[144]

The purpose of this hearing in fact was to take testimony from one of the FBI director's assistants on the general procedures of the FBI; he would explain their relationship in the case of Lee Harvey Oswald. During the hearing, one of the commission members mentioned that he had just received a copy of the British edition of *Who Killed Kennedy?*, and there followed a brief exchange of remarks on the book and its author's background. That was the extent of the portion of the "summit meeting" that concerned Buchanan.[145]

The television program, "Apostrophes," was about police misconduct in France and in America. The "conspiracy" was hardly discussed. Buchanan merely said that he could wonder at the time whether the FBI was going to kill him. He declared that in his opinion Oswald was getting money from the CIA.

Since Buchanan attacked the establishment in 1964, his name, naturally enough, appeared again in the FBI's files. But the bureau did not importune or thwart him any more than it had Mark Lane, Richard Popkin, or Harold Weisberg. If he was "discredited" after the publication of *Who Killed Kennedy?*, it was because it was recognized, when the *Warren Report* was released, as being particularly preposterous. No publisher wanted to hear his name again.

Innocently enough, Buchanan recounts in *Big Brother* that the editor in chief of *Izvestia,* Khrushchev's son-in-law, "thanked him for all [his] articles *Izvestia* had published." Buchanan had been introduced to him at a Paris hotel at which a Soviet delegation was staying.[146]

More disinformation appeared in 1985, between the covers of *Reasonable Doubt.* A "compelling" analysis, commented the *New York Times* in its review of *Reasonable Doubt,*[147] whose author, Henry Hurt, "undert[ook] to draw from the massive work of the independent critics and researchers" a "coherent and conclusive presentation."[148] Henry Hurt then ignored the fact that the House Select Committee on Assassinations had been created ten years before in order to ascertain the value of their assertions and that at a cost of $6 million, they were found worthless.

The idea of the book came to Hurt "when [he] received a telephone call from a man who stated he had participated in a conspiracy to kill President Kennedy."[149] This man, "a raging alcoholic,"[150] has been "confined in a mental hospital" since 1983.[151] "He went berserk," "terrorizing his family," who were rescued when "sheriff's deputies crashed into the house and seized him."[152] Henry Hurt found "baffling" the fact that the FBI showed "a determined lack of interest" in the alcoholic's "confession."[153] He did not recognize a typical case of ethylic mythomania.

10
Conclusion

To sum up, the Warren Commission took a third-rate *arriviste* for a mixed-up ideologue, a selfless dissenter, a terrorist. Believing he understood "Marxism," Oswald pretended to be—or even thought he was—"a Marxist." After having conceived a political platform which, as he saw it, combined the best of capitalism and Communism, Oswald had great hopes which did not materialize, and his sense of frustration deepened.

What is missing in the commission's conclusions is any mention of Marina Oswald. The commission did not want to see that if she had not affected great indifference on November 21, had not appeared to be determined about a separation from Oswald, nothing would have happened on November 22. Marina testified: "I wasn't really very angry. I, of course, wanted to make up with him. But I gave the appearance of being very angry. I was smiling inside, but I had a serious expression on my face."[1]

What took place between them on the day before the assassination, reported Marina Oswald's friend, Ruth Paine, "could certainly have affected his thinking about it." She added, "It is conceivable even that he hadn't seriously thought about shooting the President."[2] The FBI, which tapped the Paines' phones (in Michael Paine's office and the Paines' house) immediately after the assassination, heard a conversation between them. The Paines had both realized that "the explanation" could be found in the way Marina Oswald treated Oswald. Michael Paine said he felt sure Oswald had killed the president but did not feel Oswald was responsible and added, "We both know who is responsible."[3] George De Mohrenschildt told the Warren Commission: "[Marina] was annoying him all the time. Poor guy was going out of his mind."[4] The feelings of "overriding hostility" to which Oswald succumbed were directed against his wife and against himself, not against his actual victim.

On the afternoon of the assassination, given permission to make a phone call, Oswald was beside himself with rage when Ruth Paine told him his wife was no longer with her, that she had been taken somewhere else under the protection of the authorities. He could not get in touch with her anymore. He was lost without her. How could they deprive him of her?

Marina Oswald had to a great extent provoked him to prepare the attempt on General Walker's life, a brilliant feat in his eyes that would show her how great he was. Feigning resentment on the eve of the president's visit to Dallas, playing a cruel game with him, she drove him to despair and pushed him to destroy, in the person of its most prestigious representative, a world in which he was unable to find a place for himself. His dyslexia; his pressing desire during his adolescence to rise above his social condition; and then, after his marriage, his efforts to escape poverty; his maneuvers; his disappointments; and his vulnerability to his wife's moods add up to a very different criminal from the one depicted by the commission. He demonstrated to all those who had been unable to appreciate the superior being he took himself to be that he was a man to be reckoned with. He believed that his wife had left him, that he was separated from his daughters, and fate so willed that he was given the opportunity to do away with his opposite—the human being who had achieved the greatest triumphs. The senseless act of an insignificant man was taken for a deliberate, kamikazelike act.

When a national tragedy occurs, the tendency is to seek explanations as extraordinary as the event itself. It was difficult for the public to accept the fact that the most important political figure in the world had died merely because of a family quarrel between two misfits on the bottom rung of the social ladder. Led astray by piety and respect, the Warren Commission embellished the character of the wretched Oswald by ranking him among reformers and utopians. "One never speaks of this assassination without making reckless judgments. . . . The absurdity of the accusation, the total lack of evidence, nothing stops them. . . . One must read every-thing with mistrust."[5] Thus spoke Voltaire about the fables sur-rounding the assassination of King Henri IV of France.

Playing into the emotional atmosphere after President Ken-nedy's assassination was the Soviet Union. Everwatchful for op-portunities to weaken the Atlantic Alliance, the USSR did not fail to use the apparently strange circumstances surrounding the as-sassination; disinformation was sown in Europe.

Europeans belonging to the Communist party were convinced that American interference prevented their countries from enjoying the blessings of the regime they dreamed of and that right-wing Americans wanted their country to attack a peace-loving Soviet Union. Many apolitical people who believed the rumors circulated from day one by the media about Dallas were soon disturbed by the disinformation coming straight from their Communist fellow countrymen and began to wonder whether relying on America did not endanger Western Europe. President Kennedy, they were told, had been assassinated because he wanted to resume normal rela-tions with Cuba, withdraw American troops from Vietnam, go after the all-powerful CIA; the conspirators were from the extrem-ist faction of the American right-wing, the monopolies which, like the Pentagon, feared a decrease in allocations for armaments. This would make the thermonuclear attack against the Soviet Union they wanted impossible. The thesis to develop was that Western Europe would doom itself to destruction by accepting the protec-tion of a country in which power belonged to multimillionaires who controlled the police, the FBI, the CIA, and who appealed to the Mafia when they wanted to get rid of those who stood in their way, a country whose president was simply eliminated when he tried to oppose them.

The fantastic statements and mendacious assertions convinced many Europeans who, at the time Oswald was murdered by Ruby, had not believed there was evidence of a conspiracy, that the Amer-ica of Roosevelt, of Kennedy, now the America of Johnson, was about to fall apart. These allegations played an important role in the development of disaffection among America's allies. What opinion could these Europeans have of their great ally when they read stories such as the one at the end of an article in one of the January 1977 issues of *New Times*: in August 1963 "the New Or-leans police" put Oswald in jail for no apparent reason; "a former code clerk of the FBI station in New Orleans" reported that a plot to kill President Kennedy during his trip to Dallas had been hatched; the telegram was "destroyed"; Oswald was "released from jail and allowed to go to Dallas." Thus, the New Orleans police was represented as being in league with the Dallas police in a plot with accomplices everywhere.

As previously mentioned, General de Gaulle commented that the assassination of President Kennedy demonstrated America's instability and that dependence on her was a dangerous mistake. The media, when they were not supporting or contributing to the conspiracy theory, gave preference to the kind of sensational news that led people to wonder; the media influenced politicians as well as the man in the street. Finally, people generally imagined that the conspiracy had been proved. There were those who realized that no evidence was ever brought to support the theory and that the reasons for disbelieving the investigators proved, one after another, to be without foundation. Nevertheless, they thought that someday something would be available that would corroborate the allegations of the Warren Commission's detractors. However, since Oswald acted alone, nothing will ever be added to the existing documentation.

This campaign against America was not comparable to the kind of "active measures" carried out without foreknowledge of results, whose impact is left to chance, and which, easily denied, leave no trace in the minds of those who are aware of the denials. It went on for many years, until the Kremlin judged the question settled; whatever material in an interview, an article, or a book could help shake confidence in the stability of the most important member of the Atlantic Alliance was picked out and developed, thus reaching a large audience.

Among those who propagated the conspiracy theory in Europe, there were Soviet agents, such as the unknown authors of *L'Amérique brûle* or the well-connected Parisian who distributed pro-Russian newsletters. There were also misinformed, naive, or greedy people whose writings were sometimes in harmony with *New Times'* articles or Tass's dispatches. It is not easy to determine to which category the detractors of the Warren Commission belonged—except probably in Joesten's case—or the extent to which the tales fabricated by Moscow and the embellishments added to misinformation picked up in foreign newspapers helped the conspiracy theory to spread. It is difficult even to know who was the first to launch some of the disinformation published at the same time in different countries. In the end, the belief in the conspiracy spread by word of mouth, from newspapers to magazines, from magazines to books, from England to France, from France to England, from Europe to America, from America to Europe, with Soviet disinformation services watchful and active in the background. Those who believe that the investigation of the assassination was scandalous do not know themselves what convinced them of the existence of a conspiracy. Books, excellent in other respects, whose serious errors have been mentioned in previous chapters, simply echoed rumors of uncertain origin that had remained "in the air" and which their authors did not question.

The evolution in European sentiment is demonstrated by the change in attitude of the highly respected *Le Monde,* which in 1963 saw Ruby and Oswald as "two warped loners," and which in 1983 thought that many questions had not been answered. As for the Americans, *New Times* had to acknowledge in 1966 that they had readily accepted the conclusions of the Warren Commission; in 1967, however, *New Times* observed that this was no longer the case; and in 1977 it mentioned that an overwhelming majority wanted a new investigation (they wanted "the tangle of crimes which the Warren Commission failed to unravel to be untangled,"[6] in disinformation style). This development in the United States had not been really foreseen but was a beneficial side effect. As no evidence was ever brought forward at any time to justify the change in public opinion, it is apparent that it was due chiefly to the campaign of disinformation.

In a speech in Munich on December 26, 1983, the United States ambassador to Germany said: "In the years immediately following World War II, many Europeans permitted themselves to be mesmerized by American society. . . . the turning point may have come with the death of President John F. Kennedy, who was immensely popular in Europe, perhaps even more popular than in America. . . . it changed the image of the United States drastically."

The object of this study is to demonstrate that if the United States is no longer in the eyes of its allies the great country it was in the 1960s, it is in large part because of the campaign of disinformation waged by the Kremlin at every opportunity, on newsworthy topics about which opinion could be swayed along the lines desired by the Soviet Union. The guiding theme of disinformation is exposed in the Soviet encyclopedia under the heading "War": "In the U.S.A. the theory of 'absolute nuclear deterrence' is widely held, the essence of which is that the U.S.A. must establish world domination by means of using or threatening to use nuclear weapons, above all against socialist countries."[7] The disinformation on Oswald's crime, the vivid memory of which still affects the older generation, was used by this writer as an illustration of one of the techniques applied; it consists of amplifying and spreading whatever was published in foreign countries on any subject that could be interpreted as suggesting, even remotely, that the military with ties to right-wing extremists was leading America to fascism and war.

After Oswald's crime Europeans were told that a large group of Americans wanted to get rid of a peace-loving president, that Western Europe was now directly threatened and would be secure only if it renounced the Atlantic Alliance. Thus, the path would be opened up to the Finlandization of Europe, and, finally, the United States would lose interest in the fate of its present friends or allies, as it lost interest in the fate of Eastern Europe. Some of those who, twenty years ago, believed that the assassination of President Kennedy was the result of a large-scale operation mounted by his political enemies are active neutralists today. They fail to see that Russia is a militarist, imperialist, and expansionist country, and they are not aware that disinformation was used after the war to sow confusion in Russia's neighboring countries, now the satellites of a totalitarian superpower.

Those writers who in good faith circulated in Europe and then in America the conspiracy theory, and affirmed that the people behind Oswald were powerful enough to be immune from thorough investigation, served as spokespersons for the Soviet propagandists. They gave the seal of respectability to books sanctioned or concocted by Moscow, books such as *Oswald, Assassin or Fall Guy, Oswald: the Truth,* and *L'Amérique brûle.*

Those who were convinced there was a conspiracy had become enmeshed in the web of contradictory claims made by people hostile to the United States on principle, by authors hoping for a best-seller, and by serious writers who relied on chapter 7 of the *Warren Report.*

"Truth has the strength of its parts, firmly chained together, a strength which error lacks."[8] The major or minor events of Oswald's life, his frustrations, his failures, were linked, and at the end of the chain was the enormity of the crime.

Abbreviations

HC, pp.   *Report of the Select Committee on Assassinations U.S. House of Representatives: Ninety-Fifth Congress, Second Session. Findings and Recommendations* (Washington: Government Printing Office, 1979).

HC, vol.:pp.   *Hearings before the Select Committee on Assassinations and Appendices to Hearings* (Washington: Government Printing Office, 1979).

NYT   *The New York Times.*

NYT Magazine   *The New York Times Magazine.*

Schweiker Report   *Select Committee to Study Government Operations with Respect to Intelligence Activities, United States Senate. The Investigation of the Assassination of President John F. Kennedy: Performance of the Intelligence Agencies. Final Report, Book V* (Washington: Government Printing Office, 1976).

WR, pp.   *United States, President's Commission on the Assassination of President Kennedy. The Of-*

ficial Warren Report on the Assassination of President John F. Kennedy, analysis and commentary by Louis Nizer; historical afterword by Bruce Catton (Garden City, New York: Doubleday, 1964).

WR, vol.:pp.   *U.S. Warren Commission, Investigation of the Assassination of President John F. Kennedy. Hearings Before the President's Commission on the Assassination of President Kennedy,* 26 vols. (Washington: Government Printing Office, 1964).

Notes

Introduction

1. *Oxford English Dictionary,* 1st ed., s.v. "dis-."
2. Michel Heller, "La Désinformation, moyen d'information" in *Politique Internationale* (France: Hiver, 1981), 239.
3. Branko Lazitch, "La Désinformation, arme de la guerre politique" in *Est & Ouest* (March 1984): 7–8.
4. Richard H. Shultz and Roy Godson, *Dezinformatsia—Active Measures in Soviet Strategy* (New York: Pergamon Press, 1984), 134.
5. Ibid., 142.
6. Ibid., 144.
7. *Paris-Match,* July 11, 1980, cited by Shultz and Godson, *Dezinformatsia,* 135.
8. *Time,* Oct. 6, 1980, 60.
9. WR, 375–424.
10. WR, 375.
11. WR, 421.
12. WR, 423.
13. WR, 420–21.
14. WR, 9:261, 313.
15. Drew Middleton, *NYT,* Nov. 26, 1963, 12.
16. Henry Fairlie, *NYT Magazine,* Sept. 11, 1966, 54–55.
17. *L'Express,* Feb.–March 1964.
18. Léo Sauvage, *L'Affaire Oswald* (Paris: Aux Editions de Minuit, 1965).
19. *Les Temps modernes,* July 1964.
20. WR, 5:559.
21. HC, 12:682–83 (The Library of Congress, The Assassination of President John F. Kennedy, an alphabetical bibliography).

Introduction (continued)

22. Joachim Joesten, *The Case Against Lyndon B. Johnson in the Assassination of President Kennedy* (Munich: Dreschstr, 1967).

1. Disinformation in 1963

1. *Pravda,* Nov. 24, 1963, quoted in *The Current Digest of the Soviet Press,* Dec. 11, 1963, 6.
2. Gladwin Hill, *NYT,* Nov. 24, 1963, 1–2.
3. WR, 800.
4. Joseph A. Loftus, *NYT,* November 25, 12.
5. *NYT,* Nov. 26, 1963, 15.
6. *Le Figaro,* Nov. 26, 1963.
7. *Le Monde,* Nov. 27, 1963.
8. WR, 23:78.
9. WR, 354.
10. WR, 333–74, 779–806.
11. WR, 23:351.
12. WR, 25:505.
13. WR, 23:101.
14. WR, 22:887.
15. WR, 15:417.
16. WR, 342.
17. WR, 344.
18. WR, 5:191.
19. WR, 13:188.
20. WR, 219.
21. WR, 22:369.
22. WR, 13:70.
23. WR, 349.
24. WR, 5:200.
25. Radio Moscow, Nov. 24, 1963, quoted in *Communist Affairs* (Nov.– Dec. 1963): 4.
26. Deutschlandsender (East Berlin radio station), Nov. 25, 1963, quoted in *Communist Affairs* (Nov.–Dec. 1963): 4.
27. *NYT,* Nov. 26, 1963, 12.
28. *Pravda* and *Izvestia,* Nov. 26, 1963, quoted in *The Current Digest of the Soviet Press,* Dec. 11, 1963, 9, 10.
29. *Pravda* and *Izvestia,* Nov. 27, 1963, quoted in *The Current Digest of the Soviet Press,* Dec. 11, 1963, 12, 13.
30. Tass, quoted in *NYT,* Nov. 27, 1963, 19.
31. Tass, quoted in *NYT,* Nov. 28, 1963, 32.
32. *NYT,* Nov. 27, 1963, 17.
33. *Le Monde,* Nov. 26, 1963.
34. Ibid., Nov. 27, 1963.
35. *Paris-Presse,* quoted in *NYT,* Nov. 28, 1963, 32.

Disinformation in 1963 (continued)

36. *Le Figaro,* Nov. 29, 1963.
37. *L'Express,* Nov. 28, 1963.
38. *L'Humanité,* Nov. 26, 1963; *Pravda,* Dec. 1, 1963.
39. Pierre and Renée Gosset, *L'Express,* Dec. 12, 1963, 18.
40. Ibid., 20.
41. *Izvestia,* Dec. 19, 1963, quoted in *Communist Affairs* (Nov.–Dec. 1963): 6.
42. Raymond Cartier, *Paris-Match,* Dec. 28, 1963, 32.
43. *Le Monde,* Dec. 12, 1963.
44. *Stern,* quoted in *Literaturnaia Gazeta,* Dec. 21, 1963; in *Communist Affairs* (Nov.–Dec. 1963): 6.
45. Jean Raymond Tournoux, *La Tragédie du Général* (Paris: Plon, 1967), 455.
46. Ibid., 456.
47. Ibid., 457.
48. Ibid., 458.
49. WR, 122, 135.
50. WR, 6:409.
51. HC, 287–88.
52. HC, 355.
53. WR, 119.
54. John K. Lattimer, *Kennedy and Lincoln: Medical and Ballistic Comparisons of their Assassinations* (New York and London: Harcourt Brace Jovanovich, 1980), 297.
55. *Le Figaro,* Nov. 26, 1963.
56. *Le Monde,* Nov. 30, 1963.
57. Shultz and Godson, *Dezinformatsia,* 30–31.
58. Ibid., 178.
59. Ibid., 30.
60. *New Times,* no. 50, Dec. 11, 1963.
61. Ibid., 10.
62. Ibid., 11.
63. WR, 48.
64. *New Times,* no. 50, Dec. 11, 1963, 12.
65. *Le Figaro,* Nov. 25, 1963.
66. Charles Roberts, *The Truth about the Assassination* (New York: Grosset & Dunlap, 1967), 15.
67. WR, 58.

2. Disinformation in 1964

1. WR, 5:100.
2. *Est et Ouest* (Sept. 1986): 36.
3. Thomas G. Buchanan, *Big Brother: Ma vie revue et corrigée par le F.B.I.* (Paris: Editions du Seuil, 1984), 125.

Disinformation in 1964 (continued)

4. *L'Express,* Feb. 20, 1964, 9.
5. Ibid., 10.
6. WR, 72.
7. *L'Express,* Feb. 20, 1964, 10.
8. WR, 641.
9. *L'Express,* Feb. 20, 1964, 12.
10. Lattimer, *Kennedy and Lincoln,* 292–94.
11. *L'Express,* Feb. 20, 1964, 15.
12. WR, 648.
13. *L'Express,* Feb. 20, 1964, 20.
14. WR, 180.
15. *L'Express,* Feb. 27, 1964, 16–17.
16. *L'Express,* March 5, 1964, 20.
17. Ibid., 21.
18. *L'Express,* Feb. 27, 1964, 17.
19. *L'Express,* March 5, 1964, 19.
20. *L'Express,* Feb. 27, 1964, 22.
21. Ibid., 15.
22. WR, 79, 106.
23. WR, 640.
24. Buchanan, *Big Brother,* 128.
25. Thomas G. Buchanan, *Who Killed Kennedy?* (London: Sacker & Warburg, 1964; New York: Putnam, 1964).
26. Mark Lane, *Rush to Judgment* (New York: Holt, Rinehart & Winston, 1966).
27. *The Listener,* May 5, 1983.
28. *L'Express,* Sept. 5, 1986, Hugh Trevor-Roper, 64.
29. WR, 5:559.
30. *National Guardian,* July 18, 1964.
31. Jean Pouillon, *Les Temps modernes,* July 1964, 184–92.
32. Ibid., 185.
33. Ibid., 186.
34. Ibid., 187.
35. Ibid., 191.
36. WR, 5:559.
37. *Les Temps modernes,* July 1964, 191.
38. WR, xiii.
39. WR, 5:554.
40. WR, 2:32.
41. Bertrand Russell, *The Minority of One,* Sept. 1964, 6–8.
42. Ibid., 8.
43. *NYT,* July 24, 1964, 13.
44. De Lloyd J. Guth and David R. Wrone, *The Assassination of John F. Kennedy* (Westport, Conn.: Greenwood Press, 1979), 9.

Disinformation in 1964 (continued)

45. *The Times,* Sept. 3, 1970, 1, 8; Sept. 4, 1970, 1; Sept. 5, 1970, 2; Oct. 31, 1970, 14.
46. *NYT,* June 8, 1964, letter by Kenneth Nary, 28.

3. Information and Disinformation

1. WR, xi–xiii.
2. HC, 11:462.
3. Ibid., 212.
4. Ibid., 213.
5. WR, 374.
6. HC, 11:246.
7. WR, 388.
8. HC, 11:390.
9. WR, 375.
10. WR, 376.
11. WR, 383–84.
12. WR, 388.
13. WR, 390.
14. WR, 394.
15. WR, 22.
16. WR, 638.
17. *Journal of Individual Psychology* (May 1967): 19–52.
18. Ibid., 23.
19. Ibid., 34.
20. Ibid., 45.
21. Dr. D. Abrahamson, *Bulletin of New York Academy of Medicine* 43, no. 10 (Oct. 1967): 886.
22. WR, 388.
23. WR, 11:452.
24. WR, 18:101.
25. WR, 8:149.
26. WR, 9:236–37.
27. WR, 11:128.
28. WR, 9:95.
29. Ibid., 155.
30. WR, 375.
31. *NYT,* Nov. 23, 1963, 4.
32. WR, 693.
33. WR, 747.

4. Misinformation on Oswald's Background

1. WR, 678.
2. WR, 183.

Misinformation on Oswald's Background (continued)

3. WR, 26, 812.
4. WR, 26, 814.
5. WR, 381.
6. WR, 814.
7. HC, 11:239.
8. WR, 383.
9. WR, 21:501.
10. WR, 495.
11. WR, 19:315.
12. WR, 381.
13. WR, 22:559.
14. WR, 19:315.
15. WR, 1:230.
16. WR, 1:205.
17. WR, 1:190.
18. WR, 423.
19. WR, 375.
20. WR, 414.
21. WR, 686; 8:297.
22. WR, 8:240–41.
23. WR, 16:623.
24. WR, 8:243.
25. WR, 17:727.
26. WR, 26:31.
27. WR, 690.
28. WR, 11:460.
29. WR, 22:701.
30. WR, 8:288.
31. HC, 2:209.
32. Ibid., 217–18.
33. HC, 12:351.
34. HC: 61–62.
35. WR, 690.
36. WR, 8:262–63.
37. WR, 16:24.
38. HC, 12:509.
39. WR, 18:464.
40. WR, 392.
41. WR, 11:299.
42. HC, 2:460.
43. WR, 11:445.
44. WR, 16:97.
45. WR, 747.
46. WR, 18:102.
47. WR, 749.
48. WR, 16:97.

Misinformation on Oswald's Background (continued)

49. WR, 22:707.
50. Ibid., 706.
51. WR, 11:447.
52. Ibid., 458.
53. Ibid., 450.
54. Ibid., 449–50.
55. WR, 11:449.
56. Ibid., 445.
57. Ibid., 456.
58. WR, 16:98.
59. WR, 393.
60. WR, 16:102.
61. Ibid., 436.
62. WR, 752.
63. WR, 16:315.
64. Ibid., 99.
65. WR, 9:261–62.
66. WR, 710.
67. WR, 387.
68. WR, 9:255.

5. Misinformation on Oswald's Motives

1. WR, 388.
2. WR, 8:10.
3. WR, 1:200.
4. WR, 8:233.
5. Ibid., 315.
6. WR, 11:96.
7. Ibid., 96–97.
8. WR, 18:103.
9. WR, 11:452.
10. HC, 2:254.
11. WR, 9:236.
12. WR, 283.
13. WR, 9:268.
14. WR, 8:434.
15. HC, 12:49.
16. Anthony Summers, *Conspiracy* (New York: McGraw Hill, 1980), 499.
17. Buchanan, *Big Brother* (Paris: Editions du Seuil, 1984), 185.
18. WR, 20:301.
19. WR, 16:107.
20. Ibid., 422.
21. Ibid., 424.

Misinformation on Oswald's Motives (continued)

22. Ibid., 425–26.
23. WR, 16:422–34.
24. Ibid., 433.
25. WR, 25:929–30.
26. HC, 12:362–63.
27. WR, 1:22.
28. Priscilla Johnson-McMillan, *Marina and Lee* (New York: Harper & Row, 1977), 359, 456–57.
29. WR, 9:351.
30. WR, 11:478.
31. WR, 9:150.
32. Ibid., 241.
33. Ibid., 255.
34. WR, 1:70.
35. *Webster's Third New International Dictionary,* s.v. "hate."
36. WR, 11:455.
37. WR, 16:442.
38. WR, 18:602.
39. WR, 1:94.
40. HC, 2:212.
41. WR, 9:52.
42. WR, 16:429.
43. Ibid., 814.
44. Ibid., 821.
45. Astolphe Custine, *Lettres de Russie: La Russie en 1839* (Paris: Gallimard, 1975), 265.
46. WR, 391.
47. WR, 406–13.
48. WR, 1:23.
49. WR, 404.
50. WR, 9:261.
51. *NYT,* April 1, 1981.
52. HC, 1:528.
53. WR, 609.
54. WR, 16:429.
55. WR, 1:47.
56. Ibid., 21.
57. Ibid., 23, 47.
58. WR, 10:38.
59. WR, 1:24.
60. WR, 410.
61. WR, 20:262–64.
62. WR, 1:23.
63. Ibid., 24.
64. WR, 24:589.
65. WR, 416.

Misinformation on Oswald's Motives (continued)

66. HC, 2:276.
67. HC, 2:278.
68. HC, 11:139.
69. WR, 11:120.
70. WR, 11:122.
71. Ibid., 120.
72. WR, 9:233.
73. WR, 281.
74. WR, 8:394.
75. WR, 11:123.
76. WR, 8:384.
77. WR, 9:33.
78. WR, 9:33; 11:119.
79. WR, 9:252.
80. WR, 8:386.
81. WR, 9:238.
82. WR, 1:12.
83. WR, 5:388–92.
84. Ibid., 389.
85. WR, 1:63.
86. WR, 9:385.
87. WR, 3:46–47.
88. WR, 1:65.
89. Ibid., 66.
90. WR, 1:65–66.
91. WR, 9:311.
92. WR, 18:638.
93. WR, 1:66.
94. WR, 21:501.
95. WR, 9:313.

6. The *Warren Report*

1. *New Times,* no. 38, Sept. 23, 1964.
2. Information obtained under the Freedom of Information Act: Document number 890–433, Oct. 1, 1964.
3. WR, 26:79.
4. Information obtained under the Freedom of Information Act: document number 1237–499A, August 28, 1964.
5. *New Times,* no. 38, Sept. 23, 1964, 31.
6. *New Times,* no. 48, Dec. 2, 1964, 10.
7. Anthony Lewis, *NYT,* June 1, 1964, 19.
8. WR, 637–38.
9. WR, 741–45.
10. Max Frankel, *NYT,* Oct. 3, 1964, 16.

The *Warren Report* (continued)

11. Robert G. Blakey and Richard N. Billings, *The Plot to Kill the President: Organized Crime Assassinated J.F.K., the Definitive Story* (New York: Times Books-Quadrangle, 1981), 40.
12. CBS broadcast, CBS Morning News, Sept. 25, 1978, transcript, 10–11.
13. *NYT,* Sept. 28, 1964, 17.
14. *Le Figaro,* Sept. 28, 1964.
15. Drew Middleton, *NYT,* Sept. 29, 1964, 29.
16. *NYT,* Sept. 30, 1964, 31.
17. *Le Figaro,* Sept. 29, 1964.
18. *Le Figaro,* Sept. 30, 1964.
19. WR, 117.
20. WR, x.
21. WR, 374.
22. Henry Fairlie, *NYT Magazine,* Sept. 11, 1966, 54–55.
23. Jean Durr, *Le Nouvel Observateur,* March 1967, 17.
24. Wesley Liebeler, quoted in *New York,* Jan. 22, 1967, 6.
25. Anthony Lewis, *NYT,* Nov. 30, 1978, A23.
26. David Welsch, *Ramparts,* vol. 5, no. 5 (Nov. 1966): 47.
27. Edward Jay Epstein, *Inquest: The Warren Commission and the Establishment of Truth* (New York: Viking Press, 1966), 68.
28. WR, 133.
29. WR, 2:229.
30. *NYT,* Dec. 1, 1966, 33.
31. *NYT,* Jan. 30, 1967, Patrick Lord Devlin and Alexander Bickel debate, 23.

7. *New Times (Novoe Vremia)*

1. Richard H. Popkin, *Le Nouvel Observateur,* no. 93, Aug. 24, 1966 and no. 94, Aug. 31, 1966.
2. *New Times,* no. 38, Sept. 21, 1966, 30.
3. Harold Weisberg, *Whitewash: The Report on the Warren Report* (Hyattown, Md.: 1966).
4. HC, 11:443.
5. *New Times,* no. 38, 30.
6. HC, 2:122.
7. *New Times,* no. 38, 30.
8. WR, 373.
9. WR, 88–89.
10. *Le Figaro,* Nov. 23, 1963.
11. HC, 1:330.
12. Richard Warren Lewis, "The Scavengers," *New York/World Journal Tribune,* Jan. 22, 1967, 7. Lewis quotes from "The Controversy," by Lawrence Schiller.

New Times (Novoe Vremia) **(continued)**

13. HC, 11:91–95.
14. Lattimer, *Kennedy and Lincoln,* 193.
15. Edward Jay Epstein, "Who's Afraid of the Warren Report?," *Esquire* 66 (Dec. 1966): 332.
16. Fred P. Graham, *NYT,* Nov. 3, 1966, 20.
17. *New Times,* no. 43, Oct. 26, 1966, 28.
18. *New Times,* no. 39, Sept. 26, 1966, 31.
19. Léo Sauvage, *The Oswald Affair: An Examination of the Contradictions and Omissions of the Warren Report* (Cleveland: World Publishing Co., 1966), 285–86.
20. WR, 555.
21. Sauvage, *Oswald Affair,* 400–401.
22. Ibid., 323.
23. Ibid., 330.
24. Léo Sauvage, *L'Affaire Oswald: Réponse au Rapport Warren* (Paris: Les Editions de Minuit, 1965), jacket copy.
25. Richard H. Popkin, *The Second Oswald* (New York: Avon Books, 1966).
26. Ibid., 88–90.
27. P. J. McMillan, *Marina and Lee,* 617.
28. *NYT,* Dec. 8, 1977, 1, B20.
29. *New Times,* no. 43, Oct. 26, 1966, 29.
30. Popkin, *Second Oswald,* 75.
31. WR, 11:372.
32. Popkin, *Second Oswald,* 76.
33. HC, 4:477.
34. HC, 10:77.
35. Popkin, *Second Oswald,* 88–89.
36. Ibid., 109.
37. *Le Nouvel Observateur,* no. 93, Aug. 24, 1966, 3.
38. Ibid., 17.
39. WR, 143.
40. *Le Nouvel Observateur,* no. 93, 2.
41. Popkin, *Les Assassins de Kennedy* (French translation of *The Second Oswald*), 117.
42. *L'Express,* Sept. 5, 1966, 58–70.
43. *Times Literary Supplement,* Dec. 14, 1967, 1219.
44. HC, 12:682–83.
45. *NYT,* Sept. 1, 1966, 1–2.
46. *New Times,* no. 43, Oct. 26, 1966.
47. Ibid., 28.
48. Ibid., 29.
49. Ibid., 31.
50. Ibid., 29.
51. Ibid., 30.
52. *New Times,* no. 51, Dec. 21, 1966.

New Times (Novoe Vremia) (continued)

53. Ibid., 29.
54. HC, 11:89.
55. Ibid., 91.
56. *New Times,* no. 51, 30.
57. HC, 1:32–31.
58. HC, 80.
59. *New Times,* no. 51, 30.
60. Warren Hinckle III, *If You Have a Lemon, Make Lemonade* (New York: G. P. Putnam & Sons, 1974), 226.
61. Ibid., 112, 115.
62. Ibid., 117.
63. *In the Shadow of Dallas,* distributed to new subscribers of *Ramparts.*
64. David Welsch, *Ramparts,* vol. 5, no. 5 (Nov. 1966): 41.
65. Ibid., 45.
66. *Esquire,* Dec. 1966, 210.
67. *NYT,* Nov. 22, 1973, 46.
68. HC, 4:467.
69. Ibid., 464.
70. Ibid., 463.
71. Ibid., 454.
72. *New Times,* no. 51, Dec. 21, 1966, 31.
73. *Le Nouvel Observateur,* Jan. 11, 1967, 25.
74. Joachim Joesten, *La Vérité sur le cas Jack Ruby* (Paris: Casterman, 1967).
75. *Lectures pour tous,* no. 16, 1967, 88.
76. *NYT,* Oct. 9, 1966, 20.
77. *New Times,* no. 3, Jan. 1977, 29.
78. *NYT,* Dec. 30, 1967, 28.
79. NBC broadcast, "The JFK Conspiracy, The Case of Jim Garrison," June 1967, 8:00–9:00 P.M., transcript, 10.
80. Ibid., A1.
81. *Ramparts,* July 1967.
82. NBC broadcast, June 1967, transcript, 33.
83. Ibid., 45.
84. *NYT,* July 5, 1967, 83.
85. Martin Waldron, *NYT,* Oct. 20, 1975, 16.
86. Sylvia Meagher, *Accessories after the Fact: The Warren Commission, the Authorities and the Report* (New York: Vintage Books, 1976), 298–301.
87. *New Times,* no. 46, Nov. 1972, 27.
88. James Hepburn, *L'Amérique brûle* (Paris: Nouvelles Frontières, 1968).
89. John L. Hess, *NYT,* Jan. 1, 1969, 12.
90. Warren Hinckle, "The Mystery of the Black Books, *Esquire* (April 1973): 130.

New Times (*Novoe Vremia*) (continued)

91. *NYT,* Jan. 1, 1969, 12.
92. Hinckle, *Esquire,* 128.
93. Ibid., 129.
94. Ibid., 130.
95. *NYT,* Jan. 1, 1969, 12.
96. Hinckle, *Esquire,* 172.
97. Ibid., 170.
98. *NYT,* Sept. 6, 1969, 22.
99. Nora Saire, *NYT,* Nov. 8, 1973, D1, and Vincent Canby, *NYT,* Nov. 25, 1973, D37.
100. Edward Jay Epstein, *Legend: The Secret World of Lee Harvey Oswald* (New York: Reader's Digest Press, 1978).
101. Alice Van Buren, *New Republic,* April 29, 1978, 35–38.
102. Epstein, *Legend,* 170.
103. Ibid., 201.
104. Ibid., 233.
105. Ibid., 170.
106. Ibid., 172.
107. Ibid., 283.
108. Ibid., 82.
109. Ibid., xv–xvi.
110. Ibid., 334.
111. Allensbach Institute, West Germany, quoted in *The Economist,* Feb. 27, 1982, 18.

8. New Commissions of Investigation and *New Times*

1. *NYT,* March 27, 1975, 28.
2. A. de Segonzac, *France-Soir,* March 30, 1975.
3. Martin Waldron, *NYT,* Oct. 20, 1975, 16.
4. Schweiker Report, 6.
5. Eric Norden, *Playboy,* Oct. 1967, 59–74, 155–58.
6. Robert Herr, *New Republic,* Nov. 11, 1978, 10; *Time,* Oct. 2, 1978, 22.
7. *NYT,* June 12, 1977, E1.
8. Blakey and Billings, *Plot to Kill,* 62.
9. HC, 1:415.
10. *NYT,* June 12, 1977, E1.
11. Blakey and Billings, *Plot to Kill,* 64.
12. Guth and Wrone, *Assassinations,* 13.
13. Summers, *Conspiracy,* 395–96.
14. Oswald's letters: Nov. 3, 1959 (WR, 263); Feb. 5, 1961 (WR, 752); March 12, 1961 (WR, 752–53).
15. Blakey and Billings, *Plot to Kill,* xiii.
16. *NYT,* Dec. 16, 1979, 73.

New Commissions of Investigation and *New Times* (continued)

17. WNET broadcast, "The MacNeil-Lehrer Report," July 8, 1980, transcript, 6.
18. HC, 9:102.
19. Ibid., 93.
20. WR, 8:14.
21. HC, 9:96–99.
22. *NYT,* Dec. 16, 1979, 73.
23. WNET broadcast, "The MacNeil-Lehrer Report," July 8, 1980, transcript, 6.
24. HC, 18.
25. HC, 149.
26. Blakey and Billings, *Plot to Kill,* 279.
27. HC, 9:201.
28. HC, 2:75.
29. Ibid., 90.
30. HC, 501.
31. CBS broadcast, "Face the Nation," Sept. 24, 1978, transcript, 2.
32. HC, 501.
33. CBS broadcast, "Sunday Night News with Ed Bradley," 6.
34. HC, 508.
35. HC, 180.
36. *Los Angeles Times,* Jan. 27, 1979.
37. HC, 520, 531.
38. CBS broadcast, "Face the Nation," Dec. 31, 1978, transcript, 6.
39. Ibid., 4.
40. *Time,* July 30, 1979, 30.
41. George Lardner, Jr., *Washington Post,* Aug. 13, 1978, A18.
42. *New Times,* nos. 1, 2, 3, Jan. 1977.
43. *New Times,* no. 2, 1977, 27.
44. *New Times,* no. 1, 1977, 27.
45. HC, 18.
46. HC, 241.
47. HC, 266.
48. *New Times,* no. 1, 1977, 27.
49. Ibid., 28.
50. Ibid., 27.
51. Ibid., 30.
52. *New Times,* no. 2, 1977, 28.
53. HC, 169.
54. *New Times,* no. 2, 1977, 28.
55. Ibid., 27.
56. Blakey and Billings, *Plot to Kill,* 386.
57. *New Times,* no. 3, Jan. 1977, 29.
58. Blakey and Billings, *Plot to Kill,* 64.
59. *New Times,* no. 3, 29.
60. Ibid., 30.

New Commissions of Investigation and *New Times* (continued)

61. *NYT,* Jan. 14, 1979, letter by Peter B. Young, 20.
62. *New York Herald Tribune,* Dec. 30, 1978, International edition, letter by Jim Haynes.
63. Nicole Le Caigne, *L'Express,* Sept. 11, 1981.
64. Arlette Marchal, *L'Express,* April 17, 1978.
65. J. F. Revel, *Commentaire,* Summer 1983, 98.
66. *NYT,* Sept. 25, 1978, 29.
67. *Report of the Committee on Ballistic Acoustics* (Washington: National Academy Press, 1982).
68. Ibid., 1.
69. Ibid., 13.
70. Ibid., 9.
71. Ibid., 5.
72. Ibid., 18.
73. Ibid., 18–19.
74. Ibid., 20.
75. Ibid., 2.
76. *NYT,* May 15, 1982, 35.

9. Disinformation and Amateur Detectives

1. Ben A. Franklin, *NYT,* Feb. 23, 1975, 32.
2. Michael Eddowes, *The Oswald File* (New York: C. N. Potter, 1977).
3. Ibid., 211–21.
4. Ibid., 2.
5. Ibid., 122.
6. Ibid., 173.
7. Ibid., 139.
8. Robert Sam Anson, *They've Killed the President* (New York: Bantam Books, 1975).
9. HC, 8:225–389.
10. Anthony Summers, *Conspiracy* (New York: McGraw-Hill, 1980).
11. Andrew Hacker, *New York Review of Books,* July 17, 1980, 12.
12. Summers, *Conspiracy,* 130.
13. WR, 22:423.
14. Summers, *Conspiracy,* 293.
15. Ibid., 294.
16. Ibid., 95.
17. Ibid., 312.
18. Ibid., 331.
19. Ibid., 341–42.
20. Ibid., 400.
21. Ibid., 442.
22. Ibid., 13.
23. WR, 684.

Notes

Disinformation and Amateur Detectives (continued)

24. Summers, *Conspiracy,* 555.
25. WR, 697.
26. Summers, *Conspiracy,* 106.
27. WR, 6:350–51.
28. Summers, *Conspiracy,* 116.
29. WR, 165–76.
30. Summers, *Conspiracy,* 185.
31. Ibid., 205.
32. *New York Review of Books,* July 17, 1980, 11.
33. WNET broadcast, "The MacNeil-Lehrer Report," July 8, 1980.
34. Ibid., 8.
35. HC, 137.
36. Christopher Lehmann-Haupt, *NYT,* July 22, 1980, C9.
37. David S. Lifton, *Best Evidence* (New York: Macmillan Publishing Co., 1980), 678.
38. Ibid., 681.
39. Ibid., 692.
40. Ibid., 193.
41. Ibid., 350.
42. Ibid., 370.
43. Ibid., 372.
44. Ibid., 697.
45. *Time,* Feb. 16, 1981, 5.
46. Ibid., Jan. 19, 1981, 22–23.
47. Michael L. Kurtz, *Crime of the Century: The Kennedy Assassination from a Historian's Perspective* (Knoxville: University of Tennessee Press, 1982).
48. *The Economist,* July 31, 1982, 79.
49. Kurtz, *Crime,* 221.
50. Ibid., 222.
51. Lattimer, *Kennedy and Lincoln,* 123.
52. Ibid., 145.
53. McMillan, *Marina,* 609.
54. Lattimer, *Kennedy and Lincoln,* 138.
55. Ibid., 354.
56. David W. Belin, *Nov. 22, 1963: You Are the Jury* (New York: Quadrangle, 1973), 427.
57. James W. Clarke, *American Assassins: The Darker Side of Politics* (Princeton, N.J.: Princeton University Press, 1982).
58. Ibid., 107.
59. Ibid., 127.
60. Ibid., 126.
61. Ibid., 124.
62. Ibid., 114.
63. Ibid., 106.
64. Ibid., 127.

Disinformation and Amateur Detectives (continued)

65. Ibid., 110.
66. Ibid., 258.
67. CBS broadcast, "CBS Evening News with Walter Cronkite," April 25, 1975.
68. Anthony Lewis, *NYT,* Jan. 3, 1968, 18.
69. HC, 11:411–12.
70. HC, 3:653–54.
71. HC, 258.
72. HC, 257.
73. Clarke, *Assassins,* 107.
74. WR, 674–75.
75. Clarke, *Assassins,* 118.
76. HC, 142.
77. Clarke, *Assassins,* 209.
78. Ibid., 117.
79. Guth and Wrone, *Assassinations,* xxv.
80. *NYT,* Nov. 19, 1983, 9.
81. Jean Davison, *Oswald's Game* (New York and London: W. W. Norton & Co., 1983), 280.
82. Ibid., 10.
83. Ibid., 68.
84. Ibid., 295.
85. Letter to Friedrich Engels, May 7, 1870, *Oeuvres de Karl Marx I,* Maximilien Rubel (Paris: Bibliothèque de la Pléiade, 1963), cxiii.
86. J. Davison, *Oswald's Game,* 211.
87. WR, 1:24.
88. WR, 9:314.
89. WR, 21:623–24.
90. WR, 10:56.
91. WR, 21:9.
92. Davison, *Oswald's Game,* 175.
93. HC, 2:252.
94. WR, 25:929–30.
95. WR, 288.
96. Davison, *Oswald's Game,* 296.
97. Daniel Schorr, *Clearing the Air* (Boston: Houghton Mifflin Co., 1977), quoted by Davison, 211.
98. Blakey and Billings, *Plot to Kill,* 146.
99. Davison, *Oswald's Game,* 213.
100. WR, 413.
101. HC, 2:270.
102. McMillan, *Marina,* 562.
103. James R. Phelan, *NYT Magazine,* Nov. 23, 1975, 125.
104. Léo Sauvage, *Les Américains* (Paris: Magazine, 1983), 393.
105. *Le Matin,* Nov. 23, 1983, 19–20.
106. Jacques Amalric, *Le Monde,* Nov. 20, 1983.

Disinformation and Amateur Detectives (continued)

107. G. B. Graziani, *Le Quotidien,* Nov. 22, 1983.
108. *Le Monde,* Nov. 20, 1983.
109. WR, 180.
110. G. B. Graziani, *Le Figaro,* Nov. 22, 1983, 147.
111. *The Guardian,* Nov. 17, 1983.
112. *Der Spiegel,* no. 48, Nov. 1983, 144–49.
113. Buchanan, *Big Brother,* 47.
114. Ibid., 54.
115. Ibid., 71.
116. Ibid., 75.
117. Ibid., 35.
118. Ibid., 82.
119. Ibid., 87.
120. Ibid., 152.
121. Ibid., 128.
122. Ibid., 152.
123. Ibid., 166.
124. Ibid., 165.
125. Ibid., 166.
126. Ibid., 104–105.
127. Ibid., 107.
128. Ibid., 106.
129. Ibid., 115.
130. Ibid., 113.
131. Ibid., 101.
132. Ibid., 112.
133. Ibid., 154–55.
134. Ibid., 157.
135. Ibid., 158.
136. Ibid., 162.
137. Ibid., 134.
138. Ibid., 177.
139. Ibid., 185.
140. Ibid., 102.
141. Ibid., 122.
142. Ibid., 141.
143. Ibid., 125.
144. CUNY broadcast, *Apostrophes,* Nov. 28, 1985.
145. WR, 5:100.
146. Buchanan, *Big Brother,* 143.
147. Adam Clymer, *New York Times Book Review,* Feb. 23, 1986, 16.
148. Henry Hurt, *Reasonable Doubt* (New York: Holt Rinehart & Winston, 1985), xi.
149. Ibid., 7.
150. Ibid., 346.

Disinformation and Amateur Detectives (continued)

151. Ibid., 391.
152. Ibid., 390.
153. Ibid., 349.

10. Conclusion

1. WR, 1:69.
2. WR, 11:394.
3. Summers, *Conspiracy,* Warren Commission Document 206, 132–33.
4. WR, 9:233.
5. Voltaire, *Dissertation sur la mort de Henri IV,* vol. 2 (Ed. Furne, 1835), 348.
6. *New Times,* no. 1, 1977, 27.
7. *Great Soviet Encyclopedia,* 3d ed., s.v. "War."
8. Anatole France, *L'Histoire Contemporaine* (Paris: Calmann-Lévy, 1981), 69.

Notes on Sources

Many works have been written on the impressionability of crowds, publicity, and propaganda, of which disinformation is the extreme form. The most revolting example of disinformation was the one that characterized the Moscow trials of the 1930s when victim was coerced into joining executioner in spreading disinformation. The only historian who immediately understood what was happening was Boris Souvarine. After the first trial, which resulted only in prison sentences for the accused, Souvarine wrote: "Nobody could sincerely pretend to believe the fables which have no more truth in them than the alleged confessions" (from *Staline: Aperçu historique du bolchevisme.* Paris: Plon, 1935. Quotation from translation by the Alliance Book Corporation, Longmans, Green & Co., 1939, 492).

Souvarine also mentioned in his book "the modern methods of deceiving opinion and spreading myths" (491) and the "incessant repetition of various processes which goes to fashion minds and which is able to determine an effective current among the crowds" (479), adding that none of Stalin's predecessors "had dared to falsify history with so much indecency, to play tricks with the truth" (485). He thus defined *disinformation,* a term that did not exist at that time, even in Russian.

The assassination of President Kennedy was the subject of thousands of books and long articles that, with very few exceptions, defended the conspiracy theory. All the necessary information on the facts was provided by the investigative agencies of the United

States to the Warren Commission, which published them. The commission's files, deposited in the National Archives, do not give any supplementary information. The testimony of some assistant counsel, published by the House Select Committee on Assassinations, provides interesting insider's information.

Two early studies deserve a particular mention: Dwight Macdonald, "A Critique of the Warren Report," *Esquire* (March 1965); and John Sparrow, "After the Assassination," in *The Times Literary Supplement* (London, Dec. 14, 1967, and Jan. 4, 1968).

A bibliography established by the Research Service of the Library of Congress is found in an appendix of volume 12, pages 646–795, to the hearings of the assassination committee.

Another bibliography—with a useful index of *New York Times* articles—is found in the following: De Lloyd J. Guth and David R. Wrone, *The Assassination of John F. Kennedy: A Comprehensible Historical and Legal Bibliography, 1963–1979* (Westport, Conn.: Greenwood Press, 1979). Sylvia Meagher and Gary Owens compiled *The Master Index to the J.F.K. Assassination Investigation.* It was published by the Scarecrow Press, Inc. (Metuchen, N.J.) in 1980.

Index